The Last Happy Men

THE
LAST
HAPPY
MEN

*The Generation of 1922, Fiction,
and the Argentine Reality*

CHRISTOPHER TOWNE LELAND

SYRACUSE UNIVERSITY PRESS   1986

Copyright © by Syracuse University Press
Syracuse, New York 13244-5160

All Rights Reserved

First Edition

The paper used in this publication meets the minimum requirements of American National Standard for Information Sciences—Permanence of Paper for Printed Library Materials, ANSI Z39.48-1984 ∞™

Publication of this book has been aided by a grant from the Hyder Edward Rollins Fund of Harvard University.

Library of Congress Cataloging-in-Publication Data

Leland, Christopher T.
  The last happy men.

  Bibliography: p.
  Includes index.
    1. Argentine fiction—20th century—History and criticism.   2. Literature and society—Argentina—History—20th century.   3. Argentine fiction—20th century—Psychological aspects.   I. Title.
PQ7703.L45   1986   863   86-5897
ISBN 0-8156-2376-3 (alk. paper)

Manufactured in the United States of America

A Osvaldo . . .

La voz a vos debida

CHRISTOPHER TOWNE LELAND teaches fiction in the Department of English and American Literature and Language at Harvard University, where he is Briggs-Copeland Assistant Professor. He is the author of the novel *Mean Time* (1982) and *Mrs. Randall*, to be published in 1987. He received his doctorate in comparative literature from the University of California, San Diego.

Contents

Notes on the Text

Unless otherwise noted, all passages from sources in Spanish which appear in English have been translated by the author of this study.

Ellipses forming part of a text cited herein are indicated by closely spaced ellipses (...), while deletions by the author of this study are signed by normally spaced ellipses (. . .).

Any page numbers appearing in citations of the periodical *Claridad* are approximate, in that the magazine appeared unpaginated.

To avoid excessive citation, a text under analysis is cited for endnote reference only at the point of initial quotation.

Preface

THIS BOOK began, some ten years ago, as a study of Argentine fiction from 1916 to 1943, from the election of Hipólito Yrigoyen to the emergence of Juan Perón. It became apparent, however, that such an undertaking would require either an extreme compression of historical and literary analysis or an investigation of truly massive proportions. Consequently, I narrowed my field of research, closing the period with the year 1930. Similarly, I adjusted upward the date of its commencement to the early 1920s. Serendipitously, this focused my attention on one of the most fecund and remarkable periods of Argentine literature, that of a group of writers now referred to as "the Generation of 1922."

To my knowledge, there is no single scholarly text in either Spanish or English which systematically investigates the output of the young writers of the twenties, though there are studies of individual writers and publications. Hence, the most basic function of this book is as literary history, that necessary initial survey of a particular era and its literature which may serve as the point of departure for other, more finely focused criticism. Given this, it will be necessary in what follows to recapitulate a certain amount of purely historical, economic, and social data, so as to indicate how particular works speak uniquely for and from the age of their production. I have opted, in the interests of a wider audience, to translate all Spanish language citations into English. I hope those familiar with the sources will find my translations adequate and at least reasonably faithful.

Beyond this, there will be considerable stress laid upon the psychological resonances of the texts, particularly in the penultimate section—a close reading of three key works of the era: Roberto Mariani's *Cuentos de la oficina*, Roberto Arlt's *El juguete rabioso*, and Ricardo Güiraldes' *Don Segundo Sombra*. Not the least of my purposes here is to demonstrate that, in literature, the appearance of or emphasis upon certain psychological states or concerns may be historically influenced. This idea arises from a conception of the production of literature as doubly dialectical. The writer as a thinking and creative individual represents the synthesis of personal history and the history of the age. After the formation of the personality as a consequence of these two factors, the individual then confronts history once again. Out of that process—the collision of the complex individual, product of both historical determinations and his or her own peculiar overdeterminations, with history experienced both intellectually and sensitively—comes the literary text, the joint venture of world and individual, molded by both and set to paper by the latter.

Such a "psychocultural" approach to a text may be helpful not only in the analysis of the text itself, but also in explaining its reception at the time of its appearance and its subsequent popularity or obscurity. The transhistorical appeal of certain works, in contrast to the cyclic relevance of others, presents a vexing question for literary scholars, one which might well be clarified by the simultaneous acceptance of methodological tools from various critical schools of thought. By linking the appearance of a particular psychological motif to the dominant economic relations within a particular society; by seeking a possible tie between a recurrent and apparently arcane image and the history not only of certain authors but also of their class or nation, we may gain insight into the appeal of specific literary works.

One question sure to be engendered by the very title of this book is: "What of the women?" The unfortunate truth is that, in the Generation of 1922, their role was very small. Among the leftist writers who constituted the so-called *grupo de Boedo,* the only "female" figure of note was the poet, "Clara Béter," a purported prostitute from Rosario who was ultimately unmasked as an invention of the precociously talented César Tiempo (Israel Zeitlin). Among the vanguardists of the *grupo de Florida,* Boedo's opposite number, the lone woman was Norah Lange. During the decade, she produced a respectable body of work in both poetry and prose, though she herself subsequently dismissed these early efforts as superficial.

Lange is an intriguing but, nonetheless, relatively minor figure of the Generation of 1922. The twenties' most famous female writer, Alfonsina Storni, had already begun to establish her reputation before the decade began, and in any case remained aloof from the aesthetic battles which so consumed the younger writers of the century's third decade. Victoria Ocampo, the publisher of *Sur,* did not found her magazine nor undertake any significant literary efforts until the 1930s. Practically speaking, up until the end of the Second World War, the number of Argentine women seriously involved in literature remained shockingly small. This is all the more striking in view of the efflorescence of writing by women since that time, to the point that their contribution to contemporary Argentine letters is at least as great if not greater than that of their male counterparts.

Women's limited participation in the literature of the 1920s is indicative of the decade's realities. Though progress had been made, women were still largely excluded from many occupations, from serious participation in public life, from most intellectual debate. If many of the issues dealt with in this study manifest peculiarly male concerns or are framed in specifically masculine terms, this should be seen as typical of ideological conditions of the age.

In preparing this manuscript for publication, difficult choices have been inevitable. Much information collected from periodicals and interviews appears in the text, but much has been excised. Brandán Caraffa's touching story of his last walk down Avenida de Mayo with the dying Güiraldes, Nalé Roxlo's reminiscence of a cocaine-fueled spree with La Chola, an old friend and sometime lady-of-the-night, a great deal of bibliography regarding Roberto Mariani's publications in the contemporary press—these and much more have been sacrificed in the interest of a manageable and focused text, though some of this material may be found in the endnotes. Later, I hope, in a less rigorous study, there will be an opportunity to share more of the secondary but often fascinating bits of biography, bibliography, and history I gleaned in Buenos Aires in 1979 and 1984.

Any author, of course, has a multitude of ambitions for the text he or she produces. My hope is that this study may spur interest in the output of Roberto Mariani, a writer of real significance who has long been neglected. Further, it would be nice to think the analysis of *Don Segundo Sombra* is both radical and convincing enough to free that novel from the bonds which have, for years, made it the object of hagiography on the one hand and sterile linguistic exercises on the other, and hence a figure of fun for those who see themselves as "serious" critics. My third wish would be that this text might further the realization in North America that Latin American literature has not suddenly burst out of southern climes with a "Boom" in the last three decades. Cortázar, García Márquez, Vargas Llosa, Fuentes, Puig, Marta Lynch, Luisa Valenzuela—these modern writers arose out of a rich tradition of twentieth-century Hispanic letters, of which the Generation of 1922 was a large but by no means exclusive element.

Once this is understood, I believe, a very fecund area of criticism and scholarly investigation will open up, that of comparative study of the literatures of the entire hemisphere. It is my instinct that, because of the shared experiences of our young histories, the two continents have produced an aesthetic qualitatively very different from that of the Old World. The time has come, despite differences of language, politics, and culture, to search out and celebrate that unique vision of ourselves and the world which makes us all American.

Acknowledgments

AMONG THOSE who have taught me over the years, special thanks are due to Drs. Howard Young, Jaime Alazraki, Adolfo Prieto, and the late James Scobie, as well as to David Viñas, Ricardo Piglia, Josefina Ludmer, and the members of my examination and dissertation committees at the University of California, San Diego: Drs. Andrew Wright, Don Wayne, Louis Montrose, Carlos Blanco Aguinaga, Michel de Certeau, Susan Kirkpatrick, Rae Blumberg, and Jaime Concha.

I was first introduced to the literature here investigated as a result of the generosity of the Rotary Foundation, which sent an unsuspecting hispanophile off to Mendoza, Argentina, in 1974. To those I knew there, I owe special recognition to Drs. Antonio Barrera, Albert Lapeyre, Fanny Prevedello, Mabel Agresti, and Emilia de Zuleta. Too, I must thank the family which made me welcome, that of Mr. and Mrs. Antonio Castro, and my many friends both at the Rotary Club, Las Heras, and at the Universidad Nacional de Cuyo.

My research was much advanced as a result of a grant from the Fulbright Commission in 1979. During my year in Buenos Aires, a number of institutions proved extremely generous in allowing me to use their facilities, among them the Biblioteca Nacional, the Biblioteca del Congreso, the Universidad Nacional de Buenos Aires, and particularly the Library of the Instituto Ricardo Rojas, the Sociedad Argentina de Escritores (SADE), and the family of the late Sergio Provenzano. The assistance of the director of the Fulbright Commission, Rolando Costa Picazo, and of Jacobo de Diego, the librarian of the SADE, were particularly valuable, as was the interest and support shown by my friends and fellow researchers in the Biblioteca Nacional, Claudio Preti and Lea Fletcher. To those who shared their memories and insights with me in interviews, many of them now deceased, I owe a debt too great to express adequately.

In the United States, I would like to thank my friends in San Diego, particularly the changing but ever-inspiring cast of co-workers at Warren College, including the "Night Crew"—Paul Dresman, Michael Holzman, the late Brooke Nielson, and Stephanie Ramsdell. Thanks too to such pillars of support as Julia Dunn and my long-suffering roommates over the years: Peter Tiersma, Paul Katz, and Katharine Haake. At Syracuse University, the support and advice of Dr. Myron Lichtblau has been deeply appreciated.

For my parents, sister and brother, of course, a "gracias" of a most special kind.

Finally, much of the research I undertook in 1979 was of a sort impossible for an Argentine investigator of that time. It is my hope, now that Argentina has emerged from the night of the Proceso Nacional, that those who would make Buenos Aires once again "the cultural meridian of the hispanic world" will find themselves free to study, discuss, and debate all aspects of their history, literature, and national life. In that great undertaking, I like to think that, in some small way, this contribution from the antipodes may prove useful.

Boston, Massachusetts   CHRISTOPHER T. LELAND
Winter 1986

Introduction

. . . In spite of the World War, the generation to which I belong knew a
world which was still stable. Only later did the cement of that moral and
spiritual universe crumble. . . . Around 1920, the elements which made up
a sort of organic system of life had still not lost their vigor. . . . The
aggressive nihilism of the vanguardist schools which arose in that epoch can
be identified with a certain playful desire to deny the bloom on the rose.
The sense of humor of an age which worshipped Progress still survived. . . .
Without straining the facts, I can affirm we were the last happy men.

Carlos Mastronardi

That stage of Argentine civilization stretching from the years 1900 to 1930
manifests some curious phenomena. The daughters of salesmen study Fu-
turist literature in the College of Philosophy and Letters, are ashamed of
the nasty money-grubbing of their parents, and snarl next morning at the
housekeeper upon discovering a few cents missing in the change from the
market. Thus we confirm the appearance of a democracy (apparently a
dazzling one), which has inherited lock, stock and barrel the mangy avariciousness of clodhoppers and born servants, who now in their first and
second generations present us with those subspecies of thirty-year-olds of
the present day: the greedy, the gross, the clumsy, the envious, and those
dying to investigate first-hand those pleasures they imagine the very rich
enjoy.

Roberto Arlt

WHAT WAS IT LIKE? That Argentina which could call forth
such radical and different judgments—where did its essence
lie? What kind of era could offer an "organic system of life" rife
with "mangy avariciousness"? What manner of "stable world"
could be populated with such vicious individuals? Where is the truth?
Which of these two voices speaks for that nation, that age?[1]

Their very cacophony, perhaps, provides the best answer. The sociologist Julio Mafud has asserted: "Argentina has no spiritual continuity. It was born with a broken soul."[2] In the testaments of Arlt and Mastronardi, two friends separated by only a year in age, we can see that discontinuity, those fault lines which make any single vision of the world of their youth as mutable as the momentary patterns of a kaleidoscope.

Argentina, more than most nations, is a paradox, a vast collection of contradictions. Its middle class is the largest and most progressive in Latin America; its oligarchy probably still controls more square miles of land than any other in the world. Its population is among the best educated anywhere, yet the country suffers a chronic shortage of skilled technicians. Of all the nations in its region, it has always offered the greatest opportunities for social mobility; probably nowhere else in South America, however, is snobbery so rampant and overt. These sorts of disjunctures have, since 1930, sent Argentina reeling through a seemingly endless series of traumas and false dawns, so that today, the hope which the nation's new and fragile democracy engenders is shadowed by the fear of some future political and spiritual catastrophe.

In the 1920s, however, these paradoxes—verifiable in novels and memoirs and cold, unforgiving statistics—had not yet delivered the nation to crisis. Indeed, the two witnesses quoted above sometimes personified those contradictions, and with many of their contemporaries reveled in them, relished them, first felt their talents bloom in the midst of them. Mastronardi himself could play the vanguardist nihilist. Arlt's sarcastic gloom occupied his own consciousness side by side with schemes calculated to leave him "rotten with money" and free, presumably, to investigate those exotic, aristocratic pastimes. Perhaps it was the very intensity of those paradoxes within these men themselves and the world they called theirs—that sprawling city one of their friends would later christen "the head of Goliath"—which made the moment so significant, so complete for good or ill in their remembrance. In the twenties, an entire historical process which had begun in Argentina in 1916, 1880, 1853, 1810, or even 1536, appeared to approach its climax. In that decade of massive flux, not only in Buenos Aires but throughout the world, perhaps it seemed that all that was evil from all ages before tottered and needed only a feather's weight to bring it to ruin.

Mastronardi and Arlt passed their youth in an age which combined tremendous intellectual ferment, artistic rebellion, political awakening, social change, and apparent social reform with economic expansion, a growing but not yet virulent nationalism, and a superficial sense of general well-being. In Buenos Aires, these were the years of the rage of the tango, the construction of the grand diagonal avenues and the promenades along the river front, the music of Honegger, Stravinsky, and de Falla, the films of Eisenstein. The city welcomed Rabindranath Tagore, Waldo Frank, and Filippo Marinetti, La Nijinska and Josephine Baker, the Prince of Italy and the Prince of Wales.[3] There were two dozen newspapers published in the capital, along with magazines for every taste, including Condé Nast's new, *porteño* edition of *Vogue*.[4] Alfredo Palacios, moustachioed and caped like some dashing bohemian, made stirring speeches for socialism in the halls of the National Congress; Leopoldo Lugones, the poet, glorified fascism in books and articles and on public platforms both at home and abroad. The city was heady with debate in what seemed the fulfillment of the bourgeois, Liberal promise.

Of course, these were also the years in which, for many, the hope which was Radicalism withered. The "Tragic Week" of anti-foreign vigilantism was fresh in memory. The Patagonia of rebellious workers was "pacified"; strikes were smashed and the masses cowed, faceless and forgotten. British capital ran the railroads, the tram lines, the gas works, and the electric company. The Americans had begun their challenge to English hegemony with Swift and Ford and Standard Oil. The Zwi Migdal, the *porteño* Jewish mafia, controlled 30,000 prostitutes, only part of a population which made Buenos Aires the international capital of white slavery.[5] In spite of some desultory efforts in the area of public housing, most families still lived in crowded apartments, or chock-a-block in a room or two of a crumbling tenement. Even those of the middle class who managed to finance a small house on the city's periphery waited years for such public services as running water, proper sanitation, and paved streets. Despite Buenos Aires' continental pretensions, green space was at a premium, victim of the mania of uncontrolled land speculation.[6] The bureaucracy was bloated, corruption not unusual. And in the wings, the philo-German army practiced the goose step while its officers observed with more than passing interest the rise of Mussolini.

Amid this welter of contradictions, the twenties saw as well a great artistic flowering, the emergence of a mass literary culture in Argentina. The Generation of 1880, the first notable group of writers in the nation's history, produced books by aristocrats for aristocrats. The Generation of 1922—the year these young writers began to gather themselves into the factions later called "Boedo" and "Florida"—arose out of the proletariat and especially the petit bourgeoisie. It was composed of authors who wrote, in one way or another, for an audience of students and workers and clerks, teachers, and other minor professionals. This is not to say that the oligarchs had lost the power of the pen. The most famous book of the age,

Don Segundo Sombra, emerged from the imagination of Ricardo Güiraldes, whose youthful grand tour had included not only traditional European watering holes, but Constantinople, Bombay, Tokyo, and Moscow.[7]

It is through the texts of these writers—a few still famous and many more forgotten—that we will attempt to gain entrance into the Argentina of the 1920s. Primarily through their fictions, we will try to reveal the truth of both Mastronardi's and Arlt's estimations of the age. We will confront the contradictions and illusions of the era, its realities and dreams. We will ask what these people thought, what moved them, and why. Were these indeed "the last happy men"? Why the last? Why happy? What was it like?

PART I

Before

CHAPTER 1

Revolution and Radicalism

ARGENTINA is a nation not so much changed as remade. Unlike other American states, which despite wars and coups and constitutional alterations maintain some sense of continuity in their national life, Argentina's history seems disjointed, eventful, and confusing enough not just for one country but for three or four. Consequently, the world of the Generation of 1922 was markedly different from that of its great-grandfathers. A profound transformation began in 1852, on the battlefield at Caseros. There, the twenty-year rule of Juan Manuel de Rosas ended, and with it the conservative policies which had kept the nation an economic and cultural backwater. Over the next twenty years, in spite of Argentina's part in the War of the Triple Alliance, in spite of the conflicts which flared between capital and provinces, the groundwork was laid for the nation's transformation. In place of the Rosista ideology, the Liberal concepts of Juan Bautista Alberdi, Esteban Echeverría, and Domingo Sarmiento dominated national policy. These men, hounded into exile by Rosas' henchmen, the dreaded Mazorca, had been deeply influenced by nineteenth-century political and economic thought and had long dreamt of a nation on the Rio de la Plata cast in the image of the industrialized powers of Europe and the burgeoning Colossus of the North. For them, the Argentine nation as it existed was a travesty, a betrayal of the past, of the ideals of the twenty-fifth of May, of San Martín, Belgrano, and Rivadavia; and also of the future, of the endless potential of a land so richly endowed by nature.[1] Sarmiento brilliantly and brutally demarcated the lines of the battle as he saw it in *Facundo: Civilización y barbarie en las pampas argentinas*. He and his compatriots, together with Europe, industrialization, immigration, and education, constituted the forces of light; Rosas and his petty, local dictators, his *caudillos*, their trade in salt beef, the gauchos, and the customs of the provinces represented those of darkness. After years of terror, repression, and exile, the victors at Caseros had no qualms about the necessity of "barbarism's" destruction, root and branch. On the eve of battle, Sarmiento charged the rebel general Urquiza: "Spare no gaucho blood."[2]

But what did the fathers of this new Argentina propose? The new political order was ostensibly committed to two principles: "To populate is to govern" and "For us, the revolution is progress."[3] These maxims represented, for the leaders of the age, solutions to the problems which prevented Argentina from fulfilling her destiny: the vast open space of the nation, as yet unexploited, and the Hispanic heritage which infected the old Argentina with a suspicion of all that was new, European, and enlightened. Concretely, these pronouncements manifested themselves in the encouragement of immigration, the establishment of universal and obligatory education, and the importation of capital to encourage the establishment and growth of both agriculture and industry, with the concomitant development of a good transport and communications system.[4]

Such ideas were, of course, anathema to Rosas and the great landowners who supported him, and also to many among the *criollos*, the largely rural population, many of mixed blood, who, for all the poverty and brutal caprice of life beneath the *caudillos*, found some sort of community and freedom in the gaucho existence.[5] It would be tempting but incorrect to view the battle of Liberals and Rosistas as Sarmiento and his friends did. For all the noble gloss of liberal democracy, mass literacy, social expansion, and material betterment, some prophets of the post-Rosas age embraced less alluring ideas, among them this:

> It happens that the sovereignty of the people can reside only in the reason of the people, and that only the prudent and rational part of the social community is called to exercise that sovereignty. Those who are ignorant remain under the tutelage and safeguard of the laws decreed by the common consent of the men of reason. Democracy, then, is not the absolute despotism of the masses or of the majority; it is the rule of reason.[6]

Or, more overtly, this:

> The Republic will never become a fact with three million Christian and Catholic inhabitants. Nor will it be achieved with four million Spaniards from the Peninsula, because the Spaniard is incapable of establishing a republic, either there or here. If we must construct our

population to fit our systems of government; if it is going to be more feasible for us to fit the population to the political system that we have proclaimed than to fit the system to the population, we must increase the Anglo-Saxon population in our land. They are the ones who are identified with the steamship, with commerce, and with liberty, and it will be impossible to establish these things among us without the active cooperation of that progressive and cultivated race.[7]

It is, perhaps, not for us to judge the thinkers of the revolution of 1853 from our privileged vantage more than a century later. Imbued as they and their contemporaries were with the optimism of the nineteenth century, it seems neither odd nor damnable that they should equate steamships and liberty, envision progress in purely material terms, or project national regeneration through racial engineering. From a purely political standpoint, they could ill afford to cast their fate to the electoral whims of an illiterate people all too recently enamored of a tyrant who had persecuted the Liberals unmercifully. And yet it has been said that Rosas, not really intentionally, bequeathed to Argentina three legacies: the *latifundia*, a strong and authoritarian army, and an inordinately powerful central administration.[8] In the years since his fall, through presidents and dictators, the nation built upon the ideals of his successors seems not only to have accepted that inheritance, but to have expanded upon it.

Most cultures die neither easily nor quickly. They adjust, conform, surrender pieces of themselves over time until they become only a memory. One civilization in Argentina did disappear suddenly and dramatically—that of the Indians. The world of Calfucurá and the other tribal chiefs ended in the War of the Desert, the campaign of the Federal Army armed with Winchesters and the telegraph, which virtually exterminated the pampas Indians in a few short months in 1880.[9] Sarmiento's hated gaucho, however, could not be annihilated. He remained on the margin of that society increasingly centered in the capital, making compromises and singing his defiance in the words of one of Sarmiento's bitterest political enemies. José Hernández' *Martín Fierro* (1872) underwent the unusual transformation from literary to folk epic, memorized and repeated endlessly in the *pulperías* by illiterate men struggling to make their lives as they always had, while the world which was theirs slowly came apart around them, the vast, unbroken pampa now crisscrossed by fences, railroads, and telegraph lines. The gaucho suffered his gradual domestication, his long dying, while the Sarmentine dream began finally to bear fruit, massively and in forms not really anticipated.

The period 1880–1916 constitutes the golden age of what came to be called "the Oligarchy." The survivors and sons of the republican elite which had triumphed over Rosas, and some the the Rosistas as well, amassed in those years fortunes which made the Argentine *estanciero*, like the Brazilian rubber king and the American robber baron, a synonym for a capitalist prince of unimaginable wealth. They lived in incredible luxury, controlled vast estates, and remade the face of the nation, transforming Buenos Aires from little more than a dirty and disease-ridden colonial city to the "Paris of South America"—a center of commerce and culture unmatched on the continent and perhaps in the hemisphere.[10]

Yet, they did not do it alone. Indeed, they were in large part the passive beneficiaries of the successful political policies they had embraced.[11] The key to their good fortune was immigration. Between 1821 and 1932, nearly 6.5 million foreigners entered Argentina. If many of these were only *golondrinas*—seasonal workers—many more came to establish themselves, to *hacerse la América*, to make their fortunes in the new paradise on the Río de la Plata. Before 1880, in spite of occasional government efforts, the migrant population which settled permanently was but a trickle. After that date, it became a flood. In 1895, one-fourth of the population of the nation was foreign born; by 1914, almost a third was. The new arrivals concentrated in the cities, particularly in Buenos Aires, and made up the great majority of two emergent social groups: the middle class and the urban proletariat. They ran the stores, traded the goods, unloaded the ships, worked in the factories of the capital's nascent industries. For the twenty years from 1895 to 1914, foreigners comprised fifty percent of the population of Buenos Aires, including three-quarters of the males over twenty.[12]

However, it was all not quite as Sarmiento, Alberdi, and others had envisioned it. First of all, the immigration proved perhaps too massive. No country in history has absorbed the numbers of immigrants relative to its population that Argentina did in a bare fifty years' time. To illustrate this, we must recall that, though numerically the United States accepted many more foreigners than Argentina, the new arrivals never constituted more than fourteen percent of the population, while from 1869 to 1957, the percentage of foreigners in Argentina was never *less* than that.[13] Still, this might not have been so significant had those arriving indeed "populated the desert." Had the pampas been divided into small farms for individual cultivation, perhaps the cultural shock of so many new residents might have been dissipated. However, by 1880, the best land was already concentrated in the hands of a very few, the same few who controlled the government in Buenos Aires. The oligarchs were willing to accept a few shepherds here and there, a certain number of sharecroppers, but the Argentine economy by this time was firmly linked with international British capital, having found its place as a provider of beef, mutton, wool, leather, and grain. These required little labor relative to space, and the *estancieros* were certainly not willing to see their vast *latifundias* subdivided into truckfarms and orchards.[14] Hence, the immigrants congregated in the cities, and there did service as middlemen. Inevitably, barrios arose composed almost entirely of aliens, and the traditional social structure, social relations, and society itself tended to disappear completely in the urban centers.[15] Buenos Aires and Rosario in particular became cosmopolitan islands in a *criollo* sea, till even Roca referred to the former as "a province of foreigners."[16]

Sarmiento, like a fugitive from the Eliot canon, ended his days with a frustrated "that is not what I meant at all." Not only did the immigrants not populate the desert, not only did they come mostly from the lowest social classes of their native lands, not only were they of Eastern European and Mediterranean (and thus "inferior") stock, but most did not even trouble themselves to become citizens of their new homeland.[17] Citizenship promised very little: for some, a ballot to be filled out per instructions from the local ward captain; for all, the necessity of military service. Maintaining one's nationality at least permitted the hope that the resident consul might be of help in some emergency.[18] It seemed a new nation was not being built but rather that one was being layered on top of another, producing a structure both flimsy and dangerous. "One does not construct a homeland," wrote Sarmiento in his old age, "without patriotism as its cement, nor does one build as the soul and glory of nations a city without citizens."[19]

The problems which immigration created became more and more evident as one century ended and a new one began. Yet, the oligarchy, in general, refused to make any concessions which might in some way have altered the social and economic relations then prevailing and thus averted the impending crisis. They found themselves increasingly ambivalent about the whole enterprise of national regeneration, anxious to integrate the newcomers but loathe to grant them any real power.[20] A society arose which permitted a certain economic and social mobility, but whose reins were tightly held by a select few. This elite established the *unicato,* the cliquish, single-party rule of the late nineteenth century, which with the years gradually betrayed more and more the political principles it ostensibly stood for, those principles originally given voice by the anti-Rosistas. However, as very junior partners in international capitalism, the oligarchy maintained its economic liberalism, and as a consequence, accrued a vast foreign debt during the boom years of the eighties. These policies led directly to the first serious challenge to the then ruling class: the crisis of 1890. The autocratic rule of President Miguel Juárez Celman, while favorable to oligarchical interests, had pushed the middle class to the brink of ruin. In the midst of a severe financial panic, various scandals involving the administration came to light, and a peculiar coalition of groups—proto-socialists, Catholics, liberal democrats, and ex-President Bartolomé Mitre—joined together and almost toppled the government. To avert revolution, Juárez Celman stepped aside in favor of his vice-president, Carlos Pelligrini. Soon after, the odd allies of what they had dubbed the Civic Union split, with Mitre and the conservatives making their peace with the *unicato.* The more leftist factions followed Juan B. Justo into the new Socialist Workers Party. Provincial centrists eventually joined Lisandro de la Torre in the Progressive Democratic Party, while the remainder, largely composed of the urban middle class, adhered to the movement first championed by Leandro Alem, the Radical Civil Union (UCR).[21]

The history of Radicalism in Argentina, both as an opposition movement and as a party in power, is linked inextricably to one man: Hipólito Yrigoyen. Though president of the republic for eight years, and surely the dominant political presence in Argentina for twenty, Yrigoyen remains a controversial and shadowy figure, and the movement he headed likewise seems to elude precise definition. A poor speaker, a dictatorial political boss, a man who judged associates less by character than by loyalty, Yrigoyen nonetheless was a brilliant organizer and a man profoundly dedicated to his beliefs. His appeal to his constituency bordered on the messianic, and his faith in the people and the secret ballot approached the mystical. He struggled most of his life to reform the Argentine political system through "intransigency and revolution." An attempt at the latter failed in 1905 as it had in 1890, but the former—the refusal to take part in the elections sponsored by the ruling class—eventually wrought the change in electoral procedures which, it seems, Yrigoyen thought would end political strife in the nation once and for all.[22]

The movement which surrounded this singular man accurately reflected his vision. In the first years after its appearance, it seemed to the ruling class a dangerous Jacobin party, committed to revolutionary change. However, even in the midst of this hysteria, there were those in the oligarchy who recognized that the Radicals were not so fearful as they might appear at first blush. While it was true that the party's membership included many immigrants and sons of immigrants, its mass following and leadership were largely *criollo*. Further, though in its years of opposition Radicalism enjoyed and encouraged considerable proletarian support, its programs and philosophy were relatively moderate and solidly middle class. Indeed, many of its central figures represented progressive elements of the oligarchy itself. A rightist legislator of the period remarked: "Why is it that the conservatives are bent upon preventing the Radicals from taking over the administration? They represent the same interests and principles as we do. We should let the People have its way, because if not we run the risk of attracting it to the really advanced parties."[23]

The dual insight here expressed is remarkable both for its exactness and honesty. Radicalism's ultimately nonrevolutionary nature arose precisely from its composition as a middle-class movement. This social group, whether *criollo* or immigrant, owed its position and continued well-being to the primary export economy which the oligarchy had created in collusion with foreign capital. The middle class enjoyed the benefits inherent in a developed but dependent nation, benefits which might well be endangered by profound social and economic changes. Within the economy, the middle class filled positions in the service sector, in commerce, and the bureaucracy. Thus, it lacked "a commitment to the overthrow of agrarianism for the sake of its own class interests. On the contrary it appeared as a social appendix to the agrarian system, and a reflection of its development in an advanced capitalist form."[24]

Beyond this, at least certain members of the oligarchy began to see in Radicalism a political movement which might be used to lure the proletariat away from the overtly revolutionary left. Their concern was less Justo's socialists than the anarchist cells developing in the immigrant barrios of the large cities.[25] Many of the Spaniards and Italians in Argentina at the turn of the century arrived already thoroughly politicized. The rise in illegal strikes, the proliferation of *círculos de obreros*, the circulation of texts by Kropotkin, Bakunin and, to a lesser extent, Marx and Engels, raised fears in the oligarchy of an "immigrant revolt."[26] The specter of red and black flags over Buenos Aires, à la Paris, 1871, encouraged an acceptance of Radicalism by segments of the ruling class and a further turn to the right in government policy. By the "Ley de residencia" (1905), the federal authorities were given power to expel any foreigner active in "provoking social conflict." When even this failed to stem the tide of labor and political agitation, which climaxed in the attempted assassination of the chief of the Buenos Aires police in 1910, the response was the even more odious and repressive "Ley de defensa social," which severely restricted the rights of workers to organize.[27]

The year of the centenary, the anniversary of the 1810 Revolution, was the apogee of the oligarchy and its swan song. Regardless of laws and deportations and arrests, the populist tide was rising, and it became more and more evident that the ruling class faced the choice of compromise or an eventually successful uprising of professionals, bureaucrats, and white- and blue-collar workers. Its constituents opted for the former course, and in 1912, the moderate reformer, Roque Saénz Peña, established himself in Argentine history by giving his name to the law guaranteeing universal male suffrage and the secret ballot.[28] For the next four years, the Radicals marked time, aware that their hour had arrived. In 1916, by a hair's breadth, the intransigent Hipólito Yrigoyen won election as president of the republic.[29] After his inauguration, his carriage was drawn down the Avenida de Mayo by young supporters through throngs of well-wishers, and it seemed, perhaps, that Yrigoyen's estimation of himself might be correct: "There are lives through which shine all the qualities and conditions of an epoch, and such is my own."[30]

And what were those qualities and conditions? By the time Yrigoyen was elected, the "barbarism" Sarmiento so hated had largely disappeared. Since 1880, Argentina had become a developed nation with a vast railroad system, a glittering capital, extensive port facilities, and an increasingly urban population. These advances, however, had been bought at a price and created certain glaring anomalies within the social fabric. Economically, the nation had become a dependency of foreign investors. As Juan B. Justo remarked: "English capital has done what their armies could not do [during their attempted conquest of Buenos Aires in the Napoleonic period]. Today our country is tributary to England."[31] Banks in London, and to a much lesser extent Paris, owned the docks, the rail carriages, the factories and streetcars. The subway which rumbled all the way from the Plaza de Mayo to Primera Junta was, revealingly, called the "Subterráneo"—the "Underground."[32]

If the language of commerce was English, that of culture was French. The Avenida de Mayo, with its sidewalk cafés and grand sweep from the Casa Rosada to the Congreso, owed its inspiration to the Champs Elysées. The Bois de Boulogne inspired the parks at Palermo. Zola, Anatole France, the Symbolists, and Decadents provided the great literary models. French fashion reigned supreme.[33] More disturbingly perhaps, cultural life of any sort came to be more and more centered in or at least dictated by the cosmopolitan capital. The last remnants of nativist culture were disappearing, or becoming so marginalized as to be moribund. As a consequence, the entire definition of *argentinidad*, in crisis since the mid-nineteenth century, became even more problematic. Traditions underwent bizarre transformations under the impact of immigration. The *culto de coraje*, the violent machismo of the pampas, flowered anew among the *compadritos*, the dapper, knife-wielding hooligans of the crowded urban centers, if it had not already been twisted into a *culto de la potencia sexual*.[34] Argentine society, reflecting the numerical realities of the immigratory invasion, was preponderantly male. As such, it manifested various predictable characteristics: intense male bonding, a deprecation of women and of love, a deification of the mother, a proclivity toward and lionization of violence, all masking a pronounced adolescent homoerotic strain.[35] These tendencies were exacerbated by the fact of immigration itself—the constant confrontation of new arrivals with the established immigrant community, itself at odds with the better integrated second and third generation hyphenated Argentines and with the *criollos* themselves. Beyond this, the middle and lower classes suffered, in an odd way, from the "dream of Argentina." The legend of the silver land, the desire to *hacerse la América*, brought many to the Río de la Plata in the first place. Once there, the internal pressure for financial betterment received impetus from the political impotence of the laboring classes. As a consequence, there arose a society brutally materialistic in its values, cliquish and competitive, drawn into a cult of money, status, and academic title, inevitably characterized by "opposition and exclusion."[36]

This is not what Yrigoyen claimed or wished to typify. The Radicals wanted to create a unitary rather than a pluralistic society, remain a "movement" rather than become one political party among many. "The UCR is not hostile to any legitimate interest, and on the contrary there is room in its ranks for all those who wish to put themselves sincerely at the service of their country."[37] Nonetheless, Yrigoyen in his first term made numerous enemies. In the early years of his administration, the proposition of various moderate reforms—an income tax, an agricultural bank to encourage colonization, and a temporary tax on agricultural exports to help alleviate unemployment—earned the president the enmity of the oligarchy. He further alienated these sectors by his determined neutrality during World War I, even in the face of considerable Allied pressure. His ruthless use of presidential interventionary power in provincial governments, by and large still controlled by conservatives, further irritated the ruling class, though in a sense Yrigoyen had little choice but to use his constitutional prerogatives. The national senate was chosen not by popular vote but provincial legislatures, and until the Radicals controlled them, there was little chance of meaningful reform.[38]

Nonetheless, the class which suffered the cruelest disappointments under Yrigoyen was the urban proletariat. Wooed aggressively by the Radicals, it had hoped for an improvement in working conditions, broader rights to organize and strike, and even a meaningful redistribution of wealth. It confronted instead federal labor policies which were "indecisive, moderate and contradictory."[39] This is not all that surprising. The Radicals claimed, after all:

> Nor do we accept class differences, or that there are any classes in the Argentine Republic. . . . We do not fail to see that there are conflicts between Capital and Labor, but we do not accept that there is a proletarian or a Capitalist class, even if ninety-five per cent of the Argentines were to fall into what in Europe is called the proletariat. Nor is it right to bring into our new America, where new ideals of human solidarity are being formed, such sentiments of hate on account of differences of race, religion or class.[40]

Still, it would be wrong to brand Yrigoyen's regime as systematically antilabor. Rather, the president saw himself obligated to defend "national" interests, which oftentimes seemed at odds with the cosmopolitan and universalist ideals of the organized Left. Further, his options were severely limited by the continuing economic power of the oligarchy and of foreign capital, which were unalterably opposed to unionization or any other capitulation to worker demands. The end of Radicalism's courtship of the workers came finally in 1919, in the chain of events known as the *Semana Trágica*. An inflation of varying intensity had afflicted Argentina throughout the period of the First World War and worsened after the Armistice. The working class endured the greatest hardship as a result of this condition, while it actually proved beneficial to the landed interests, both because it made their exports cheaper and because many of them held large sums in foreign currency. Urban laborers, however, suffered a notable decline in real wages. Further, the president had to consider a growing challenge from the Right in the form of the proto-fascist Argentine Patriotic League and the power of European interests no longer distracted by the war effort. Thus, when he sought to repress with federal authority a metallurgical workers' disturbance which had blossomed into a general strike, Yrigoyen inadvertently unleashed all the dark energies which the social transformation of Argentina since 1880 had engendered: violent nationalism, racism, paranoid anti-Leftism, rabid anti-Semitism. Trams burned, barricades appeared in the streets, shots were fired. Gangs of thugs—an odd mix of wealthy *señoritos*, middle-class *porteños*, and the lumpen—invaded worker barrios to hunt down, terrorize, beat, and kill "Jews" and "Bolsheviks." Order was finally restored, but it promised little to the proletariat. [41] As Pedro Orgambide has noted:

> From the very beginning of the twenties—with the workers' rebellion of the Tragic Week having been suffocated in blood and flame; the Anarchist workers' centers obliterated; the anti-immigrant and anti-Semitic nationalist pretty-boys emboldened; the workers' movement itself infected with socialism's moderate tendencies—the immigrant proletariat found itself abandoned before reaction. Many of their champions were in jail in Ushuaia and the *ley de residencia* had been invoked against others . . . the timid petit bourgeois mentality attempted, modestly, to ascend to power. Radicalism channeled that force, sustained it, and as they said at the time, the movement's fate was the proof of the pudding. [42]

The failure of the minimal economic reforms proposed by Yrigoyen created for his administration its most serious problem: how to fulfill the promises of Radicalism to its most ardent supporters, those of the middle class. The solution was found in the elaborate patronage system established by the party, greatly strengthened and expanded by the UCR's access to the federal treasury. State spending increased dramatically during Yrigoyen's first term, from 375 million pesos in 1916 to 614 million pesos in 1922. In 1919, there was a major party purge to make way for "new blood," and to reward or punish its members for their allegiance to or disobedience of party dictates. With the opening of the universities to the middle sectors as a result of the Reform of 1918, greater and greater numbers of graduates sought entrance into the bureaucracy, and the UCR saw in its patronage system not only a means to absorb these upwardly mobile elements into the labor force but to cement them to the party as well. Government borrowing, however, raised interest rates and dried up credit sources. Consequently, the landed interests, who had originally profited from the Radical policy through the issuance of short-term loans, grew increasingly less enamored of the practice, particularly during the recession which set in with 1922 and persisted for two years. [43]

When Yrigoyen retired from the Casa Rosada in 1922, he left the nation superficially altered but essentially unchanged. The working class had gained little under his aegis; the oligarchy found him less and less to its liking; the nation remained locked in its dependent status.[44] Yet perhaps it is too much to expect basic social change to come about in a bare six years in any but the most overtly revolutionary situation. Certainly for the petit bourgeoisie and the professional classes, it appeared that a tremendous shift in power had taken place in Argentina. The landed interests rather less sanguinely perceived what they also took to be significant alterations in the national life.[45] Among his supporters, who remained legion, Yrigoyen was still a semi-divine figure, the man of the hour in Argentina. Though he had left the presidency, they anticipated he would continue to wield vast power under the cover of his hand-picked successor. That successor, as it turned out, had rather different ideas, probably even as he took the oath of office to preside, unwittingly, over the age of "the last happy men." His name was Marcelo de Alvear.

CHAPTER 2

The Literature of Liberalism

UNLIKE RUBÉN DARÍO, who sprang unanticipated and monstrous out of the literary void of Nicaragua, the Generation of 1922 formed part of a long and distinguished literary tradition. Though lacking any colonial artistic heritage, Argentina produced writers of note from the first decades after independence. Esteban Echeverría and José Mármol chronicled the repression of the age of Rosas in *El Matadero* and *Amalia*. Sarmiento contributed the generically perplexing *Facundo*—part political essay, part character study, part sociological treatise, part prose poem. Then, of course, came Hernández, the creator of Martín Fierro, the wright of the national myth. Still, it might be said that Argentina finally achieved some sort of literary maturity only after 1880, with the emergence of a generation of novelists, most sons of the oligarchy and many enchanted with the aesthetics of the Goncourts and Zola. Among the most successful of these writers was the young Julio Martel (José María Miró), whose *La Bolsa* of 1890 captures the wild faith in speculation of the eighties which brought about the fall of the Juárez Celman government, and also, quite as significantly, reflects the virulent xenophobia and anti-Semitism already afflicting *fin de siècle* Buenos Aires. Miguel Cané, José Antonio Wilde, and Lucio V. López were all roughly contemporary to Martel, along with Eugenio Cambaceres, perhaps the most important and original voice of *los de ochenta*.[1] *Sin rumbo*, his best work, relates the life and eventual suicide of a jaded and decadent *estanciero*, though *En la sangre* is perhaps more attuned to the social attitudes of the day, with its emphasis on a gloomy social Darwinism and its vision of the immigrants as of that "most backward and corrupt" part of humanity.[2]

By late in the century, Buenos Aires was established as the literary capital of Latin America. Darío made his way there from Santiago in 1893, bringing with him the doctrines of *modernismo*, the first indigenous

15

American movement in Hispanic literature. Its cosmopolitan vision and verbal sumptuousness set well with the city's young bohemians, among them a wild-eyed young *cordobés* intoxicated with poetry and revolutionary politics: Leopoldo Lugones.

Lugones, for a quarter century, was the dominant literary presence in Argentina. From his beginnings as the enfant terrible from the hinterlands, artistic rebel, and socialist, Lugones gradually assumed the position of unofficial poet laureate. His politics likewise underwent a transformation, as he moved from his early revolutionary posture through liberalism and then conservatism to the bellicose and chauvinistic fascism of the last decade and a half of his life.[3] He started out a dedicated *modernista*, and remained a good friend of Darío's. Nevertheless, he grew as an artist beyond the limits of that movement in such works as *Lunario sentimental*, which in its concern with metaphor presages much of the poetry of the Generation of 1922. Remarkably prolific, he produced over a forty-year career ten volumes of poetry and more than twice that number in prose, experimenting in almost every form: from mystery and a sort of proto-science fiction in *Las fuerzas extrañas* and *Cuentos fatales*, to history and biography (*El imperio jesuítico*, for example, and *Roca*); from the complex and nearly unreadable epic, *La guerra gaucha*, to the rhetorical and disturbing political philosophy of *La patria fuerte* and *El estado equitativo*.[4]

If Lugones had a rival in influence in the century's first twenty years, it was Manuel Gálvez. Son of an old and comfortable family in Paraná, Gálvez first tried his hand at the impressionistic essay and modernist poetry. He found his niche only in 1914, at age thirty-two, when he turned to the novel. His first effort, *La maestra normal*, remained unheralded until it was praised by Miguel de Unamuno in a note in *La Nación*, after which it sold well and became the center of a national controversy. In its presentation of the suffocating life of La Rioja, it provoked the ire of both the provincial citizenry and nationalistic intellectuals, including Lugones. The book was construed as everything from pornographic to a tract against lay education. Despite its stormy reception (or, perhaps in part, because of it), it has remained one of Gálvez' best-known works, and one which well illuminates both his literary methods and his ideological concerns. In weaving the tale of the seduction of Raselda, the schoolteacher, by Solís, the *porteño* rake sent to La Rioja to recover his health, Gálvez mixes a highly realistic style with a solidly moral content. This latter, however, is not the smug and judgmental piety of middle-class Argentine Catholicism, but rather a religious faith tinged with Tolstoian mysticism and a strong sense of social responsibility. Gálvez, though for most of his life a devout Christian, nonetheless had imbibed enough of the millenarian anarchism so prevalent in bohemian circles of turn-of-the-century Buenos Aires that it colored his beliefs throughout his life.

Gálvez' concern for the Argentine underclass emerged much more forcefully when he turned his attention to the urban scene. Certain moments of *El mal metafísico,* an evocation of the bohemia of the author's youth, focus upon the misery of the *porteño* workers. But it was only in 1919, with the appearance of *Nacha Regules,* that Gálvez had the opportunity to represent his social doctrine overtly. This novel, with its strongly naturalistic tone, is in some ways peculiarly anachronistic. By the time of its appearance, the zenith of Zola's influence had long passed. Nonetheless, it became a best seller and remained Gálvez' best-known work internationally. In relating the mutual redemption of Nacha, the prostitute, and Monsalvat, the idealistic and ultimately broken reformer, it set the tone for a number of social novels which followed over the next two decades.

Still, *Historia de arrabal,* a later and much slighter novel than *Nacha Regules,* exerted perhaps an even greater influence upon some of Gálvez' immediate literary descendents. In this piece, the salvation often anticipated in Gálvez is aborted. Rather, the tale emerges as the unsparing account of a girl of La Boca, victimized by all around her and finally mesmerized into murdering the one man who has offered her love and a chance for a decent life. Gálvez pays tremendous attention to naturalistic detail, taking a great care to evoke the desolation of the industrial slum. Interestingly, he also attacks the ever-present *criollo* racism by drawing the heroine's Italian mother as a hard-working and sensitive woman, in contrast to the alcoholic brutality of her native father. In no other book are both the sincerity and limitations of Gálvez' passion for social justice so evident. As will become apparent, many of those same limitations were at work among his literary successors as well.[5]

Beyond Lugones and Gálvez, a number of other Argentine writers exercised influence over the next generation. Hugo Wast (Gustavo Martínez Zuviría) penned fast-paced and entertaining novels, often repetitious but extremely popular. A much more significant and little studied talent was the reclusive Benito Lynch, from whose *estancia,* between 1916 and 1933, a series of books about life on the pampas emerged, including the well-received *El inglés de los güesos* and the psychologically astute *Los caranchos de la Florida.* Another eccentric was Horacio Quiroga, fantastical and morbid, the quintessential bohemian in his quirky clothes and bushy beard, equally at home in the capital's polyglot bistros and the jungles of Misiones. He held contemporaries spellbound with such unique works as *Cuentos de la selva* and the collection whose title speaks the dark course of Quiroga's own destiny, *Cuentos de amor, de locura y de muerte*.

Roberto J. Payró, meanwhile, rivals Gálvez as the best exponent of realism in the Argentine fiction of the early century. His contemporary picaresque novels, such as *El casamiento de Laucha* and *Divertidas aventuras del nieto de Juan Moreira*, demonstrate both his deft artistry and a profound commitment to social change. Unsurprisingly, he, along with Lugones and the essayist José Ingenieros, was among the founders of the Socialist Workers Party and a leading contributor to its newspaper, *La Vanguardia*.

Generally, it may be said that the Argentine works produced after 1880 which had the greatest impact upon the poetry of later years were those of Leopoldo Lugones and, to a lesser extent, those of Almafuerte (Pedro B. Palacios), the pioneer of urban social verse along the Río de la Plata. In prose, meanwhile, the most significant influences were realistic and naturalistic novels of city life, most often concerned with the poor, particularly the most marginalized members of society—prostitutes, pimps, *compadritos*, and bohemians. There seems to be a certain obsessive interest in the monstrous in these works, along with an ambivalent fascination with cosmopolitanism. Beyond Gálvez and Payró, authors of this type include Francisco Sicardi, Fray Mocho (José Sixto Alvarez), Luis Pascarella, Juan Palazzo, and Héctor Blomberg.[6] Also to be considered, of course, are figures from the Argentine theater, particularly Florencio Sánchez, whose plays from the first decade of the twentieth century were the first real examples of a national, urban drama. Too, the *sainete*, the odd, seriocomic popular entertainments of the era, wrought a certain influence in the 1920s, though the young writers of the era would surely have denied any connection.[7]

This diverse group from the early 1900s generally shared a certain ideological tilt. They professed, or were at least attracted to, a kind of romantic anarchism with eschatological overtones. They were intrigued by the concept of the sociological bases of character formation and with social questions as a whole, though the ardor of many for radical solutions cooled with the years.[8]

Another feature of the late 1800s and early 1900s is supremely important in understanding the work of writers of the 1920s: the gradual development of mass literacy and the concomitant growth of publishing. These years saw the multiplication of dailies and weeklies, challenging the journalistic hegemony of the great traditionalist organs, *La Prensa* and *La*

Nación. Newspapers of every political stripe and in a variety of languages competed for readers' attention, and almost all featured a weekly literary page or supplement which gave many young writers and poets their first experience in print. Often journalism provided these writers with their daily bread. Payró, Lugones, the Jewish immigrant novelist Alberto Gerchunoff—all depended for a good part of their lives on newspaper work to pay the rent.

In these years as well, the first mass circulation magazines made their appearance. Some, such as *Caras y Caretas, El Hogar,* and *Plus Ultra,* built up tremendous circulations and continued for many years.[9] In addition to social notes, news, personality profiles, and household hints, such journals consumed vast amounts of creative material of all levels of quality. The same was true of the various "weekly novels." *La novela semanal,* which first hit the stands in 1917, quickly spawned a host of imitators. Most featured soggy and eminently forgettable melodramas, but many young writers, Roberto Mariani and Alfredo Bufano among them, made more money from their attempts at *novelitas rosas* than from their more serious literary efforts.[10]

However, the most meaningful publishing efforts of these years were surely the little magazines—most underfinanced, most ephemeral— which first began to appear in the nineties, growing in number as the new century passed from infancy through adolescence. The variety and fortunes of these journals are well described in the pioneering, largely bibliographical work of Héctor Lafleur, Sergio Provenzano, and Fernando P. Alonso: *Las revistas literarias argentinas (1893–1960).* One magazine in particular, however, demands special mention, not only for its quality and longevity, but for its early recognition and support of the young writers of the twenties.

Nosotros, "the most important document of Argentine intellectual life of the first four decades of the century," is rivaled in its historical significance only by *Sur,* which finally replaced it as the national magazine of ideas.[11] Founded in 1907 by two ex-classmates from the National University, Roberto Giusti and Alfredo Bianchi, *Nosotros* published over the thirty-six years of its life virtually every important writer Argentina produced, as well as pieces by and about many foreign talents as well. Moderately socialist in outlook, it nonetheless provided a forum for diverse perspectives: Lugones' nascent fascism, Leónidas Barletta's leftism; C. Villalobos Dominguez' quixotic Georgism. In its pages, the "Ultraist Manifesto" authored by Jorge Luis Borges first reached a large public, and the magazine, though its editors were profoundly skeptical that there was much new in the "new sensibility" of the young writers of the early twenties, conducted the most complete series of interviews with them ever assembled, in consecutive issues in 1924.[12] Bianchi in particular was influential in fomenting the establishment of the new generation's first magazine, *Inicial*, though he was balefully unimpressed with the results.[13]

In many of their ideals and ideas, it may seem that Gálvez and Payró, Bianchi and Giusti, and their contemporaries did not differ much from those writers who first came to prominence in the 1920s. These younger authors, like others before them, claimed that their generation would be the one to transform art and society. Their insistence on their "new sensibility" may seem simply their confusion of radical aesthetics with youthful enthusiasm. However, a chasm separates them from previous generations, one formed in part by such national occurrences as the Yrigoyen victory and the University Reform of 1918. But particularly, it is the product of two international events: the First World War and the Russian Revolution.

PART II

The Generation of 1922

CHAPTER 3

The City and the Age

We are living the most glorious days, incomparable to those of any other epoch of human history—better than the trumpeted century of Pericles; better even than the Renaissance, that crabbed era of graverobbers sniffing the dead.

Eduardo González Lanuza

MARCELO DE ALVEAR, "Marcelino," as he was called, was a dumpy, dapper man, philosophically inclined to "let things happen, let them go."[1] He surely lacked the magnetism and sense of mission which possessed Yrigoyen, but that perhaps made him all the more appropriate a leader for the 1920s. The preceding six years had produced a number of changes in the social climate of the nation and particularly of the capital. Movie houses and restaurants proliferated, the municipal bathing beaches opened, the Federal District continued its modernization and beautification. Women had begun to play a greater role in the national life, if not so overtly as their sisters in North America and Europe. The very fact that they now attended social events unescorted and appeared on the streets after ten o'clock represented considerable progress in a nation which had traditionally believed a woman out alone at night must be one of two things—a lunatic or a prostitute.[2] The *sainetes* and the tangos of the period well captured the era's freer, more open, more relaxed style of life, genially presided over by Alvear and his opera star wife, friends "of the social scene, of the artistic whirl, of the glittering bustle of the city."[3]

Politically, however, all was not quite so peaceful as it might have first appeared. The writer Eduardo González Lanuza sees Alvear as a man both "balanced and prudent in his equidistance from the impulses of

23

plebeian Yrigoyenism and obsessions with manners and fortunes of the Jockey Club."[4] Such determined moderation, however, placed great strains upon the Radical Civic Union. From early in his administration, Alvear rejected the central policy of Yrigoyen's regime—the constant expansion of patronage and state spending. He preferred to limit expenditures and ease the credit pinch which Yrigoyen's activity had created. Such a course was quite popular with oligarchical interests but appalling to the middle sectors.[5] After only one year of Alvear's leadership, the Radical party had begun to split, quite obviously along class lines. The progressive elements of the oligarchy who had joined the ranks of the UCR now tended to side with Alvear while the mass middle class continued loyal to Yrigoyen, who still controlled the party machinery. In 1924, the division became formal, with the more conservative elements forming the Anti-Personalist Radical Civil Union. They rejected what they termed the *caudillismo* of Yrigoyen and claimed to oppose patronage, though there was an attempt to employ it soon after the schism to wrest the movement's membership out of Yrigoyen's orbit. These efforts were unsuccessful, both due to the old leader's popularity and power and to Alvear's refusal to raid the treasury for the sake of his new party. The Anti-Personalists achieved significant sway in Entre Ríos and Sante Fe, always bastions of anti-Yrigoyen sentiment, but the orthodox Radicals maintained their grip on the city and province of Buenos Aires.[6]

The secession of the oligarchical elements greatly affected party policy. By 1928, nationalization of the oil industry, together perhaps with the public utilities, was openly proposed by the Radicals, an idea clearly demonstrating their middle-class orientation. Such a course had nationalistic appeal, and quite obviously would increase the federal government's purse and allow for an expanded bureaucracy. Even more dramatic evidence of the effect of the intra-party split could be found in the legislature itself. While at the outset of Yrigoyen's first term "almost all Radical members of Congress were recruited from among traditional elite groups, [in 1928] a large proportion were of middle class background and of immigrant family origins."[7]

Too much emphasis upon such political infighting, however, plays the age false, for in general Alvear's years as president were characterized by the same sense of heady well-being found in the United States of that era, or internationally for that matter. We know now the consequences of the First World War's shattering of the nineteenth century, and even in the early twenties there certainly existed among many artists, writers, politicians, and ex-combatants a consciousness of its possible ramifications. Nonetheless, our conception of the age has been skewed by our awareness of what came after—the Depression, the Purges, Francisco Franco, the horror of Nazism and the Final Solution, another even more devastating war, and finally the atomic bomb. But we must not forget that, particularly in 1922 and even as late as 1929, the future appeared to be a bright one. The "war to end all wars" was over, Europe was in the midst of economic recovery, the more restrictive aspects of nineteenth-century respectability seemed happily past. The 1920s were years of "the spirit of Rapallo," of the Kellogg-Briand Pact, of economic boom. If jarring notes sounded—general strikes and Chinese conflicts and the rise of Mussolini—they were few, their implications yet unrecognized. In spite of articulate doubters, the twenties were generally an optimistic decade, regardless of one's nationality, social status, or political proclivities. For the traditionalist, the Red Menace appeared to be at bay, whether in Germany, the United States, England, or Argentina. For the leftist, the new world was abuilding in the Soviet Union: with the imperialist war ended, preparations could now be made for the last revolution.

In 1920, Buenos Aires had a population of almost two million, and the nation would absorb another tremendous wave of immigrants over the next ten years, after the hiatus caused by World War I. Argentina was now over one half urban. The old battle between the provinces and the capital—the root of constant strife throughout the previous hundred years—had definitively ended. The city had won. Its forced federalization in 1880, intended to limit its power, had instead assured it.[8] If certain national events might still have their genesis elsewhere—the University Reform which began in Córdoba, for example—it was only after their impact upon the capital that they achieved their full resonance. All the significant railroads spread like spokes from stations on the city's plazas; Buenos Aires was by far the nation's greatest port; what national industrial production there was largely concentrated in and around the Federal District.[9] It is as if New York, Chicago, Washington, and Pittsburgh had all coalesced in one location. Bonarense universities were the most important, its shops by far the most elegant. Through the capital the national wealth ebbed and flowed. As Ezequiel Martínez Estrada wrote: "Buenos Aires absorbed the whole Republic; it is the breach by which the Republic, flowing through rivers and railroads, hurls itself into the ocean towards Europe."[10]

Culturally as well the capital had no rivals. A few eccentrics— Dávalos in Salta, Benito Lynch on his *estancia* in Uruguay—might make their homes elsewhere. Some, for reasons of health, might be ensconced in the Córdoba hills or in Cuyo. But Buenos Aires was the magnet, and any Argentine serious about creative work inevitably was drawn to it. No urban area in the nation could compete. There could be no "Mendoza School of Architecture" à la Chicago, no "Fugitive Poets" sheltered in some university in Bahía Blanca. *Porteño* culture *was* Argentine culture.

For the arriving provincial, as for the arriving immigrant from overseas, the city must surely have dazzled. Trolleys and interurban trains clattered all over the Federal District; such outlying neighborhoods as Almagro, Caballito, and Belgrano now became part of the city's sprawl.[11] High culture flourished at the Colón and Coliseo theaters, while along Calle Lavalle the movies delighted larger and larger audiences. A block over, along and just off Calle Corrientes, elaborate theatrical reviews and other entertainments packed such houses as the Maipú-Pigalle with its "all-girl" orchestra.[12] "Corrientes *angosta*," still only two lanes wide, was "the street that never slept," its cafés and bars open all night. At its foot was El Bajo, the lively, often dangerous district of strip joints, brothels, pool halls, and gambling dens, the preserve of sailors, gangsters, pimps, and thrillseekers.

Buenos Aires in the 1920s was like Chicago of the same era, a city consciously flamboyant in its sin. No rage of Paris or Berlin was too extreme or exotic for the *porteño*. Nude follies, transvestism, "cocaine mania"—all formed a part, at least for the moment, of bonarense nightlife.[13] They brought in tow, of course, the concomitant human suffering, the wages of gambling and drug addiction and prostitution. The Mafia flourished, and the Zwi Migdal continued to trade on the hopes of young Jewish girls of Slavic Europe, luring them to America with the promise of marriage and then installing them in one of the multitudinous brothels it controlled.[14]

Still and all, it must be borne in mind that this glittering city of jaded pleasures, the languid life of late nights and the tango, was that of only a small percentage of the population. Among the monied classes, there were those who never wandered into Corrientes' racier establishments, much less descended to the truly amoral precincts of El Bajo. The same was even truer of the self-consciously upstanding middle strata.[15] Certainly too, those sectors and the proletariat rarely if ever had either the funds or the leisure to take advantage of the *porteño* wild side. The typical worker's recreation during the era was much more likely to involve a visit to a neighborhood tavern, or a family outing to the zoo or the Isla Maciel on the far side of La Boca.[16] All-night revels were hardly practical for men and women who put in a five-and-a-half or six-day work week and had families to support.[17]

Too, in spite of its burgeoning population and widely varied culture, Buenos Aires oddly remained *la gran aldea*, "the great village."[18] It was a city of personal relationships, one where a job or an invitation or a publishing contract might still be had through the good offices of a friend or a friend's father or the friend of a friend. Pacing petitioners filled the Casa Rosada of Yrigoyen and Alvear, and the president of the republic not infrequently walked alone across the Plaza de Mayo to sip a demitasse at the Gran Café Tortoni.[19]

On some levels, the city seemed to wear its chic uneasily. *Porteño* boosterism was sometimes shrill, as if the Paris of the Americas might not be immediately recognized as such. The Spanish suggestion that Madrid was the "cultural meridian of the Hispanic world" brought howls from the banks of the Río de la Plata, the sort which belie that absolute self-assurance citizens of a world capital assume as birthright.[20] In Buenos Aires itself, aesthetic battles of the age were often rendered slightly absurd as opponents cast aspersions on one another's masculinity. There was a terror threading through the polemics of one's art being misconstrued as *fifí, amariconado*—"sissified." It was as if all wished to be considered radical but were uncomfortable with the sorts of accusations vanguardism seems inevitably to call forth, as if beneath the cosmopolitanism lurked the fear that it had been a mistake to abandon the simpler, more earthbound, "masculine" virtues which ostensibly formed part of the gaucho inheritance.[21]

The middle classes now comprised over a third of the economically active population.[22] Some shopped alongside the well-fixed at Harrod's and Gath y Chaves' on Calle Florida, or at the Tiendas San Miguel on Mitre. Others surely joined the working class in the vastly expanded commercial district in Once, where small businesses run by Jewish, Spanish, and Italian immigrants provided a less expensive center for shopping and entertainment.[23] It is out of this general area, out of the bars off Corrientes beyond Pueyrredón, that perhaps the most famous Argentine of the decade appeared: the immortal tango singer, Carlos Gardel.

In the twenties, more than two-thirds of the Argentine population was literate.[24] The press, both in Spanish and other European languages, continued booming, with the venerable *La Nación* and *La Prensa* confronting severe competition from such periodicals as Natalio Botana's *Crítica*. Publishing reflected the effects of a mass readership, and those one-time rebels of earlier generations—Lugones and Gálvez and Hugo Wast—saw their artistic leadership challenged, at first quietly, then ever more forcefully, by a new group of writers preaching a "new sensibility." These young artists were divided among themselves as to what such a "new sensibility" implied, but they were perfectly willing to do battle with one another and with the literary idols. In 1921, the "mural magazine" *Prisma* suddenly materialized, plastered on walls down the length of the Avenida Santa Fe in Palermo and Barrio Norte. In the literary contest sponsored by the newspaper *La Montaña*, four largely unknown writers swept the competition in fiction. Retrospectively, it has been recognized that the diverse group emerging in print in that period comprised the distinct artistic movement which we now know as "The Generation of 1922."

CHAPTER 4

The Movements

MARTIN FIERRO feels the absolute necessity of self-definition, and of showing all those able to understand that we find ourselves in the presence of a NEW sensibility and a NEW comprehension, that . . . presents us unimagined panoramas and new media and forms of expression.
—from the "Manifesto de *Martín Fierro*" (May 1924)

Claridad aspires to be a magazine whose pages reflect the restlessness of leftist thought in all its manifestations. We want to be nearer to the social struggle than to purely literary battles.
—From *Claridad,* Number 1 (July 1926)

SOUTH AND WEST of downtown Buenos Aires, the city spreads vast and seemingly infinite in a great, gray monotony. The river, the parks of Palermo, the luxury flats of Barrio Norte and mansions of Belgrano, the middle-class comfort of Villa del Parque—these all lie in the opposite direction. South of Calle Rivadavia— the "longest street in the world," the street that bisects the capital and stretches into the suburbs—are workers' homes, the stockyards, slaughter houses, heavy industry. The barrios here—Nueva Pompeya, Flores, Mataderos—all have their own major avenue, their shopping districts, their neighborhood clubs and pubs and loyalties. Of them all, perhaps one is the quintessential proletarian enclave. It is just beyond Once, at that point where Buenos Aires fans broadly across the endless pampa. It takes its name from its major thoroughfare: Boedo.

On this street, named for a representative to the Congress of Tucumán, a man named Lorenzo Raño had the printshop which, during the 1920s, would handle the business of a new publishing house called Claridad. Meanwhile, in one of those peculiar coincidences of history, on

Calle Tucumán itself were editorial offices of quite a different sort, those of the magazine *Martín Fierro*. In the very heart of the city, they were but steps away from what, in those years, was likely Buenos Aires' most famous street, one a mere dozen blocks in length which had enjoyed, like Fifth Avenue, a reputation first for fine houses and then for fine stores. Its tone was so rich that, until the Peronist era, men without jackets were not allowed on its sidewalks. This "street of elegance and good taste" is Calle Florida.[1]

Traditionally, the names of these two streets divide the Generation of 1922 into two antagonistic groups—Boedo, the champion of social change, the working class, and art at the service of the coming revolution; and Florida, the aesthetic vanguard, dedicated to art and its redefinition. Boedo's spiritual home, so the story goes, was Moscow; Florida's, Paris. One gets the impression of two armed camps, each glowering belligerantly across the city at the other.

This characterization, if convenient, is not quite accurate. While the pronouncements of both groups were noisy indeed (and grew increasingly fulsome as the decade progressed), it was initially a bit difficult to determine which of the young writers who broke into print in the first years of the 1920s belonged to which group. With some, such as Raúl and Enrique González Tuñón and Roberto Arlt, the problem of meaningful categorization remains to this day.[2] The assignment of an author to Boedo or Florida is sometimes more the result of whim than critical judgment, particularly in such polemical works as Leónidas Barletta's *Boedo y Florida: Una visión distinta*[3] or González Lanuza's *Los martinfierristas*. While sources of valuable material, these books seem in many ways written less to illuminate the history of Argentine literature than to settle scores thirty or forty years after the fact.

Nonetheless, it is equally incorrect to pretend that Boedo and Florida were, beyond the most superficial differences, interchangeable in membership and philosophy, a view promulgated ex post facto by Jorge Luis Borges and others.[4] As Argentina moved toward the debacle of 1930, the two groups did establish themselves as antagonistic, even if their constituents drank together, favorably reviewed one another's works, and published occasionally in each other's journals. Their conflicts were not conducted in private, nor was knowledge of them limited to the coteries of the vanguardist or leftist literati. Readers of *La Nación* and *Crítica*, of *La Vanguardia* and *La Razón*, were kept informed of the various polemics and panegyrics, and the issues and arguments raised in these interchanges were very real and indicated profoundly different approaches to life and art. If the members of one group maintained, in the end, an allegiance to those of the other, this perhaps arose from their common goal of the alteration of literature, of a rupture with the past, with the art and vision of preceding generations.[5] Where the form and function of the new art were concerned, however, their ideas were radically distinct.

Argentina in 1920 was ripe for a new aesthetic. Yrigoyen's presidency was more than half over, and the Semana Trágica had now illustrated the acceptable limits of social revolution. The University Reform had provided the young, particularly the students of La Plata and the capital, with a new sense of power, as well as a thirst for new ideas. Out of Europe, isolated first by war and subsequently by the first steps of recovery, news now arrived of burgeoning vanguard movements in literature and art. Up to this point, Argentina had remained virtually ignorant of such phenomena as futurism and cubism. Buenos Aires had enjoyed no Armory Show to serve as introduction to the Parisian new wave. There were cognoscenti, of course, but it was not really until the twenties that the pre-war movements, along with dadá and expressionism, first made an impact on the Argentine consciousness.[6]

The impetus for the "new generation" came initially from young intellectuals of the period, many of whom were associated with the Ateneo Universitario: Julio V. González, Abilio García y Mellid, Aníbal Ponce, Héctor Ripa Alberdi, José Gabriel, and Jorge Max Rohde.[7] These young men—some dilettantes, some destined for notable careers in criticism, none an artist of any great moment—formed salons, debated philosophy, aesthetics, and political theory, and, if none too radical in their ideas, prepared the soil for more innovative minds and talents.

One was not long in arriving. Jorge Luis Borges sailed into Buenos Aires harbor in 1920, his family's inadvertent European exile at an end.[8] Unwilling to chance the sea lanes to return home during the war, they had remained for five years on the continent, where their peregrinations brought them finally to Madrid. There the young Borges, already charged with vanguardist ideas absorbed elsewhere in his travels, embraced Spain's version of the new aesthetics: Ultraism.[9]

This movement, as preached by such Iberians as Rafael Casinos Assens and Ramón Gómez de la Serna, involved "the tenacious use of metaphor, the adoption of free verse, and the rejection of the auditory pleasures arising from rhyme."[10] The anecdotal and descriptive was displaced in favor of phenomenological experience—the succinct capturing of the thing in itself through metaphor. Emphasis was placed on "mental rigor and dignity," with the development of a "new lyric" stressing "the image, the *sententia*, the epithet, all strikingly concise."[11] The movement found its literary ancestors in Whitman and Rimbaud, its contemporary heroes such figures as Apollinaire, Cocteau and Reverdy, Valery Larbaud, and the Franco-Uruguayan Jules Supervielle.[12] Anathema to this "new sensibility" was *modernismo*, particularly as that school was supposedly personified in Leopoldo Lugones.

The emphasis of ultraism on concision naturally made it more applicable to poetry than to prose. Its adherents were thus largely devoted to verse, and its publications reflected that prejudice. González Lanuza sees this in broader terms, as something beyond mere intellectual predilection or the dictates of association with an aesthetic movement. For him, the group's preference for poetry arose from youth, from the desire to achieve the greatest force of feeling in the fewest words.[13] Prose was useful to these writers as a polemical medium, but poetry seemed the genre for the regeneration of art, to advance the idea that "every line, every stanza, should be the vehicle of surprise and an incontestable victory."[14]

In pursuit of such unmitigated triumphs, Borges, with his cousin Guillermo Juan (also surnamed Borges, although he usually omitted that name), Guillermo de Torre, and Eduardo González Lanuza, launched the "journal" *Prisma*, really a broadside. The text of the first issue (December 1921) consisted of a rabble-rousing manifesto by Borges, accompanied by some brief poems by Spanish ultraists. A second (and last) number appeared in March of 1922.[15] *Prisma* was followed by another, equally mortal periodical, *Proa*, which in its first incarnation emitted three issues. It remained a determinedly ultraist publication, though its circle of contributors widened somewhat to include Macedonio Fernández, Norah Lange, Roberto Ortelli, and the ill-fated Sergio Piñero. Norah Borges, sister of Jorge Luis, served as the artist for the group.[16]

Meanwhile, in the same month that *Prisma* appeared, *Nosotros* published an essay on ultraism by Borges ("the very young Argentine writer"), the movement's debut, as it were, in the national intellectual world.[17] This was followed, in September of 1922, by the appearance in the magazine of a brief ultraist anthology, featuring poems by Borges, Piñero, Lange, Ortelli, Guillermo Juan, and two women lost to literary history, Clotilde Luisi and Helena Martínez.[18] By the time of *Nosotros'* "Inquiry Concerning the New Literary Generation" (May–September 1923), it still seems that the ultraists remained the only recognizable group of writers in the city who were committed to a specific vanguardist aesthetic.[19] The critical circles gradually forming around Rohde on the one hand and Gabriel on the other exchanged some sterile snipes, and there was obviously a nucleus taking shape on the Left.[20] Many in the former groups had an interest in the appearance of a new journal out of the national university in La Plata, *Valoraciones*.[21] The "Inquiry" itself seems to have provided the impetus for yet another journal, *Inicial*.

The history of *Inicial* points up, in a number of ways, the kind of confusion and infighting to which the new generation was prone. Directed at first by Homero Guglielmini, Roberto Ortelli, Roberto Smith, and Alfredo Brandán Caraffa, the magazine appeared the month after the *Nosotros* series concluded, October of 1923. Whatever it may have lacked in coherence *Inicial* made up in shrillness. After a blunderbuss manifesto, in which the editors place themselves in opposition to (among other things) communism, Pan-Americanism, cynicism, and dilettantism, while affirming their belief in "life, love and truth," the first article, Brandán's "Pizzetti y el Dios único," seems an augury of a dismal future.[22] Departing from a commentary on Hildebrando Pizzetti (a composer who has since plummeted from obscurity into oblivion), Brandán undertakes a review of the civilization of the last few centuries, divisible into the forces of darkness (which are Jewish, capitalist, Puritan, Communist, Wagnerian, and centered in Moscow and New York) and those of light (Italo-French, Catholic, and anti-democratic, musically represented by Debussy and Beethoven, with capitals in Rome and Paris).[23] Precisely what one is to make of this mishmash is unclear, except perhaps to dismiss it as a bizarre attempt by an apparently intelligent young man to systematize, however absurdly, his prejudices of the moment. Its superficial erudition, its fantastic juxtapositions, and its baiting tone certainly had an effect. Along with the manifesto, the piece provided Bianchi with more than enough ammunition for his assault on *Inicial* in the next month's *Nosotros*.[24] González Lanuza was so appalled by it that, when Borges appeared with Brandán in tow for a lecture at a local Jewish center, he broke with the ultra group and remained estranged from Borges for years.[25]

Inicial remained strident, invoking in its second issue Spengler and Ortega y Gasset to justify itself and redoubling both its anti-Communism and anti-Semitism.[26] Nonetheless, the same issue carried articles by two figures associated with the Left, Santiago Ganduglia and Luis Emilio Soto, and in the section "Comentarios sobre la política," the editors asserted flatly that they were antifascist, applauding Mussolini only because, as Spengler had suggested, his government signified the bankruptcy of capitalism and parlimentary democracy.[27] In its third number, *Inicial* presented an article by Borges, insisting that the Jewish tradition is the carnal and sensitive one, and hence much more in tune with the new sensibility than the dominant rationalist, intellectual heritage of western Europe.[28]

Behind the scenes at *Inicial*, it seems there was a battle brewing, which exploded publically when Brandán Caraffa returned from a three-month sojourn in Europe. In April of 1925, *Inicial* number 5 hit the newsracks, listing an editorial board which included Raúl González Tuñón, Luis Emilio Soto, and Roberto Cugini, but neither Smith nor Guglielmini.[29]. This edition contains work by even more leftists, including a pillar of Boedo-in-formation, Alvaro Yunque (Arístides Gandolfi Herrero). The next month, yet another *Inicial* number 5 appeared, this with the original editorial board sans Brandán, and featuring, interestingly, an article by Elías Castelnuovo, Yunque's sometime companion and the authorial voice of Argentine anarchism.[30]

It was this latter *Inicial* which sired a line of descent. Brandán cut all ties with the publication, and by number 8 of the ten issues which comprise the complete collection of the journal, Guglielmini was identified as director, and the editors consisted of a safely nonleftist lot.[31]

An explanation for this brouhaha was never provided to *Inicial's* readers, but the falling out among the editors was apparently political. According to Brandán, the publication was, like most of its ilk, chronically short of money. Guglielmini, well-connected in the *porteño* Italian community, arrived at the office one day with a proposition which would have afforded the magazine financial security and even its own book publishing division. There was only one condition: that *Inicial* become an overtly fascist publication. Brandán refused, and though Ortelli and Smith supported Guglielmini in the battle over rights to the magazine's title and format, Brandán doubts either, particularly the latter, harbored much sympathy for Mussolini.[32] Both, in any case, soon left the board of *Inicial*.

Brandán Caraffa, meanwhile, moved on to another journal, the second incarnation of *Proa*, which appeared in August of 1924. Along with him at the helm were Jorge Luis Borges, Ricardo Güiraldes, and Pablo Rojas Paz, and among its regular contributors were many who had published in the renegade *Inicial* number 5. By this time, the two literary groups of Boedo and Florida had gelled. Indeed, the previous month, Roberto Mariani had fired the first salvo in what would become the polemic between the two in the weekly *Martín Fierro*.[33] *Proa* envisioned itself as a bridge between the two tendencies and to an extent was successful in its effort, even though its directors were all quite visibly men of Florida. Articles by Luis Emilio Soto and Mariani, César Tiempo (Israel Zeitlin) and Pablo Neruda were published alongside pieces by such conservative figures as Francisco Luis Bernárdez and the very young vanguardist, Eduardo Mallea. *Proa* scored some remarkable editorial coups: the first translation into Spanish of a selection from *Ulysses* (by

Borges), and the introduction of two fragments from a novel tentatively called *Vida puerca*, better known by its final title, *El juguete rabioso*.[34]

Florida produced other journals of note: the short-lived *Revista de América* and Xavier Boveda's *Síntesis*, which attempted to fill the void left by *Proa's* failure in the summer of 1926. Perhaps its most unique effort was the *Revista Oral*, which produced sixteen "issues"—oral readings or performances—most of them at the Royal Keller, a café just off the later-renowned corner of Corrientes y Esmeralda. Brainchild of the Peruvian poet Alberto Hidalgo, this sort of *tertulia* presented aloud polemic, poetry, and many of Florida's most outrageous satires: the "trials" of Leopoldo Lugones and Alberto Gerchunoff (neither of whom appeared to hear the arguments or verdicts); a party for Ernest Ansermet at which everyone wore false whiskers in honor of the well-bearded maestro; and a raucous reception for Marinetti, which ended with the chant:

> Non e vero che l'é morto Marinetti, Pun!
> Marinetti, Pun!
> Marinetti, Pun!

However, surely the journal which had the greatest currency and has remained in the public mind was that edited by Evar Méndez (Evaristo González): *Martín Fierro*.[36] This publication was conceived in the autumn of 1923, when the editor and writer Samuel Glusberg suggested the idea to Méndez. He, in turn, broached the subject with Oliverio Girondo, whose *Veinte poemas para ser leídos en el tranvía* had appeared in January of 1922. From this, over endless coffees and *copas* at La Cosechera on Avenida de Mayo and at the Richmond on Florida, the core of the group which founded *Martín Fierro* took shape: Pablo Rojas Paz, Ernesto Palacio, Conrado Nalé Roxlo, Luis Franco, and Cayetano Córdova Iturburu, plus, of course, Girondo and Méndez.[37]

In the summer of 1924, *Martín Fierro* threw down the gauntlet to the literary establishment with a flaming indictment of "anachronism and mimetism" in literature, of both *modernismo* and provincialism, offering instead a new vision of art and artist which seemed to borrow a bit from the Dadaists here and the Futurists there, a promise of an optimistic, honest, and outrageous assault on the dominant presumptions of Argentine letters and society.[38]

The self-imposed challenge was perhaps too great, and yet *Martín Fierro* did, over less than four years, present to its readers a literate and exciting commentary about the art of the age. If, at times, its satire was heavy-handed and its humor sophomoric, this at least demonstrated the risks that its contributors were willing to take. At its best, it provided some of the era's cleverest writing and most searching criticism. It was particularly strong in its consideration of the plastic arts and architecture, which to that date had elicited relatively stuffy commentary elsewhere, if any commentary at all.[39] *Martín Fierro* was one of the major vehicles for the development of an entire school of Argentine writers, and reflects accurately both their strengths and weaknesses.

That school, Florida, which embraced such diverse talents as Borges, Girondo, Güiraldes, Rojas Paz, and Bernárdez, had obviously long since grown beyond the ultraist mode. Indeed, almost immediately after the great debates sparked by Borges and company regarding the new sensibility, he and his colleagues began to move away from a number of the principles enunciated in *Prisma* and the first *Proa*. Neither of the premiere collections of vanguardist poetry—Borges' *Fervor de Buenos Aires* (1923) and Girondo's *Veinte Poemas*—can be considered strictly an ultraist work. Rather than poetry which stands as the unromanticized monument to the moment of its own creation, even this early work reflects a concern for the resonances of the image, a concern which emerges ever more strongly in the *poesía de arrabal* which became more and more typical of Florida in its later years. The search for a sort of local color, an unspoken awareness of history, gave the vanguardist poetry of the period an almost *costumbrista* cast and remains one of its most notable elements.[40]

Such eclecticism created a certain paradox within Florida itself, one apparent in the very title *Martín Fierro*. Hernández' hero represents, of course, the quintessence of *criollismo*, and yet the magazine's major talents prided themselves on their dedication to a "universalized" art, literature connected not with any nation or particular tradition but arising from the process of creation itself and associated with the regenerate postwar sensibility. For some on both the right and the left, this represented little more than another attempt to "Europeanize" the national literature.[41] And the tension between the universal and the specifically Argentine seemed to grow more problematic for Florida as well. To a greater and greater extent, the significant works of the group drew on Argentine history and traditions, a tendency obvious in Borges' 1925 *Luna de enfrente*, and perhaps climaxing in the most famous single product of Florida: *Don Segundo Sombra*.

A different but related division of heart in Florida is manifested in a specific issue: the response to Leopoldo Lugones. From the pages of the organ of Argentine respectability, *La Nación*, Lugones attacked and berated the young writers. They answered in kind, though Borges, Mastronardi, and González Lanuza all admitted that, in retrospect, their relationship with the older poet was very much two-sided.[42] On the one hand, as the nation's greatest exponent of *modernismo* and the determined defender of rhyme, Lugones had to be confronted, battled, and subdued. However, his genius was evident and, further, he himself had experimented in works from the early 1900s with metaphor, the keystone of ultraism. One member of Florida remarked: "The *cordobés* poet has influenced three generations. For our part, we admire him a great deal, but we have the obligation to be different."[43]

This ambivalence towards Lugones assumes broader significance when we consider what Lugones represented on other than an artistic plane during the 1920s. By that time, he had written the bulk of his memorable work and had turned his hand to other projects, most notably the exposition of a political vision so overtly fascistic that it was apparent even to his most ardent admirers. His tracts bristle with anti-Semitism, nationalism, and militarism. He preaches Argentine redemption with "the soldier, the artist, and the farmer" forming the phalanx.[44] Equality, he asserts, is "anti-natural and anti-scientific."[45] It is all there: a home-grown variant of Mussolini's corporate state, complete with xenophobia and imperial illusions. More disturbingly, Lugones hints at the sort of extreme repression associated not with Italian fascism but with the then still-nascent German variety.[46]

The vanguardists had had to defend themselves against charges of fascism (or, at least, philofascism) from the very first. *Inicial* had certainly provided grist for the mill, and as the Boedo group grew more and more defined, the attacks on Florida became more frequent and extreme. But the charges echoed not only from the organs of the Left. Bianchi had implied a political tilt in his early critique of the new sensibility, and in *Nosotros* in 1924, Juan Antonio Villodo made the charge outright that the editors of *Proa* (II) were Lugonian in aesthetics and fascistic in politics.[47] Borges felt compelled to reply both in *Nosotros* and also on the pages of *Proa*.[48] The vanguardists' admitted debt to futurism; their admiration for certain Italian writers associated with Mussolini (Marinetti, Pirandello, Malaparte); their own sometimes ill-thought-out attacks on liberal democracy, which, if disappointing, certainly seemed preferable to Black Shirts and neo-Roman pretensions—all these encouraged the kind of attacks which obviously caused the members of the group not only irritation but pain.[49] *Martín Fierro*, after jousting with its detractors briefly, simply proclaimed itself in its fourth issue determinedly apolitical, a stance which became even more solid after further assaults by the Left.[50]

As the decade waned, however, it became obvious that maintaining the distance between politics and art was not so simple, and perhaps not so desirable. In 1927, *Martín Fierro* ceased publication. While surely the increasing maturity and individuality of its contributors affected this occurrence, the immediate cause was the attempt by the Yrigoyenist Committee of Young Intellectuals, which included Borges, Raúl González Tuñón, and Leopoldo Marechal, to force the publication to endorse the UCR in the 1928 elections. Dissension over the point convinced Méndez, the editor, to close the journal.[51]

Perhaps one of the keys to the happiness of these last happy men was that the possibility (or at least the illusion of the possibility) of an art divorced from political reality still existed. The demise of *Martín Fierro* over precisely that issue certainly opens the question to debate. Across the city, of course, was that other group of writers whose vision of art and politics was diametrically opposed to that which prevailed on Florida. For the writers of Boedo, the two were not exclusive: they were inseparable.

Boedo lacks a seminal figure comparable to Borges. None of its eventual constituents arrived from Paris or Petrograd bearing news of artistic and intellectual ferment. Perhaps this was not necessary, for the group found inspiration more in political than aesthetic doctrines, and the former had long before had a foothold in Argentina. Anarchism came with Spanish and Italian workers; socialism, both Proudhonian and Marxist, had been significant if not powerful since the 1890s; Leninism appeared on the scene in 1920, when a faction of Justo's socialists joined the Third International.[52] Artistically, meanwhile, the group drew its models less from the "new sensibility" of postwar France and Germany than from the nineteenth-century masters of realism. Zola was obviously an influence, though Boedo demonstrated its greatest affection for the Russians: Tolstoi, Dostoyevski, Chekov, Gogol, Andreiev, and Gorki. Further, it claimed the inheritance of such Argentine writers as Almafuerte, Rafael Barret, and Juan Palazzo, those who earlier in the century had turned their attention to the plight of the underclass. Gálvez and Payró, and to a much lesser extent Wast, provided models as well, though all but Payró was ultimately rejected. In spite of the here-obvious difference in literary ancestry claimed by Boedo and Florida, it should not be forgotten that those of the latter group were well versed in the realist tradition, and that, for example, Boedo's Roberto Mariani was one of Argentina's most vociferous and dedicated partisans of Marcel Proust.[53]

Boedo's members were young, like Florida's, and just as "intelligent, noisy, audacious" as their compeers.[54] They also shared a similar though not identical class background, for the vast majority of the Generation of 1922, regardless of their allegiances, arose out of various sectors of the middle class.[55] Further, both groups were determined to wreak changes in the dominant culture. They differed, however, in that "those of Boedo wanted to transform the world and those of Florida were satisfied with transforming literature. The former were 'revolutionaries.' The latter, 'vanguardists.' "[56] Leónidas Barletta puts it even more succinctly: "Art for the Revolution" or "The revolution for Art."[57]

Such proclamations of radical intent must be seriously if not uncritically received. The young writers of the group certainly were sincere in their pronouncements. However, just as the ultraist rhetoric of the *vanguardia* did not prevent it from embracing the verse of almost every school which seemed vaguely avant-garde (and a good deal else besides), so Boedo's definition of what constituted the "revolutionary" was quite broad indeed. This is not surprising, for both internationally and especially in Argentina, the political left was in the midst of a profound redefinition and reorganization under the impact of the Russian revolution. A number of modern critics—Adolfo Prieto, David Viñas, and Carlos Giordano among them—have questioned the very description of Boedo's production as specifically "leftist" as the term is understood today, though it surely has influenced the development of "committed literature" since the 1920s.[58]

At the time, however, it did not seem so unusual to find socialists, Communists, undifferentiated Marxists, anarchists, Georgists, and plain reformists and idealists gathered together around the banner of revolution—all anxious for social change, inspired by the events in Petrograd and still affected enough by the last century to believe they might act somehow as the world's unelected legislators. Sectarian issues could be put aside in the hope that Bolshevism might not be limited to victory in one country, in spite of the disappointments in 1919 in Germany and Hungary. Such hopes began to fade as the decade progressed, as increased infighting in the group suggests, but the frustration was perhaps salved by the increasing definition of Boedo as a group and a literary force within the contemporary Argentine culture. Additionally, there seemed to be an increasing awareness, unadmitted surely, that the tradition of leftist politics in the nation was in the twenties so weak that the best that might be hoped for in the immediate future was "a literary leftism, not a social leftism."[59]

This desire for politically relevant and informed art obviously influenced Boedo's production, even on so basic a level as genre. Its muse, unlike Florida's, was prose. Just as ultraism's emphasis on concision and metaphor favored verse, the concerns of Boedo's members encouraged them to choose as their media novels and particularly short stories. Beyond the purely aesthetic advantages of fiction (the opportunity it offered for a more complete exposition of plot and, hence, of social conditions), the genre also seemed a sensible choice for its directness. These writers eschewed excessive literariness of language and experimentation with form, which might make their works inaccessible to the working class. In an era when writers like Joyce and Faulkner were only beginning to transform the novel, poetry seemed far more susceptible to such infirmities than prose.

Boedo's origins are obscure. Unlike Florida, it seems to have no agreed upon "official history," and various of its members recall the same events in wildly different ways. As with the other group, the intellectual and artistic ground for Boedo had been prepared by other writers, as well as by such events as Yrigoyen's election, World War I, and, here especially, the October Revolution. The expanding opposition press—the socialist *La Vanguardia* and anarchist *La Protesta*, joined by such unaffiliated progressive organs as *La Montaña* and *Nueva Era*—encouraged on their literary pages the political passions and the politically engaged art of various *porteño* writers. January 1919 brought the galvanizing experience of the Semana Trágica, while the 1918 exhibition of the self-proclaimed "Artistas del Pueblo"—Agustín Riganelli, Guillermo Facio Hebequer, Abraham Vigo, and others—provided an example for authors and poets of similar persuasions.[60] By the early 1920s, the central figures later associated with Boedo had begun to establish some personal contacts, though no group as such would emerge for another two or three years.[61]

The key event in Boedo's coalescence was probably the literary contest sponsored by the newspaper *La Montaña* in the summer of 1921–22. Castelnuovo, Barletta, Mariani, Yunque, and Lorenzo Stanchina—those who would later form the group's core—had all been publishing poetry, stories, and essays in various dailies during the previous year or so.[62] Nonetheless, they apparently did not make each other's acquaintance until after three of them—Castelnuovo, Barletta, and Mariani—won first, third and fourth places in *La Montaña*'s fiction competition.[63]

At this point, the sequence of events becomes quite murky. Castelnuovo, who in later years fell out with both Yunque and (violently) with Barletta, variously indicates that the initiators of Boedo were he and Barletta, brought together by Nicolás Olivari, or he and Stanchina, again with Olivari as the point of contact.[64] The latter, the *poet maudit* of the era, apparently the midwife of Boedo but later associated with Florida, was one of only two members of the left group-in-embryo questioned in the winter 1923 "Inquiry" of *Nosotros*. From his remarks, and those of the other proto-*boedista* polled, Stanchina, it appears that neither Barletta nor Castelnuovo, who are highly praised in both interviewees' responses, was particularly well known to a wider public.[65] Barletta, for his part, insists it was he who brought the group together, gradually drawing more and more newcomers into a circle developing at the print shop located at Boedo 837.[66]

It seems likely that in all these self-aggrandizing recollections there is a germ of truth. The "founding" of Boedo can probably be attributed to any one of its early central figures, depending on which perspective one takes and at what moment one decides that a network of friendships has gelled into a recognizable literary group. Olivari's testimony indicates that, by the winter of 1923 (more than a year after the *La Montaña* competition), he, Barletta, Castelnuovo, and Stanchina were friends, though he appears not to have yet met Enrique Amorim or Roberto Mariani.[67] Within a year of that, however, Mariani had been integrated into the circle, as indicated by the list of contributors to the short-lived publication *Extrema Izquierda*, which appeared only twice.[68] By that time, he had also presented his famous attack on Florida, "*Martín Fierro y yo*," in the magazine of the same name, accusing the editors of francophilia, a lack of commitment to a national literature, and softness before the reality of Lugones' fascism. Boedo was now assuming definite shape. Still and all, it seems that only after New Year 1925 did the last central figures of the group definitely align themselves with it. According to César Tiempo, he, along with Alvaro Yunque and Luis Emilio Soto, went to Castelnuovo's apartment at 11 Sadi Carnot (now Mario Bravo) to discuss literature and politics, from that day forward becoming some of Boedo's most dedicated and distinguished contributors.[69]

If there is a single figure who forged the writers of Boedo into a group to be reckoned with and helped them become, however briefly, the youngest and most serious bestsellers in the nation's history, it was a man whose own writing never transcended journalism. For Boedo, he was a combination of Evar Méndez and the booksellers Manuel Gleizer and Jacobo Samet, whose subsidy presses published the first texts by the young authors of Florida. In 1922, this labor reporter of *Crítica* hit upon the idea of a 15 × 21 cm. bound, two-column format, which would allow him to publish great classics of Western literature in low-priced pamphlets of thirty-two pages. On February 22 of that year, the first issue of *Los Pensadores* rolled off the presses. A new publisher, Antonio Zamora, was in business.[70]

In the years since, Zamora has become a controversial figure. According to Yunque, the most generous of Boedo's members, he was "a good merchant and a bad man," exploiting the writers he dealt with unmercifully.[71] Yet, it was Zamora's capitalist shrewdness which provided Boedo with two successive periodicals, one of which enjoyed a fifteen-year life span. His dedication to inexpensive editions had a profound impact upon other Argentine houses, and it won his authors a large and loyal public, including a significant proletarian and lower-middle-class audience, the very social element they sought to address. If the series of paperbacks on sexual hygiene he introduced during the twenties was, in effect, the closest to soft-core pornography he could get away with, it assured that the accounts would balance and allowed him to take risks on more serious efforts which other publishers would have rejected or gone bankrupt producing.[72] Of course, certain of those efforts did not sell badly. Editions of ten or twenty thousand copies were not unusual, this in an age when *El juguete rabioso* had an initial press run of one thousand, and *Don Segundo Sombra*, three hundred![73] "Clara Béter's" *Versos de una...* sold fifty thousand copies, likely still the best-selling book of serious verse in Argentine history.[74]

Zamora's *Los Pensadores* continued with the same format, appearing weekly for one hundred issues. He had, meanwhile, set up his book publishing venture, featuring two series, the aforementioned "sexology" texts and "Los Poetas," featuring new poets. The latter he codirected with Castelnuovo and the ill-fated Gustavo Riccio (d. 1926), indicating that, by 1924, Zamora and these two left writers were well acquainted.[75] The books emerging from the print shop on Boedo (the editorial offices were actually on the Avenida San Juan) appeared under the imprimatur of the "Editorial Claridad," the name taken from the "Clarité" group of Henri Barbusse and Romain Rolland in Paris, which the Argentine left greatly admired.[76]

In its one hundred and first number, *Los Pensadores* underwent a notable transformation. After a year and a half of reprints of Anatole France, Gorki, Tolstoi, Almafuerte, Knut Hamsun, and Lenin, among others, the journal now became one of "Art, Criticism and Literature." By this time (December 1, 1924), Boedo was a reality, and it was from the pages of the second incarnation of Zamora's magazine that the battle with Florida began to be waged in earnest. The publication ran twenty-one numbers before changing not its content but its title. After June 1926, it adopted the name of its publishing house: Claridad.[77]

Claridad suffered from the same ills which often affected the magazines of Florida, from *Inicial* to *Martín Fierro*. It too often shrieked. Its humor was frequently leaden or mere nastiness and macho posing. Its contributors, particularly Barletta, always seemed to be involved in a duel with someone, either of the opposite camp or of his own.[78] The publication often had to defend itself against accusations of favoritism toward one left group or another: Communist, socialist, anarchist.[79] Like *Martín Fierro*, it printed relatively little creative work, and it lacked the other journal's sophisticated graphics and printing. This last, of course, was no accident. *Claridad* had no particular desire to please the eye. Its function was to enlighten the masses.

For all its faults, it did provide an inexpensive and broad forum for the exchange of information and opinion of those on the left. The criticism of such contributors as J. Salas Subirat and Luis Emilio Soto was of exceptional quality, and the editors took seriously their responsibility to keep their readership informed of events of import not only in Argentina, but internationally as well. *Claridad* printed articles by Unamuno and Upton Sinclair, commented at length on Sacco and Vanzetti and the military coup in Chile, and reviewed contemporary literature and art for a large and progressive working-class audience.[80]

Boedo lacked a purely literary magazine like *Proa*, but much more significantly it had Zamora's Editorial Claridad. Before 1924, a few of these writers had managed to publish books: Mariani (*Las acequias y otros poemas* by the press run by *Nosotros* in 1921), Castelnuovo (*Tinieblas* by the Editorial Tognolini, 1923), as well as Amorim's *Amorim* and Barletta's *Canciones agrias* (1923 and 1924, respectively). With the establishment of the series "Los Nuevos," however, Claridad opened its doors not only to the verse but to the prose of its young "thinkers." In four years, the house published ten books, two of poetry, eight of fiction, in inexpensive editions which provided writers like Mariani, Barletta, Stanchina, and Alberto Pineta with a mass public they had only dreamed of.[81]

In the glory days of the Generation of 1922, 1924–28, Boedo produced one other journal of note, *La campana de palo*, which had two incarnations: June to December, 1925, and September 1926 to October 1927.[82] Founded by two journalists, Carlo Giambiaggi and Alfredo Chiabra Acosta, *La campana de palo*, like *Proa*, attempted to bridge the gap which existed between the two artistic tendencies of the era, going to great lengths to deny its connection with Boedo.[83] Nonetheless, in both perspective and its list of contributors, it was unquestionably aligned with the young left. Mariani, Riccio, and Yunque, particularly the latter two, were active in the journal, though their exact contribution is difficult to measure, given that articles and reviews often appeared anonymously. *La campana de palo* strove for a certain tone in its pieces, less aggressive than *Claridad,* less boisterous than *Martín Fierro*. It represented "a serious expression of intellectual maturity," a kind of even-handedness and complexity of thought too often lost in the fireworks of the other publications.[84] This is well illustrated by Yunque's attack on Pablo Rojas Paz's review in *Crítica* of Antonio Gil's *Cielo de Algibe*. In his article, Yunque uses the poetic practice (as opposed to the stated aesthetics) of Rojas Paz's co-Floridian, Borges, to illustrate how the *martinfierristas* rejected in their criticism what they employed in their own poetry. It is a well-honed argument and one which, in passing, registers Yunque's admiration for many of Borges' efforts.[85]

Yunque's essay provides an essential reminder as regards the Generation of 1922. The two groups may seem unalterably opposed, their self-defined differences tremendous. Boedo was radical in politics and relatively traditional in aesthetics; Florida was the opposite. Boedo was the *arrabal:* the outskirts, the workers' neighborhoods. Florida represented downtown, Barrio Norte, Palermo. Boedo favored prose; Florida, poetry. Boedo read *La Protesta* and *La Vanguardia;* Florida, *Crítica* and even *La Nación*. Yet, under all the thunder—much of it from sincere disagreement, some from an overabundance of energy and youthful hypersensitivity—the constituents of both groups shared a common vision of revolt against the old, a commitment to change. They could, even publicly, admire each other's efforts and cede supremacy to one another in certain areas.[86] On the neutral ground of certain cafés—the Tortoni and La Cosechera downtown, La Perla near the Plaza Once—they drank and chatted and listened to one another's opinions, or, more formally, to one another's lectures. In subsequent years, as youthful friendships faded, members of each group found themselves in close contact with men who, at twenty-five, they had berated as representatives of the worst politics and aesthetics imaginable.

But here, the subsequent history of the Generation of 1922 is not our concern. Rather, we will turn to the works by authors of both Florida and Boedo, produced in the years of the greatest significance and optimism for both—the mid-1920s. Out of this investigation, perhaps the strengths, weaknesses, and most especially the paradoxes of the individual authors and the movements they represent will become apparent, and will allow us to speak with greater specificity of that peculiar decade of happy men.

The Writers

TURNING FINALLY from history and literary heritage, publications, and personalities to the actual work of the Generation of 1922, one faces a daunting task. The sheer volume of production of these young writers is impressive. Borges in the decade of the 1920s published three volumes of poetry and two of essays; Mariani, three of short stories and one of poetry; Norah Lange, two collections of poems and a novel; Barletta, two books of stories, one of verse, and four novels; and so on down the list. In addition, these authors were contributing book, music, and theater reviews, political and philosophical analyses, literary criticism, translations, and creative pieces never anthologized to their publications of choice. Most of them were simultaneously working full time in a variety of jobs: Arlt as a journalist, González Lanuza as an industrial chemist, Barletta as a customs expediter, Castelnuovo in a linotype shop, and Mariani in the office. Their energy seems to have been nearly inexhaustible. Selecting which examples of this tremendous creative outpouring to analyze requires some organizing principle.

A first, albeit perhaps draconian, measure is to limit our attention to prose. While such a step can perhaps be defended on the basis of a critic's personal preferences or expertise, there are more fundamental reasons for emphasizing the decade's fiction over its verse. In the first place, in spite of the vast amount of poetry turned out by both Boedo and Florida, the Generation of 1922 produced no monumental work in that genre. There is no watershed book like *Lunario sentimental*, much less a *The Waste Land*, dividing poetry which precedes it and that which follows. There is no Darío or Neruda to transform inalterably the poetic landscape. Ironically, though poetry was what the new generation spent most of its polemical energy arguing about, it was in prose that its most significant works appeared. The roots of *Fervor de Buenos Aires* and *Veinte poemas*, of *Versos de la calle* and *Un poeta en la ciudad* can be found finally in

45

Lugones, Carriego, Almafuerte, and Calou, in the young Güiraldes, in the *posmodernistas* and symbolists of the decades 1900–1920.[1]

It is not that the young poets added nothing. To the contrary, their determined emphasis on the importance of free verse and metaphor strengthened and finally legitimated the break from rhyme and anecdote necessary to propel the national poetry into the new century. The stress on modern life, modern technology, and the modern metropolis reflected accurately the national transformation Liberalism had wrought, and swept away the last cobwebbed swans and mythic heroes who had still had a place in the preceding decade. However, this impulse was already there and had been accumulating force before the new generation arrived on the scene. Ultraism, in the end, was less a sharp break with the past than a banner around which young poets, regardless of aesthetic philosophy, could muster. In terms of influence, ultraism burned out very quickly. Borges, its champion, had abandoned any strict adherence to it by 1923. González Lanuza did his best to produce an ultraist book with his poetry in *Prismas* (1924), but soon left the philosophy behind in his verse and, as Guillermo Ara has pointed out, probably produced a more realized ultraist book in his prose *Aquelarre*.[2] In general, the poetry of the age is intimate, highly influenced by the subjective consciousness, personal obsessions, and eccentricities of the poets in a way that the prose is not.

In fiction, conversely, there appeared works distinct from any that had come before. If Argentine readers were familiar through translations with Gogol, no writer in Buenos Aires had employed office workers and petty bureaucrats as the dramatic center of a work of fiction until Mariani wrote *Cuentos de la oficina*. *Aquelarre* was a departure from anything extant in the national canon. *El juguete rabioso*, with its raw presentation of the anomie of urban petit bourgeois youth, broke radically with the traditional *Bildungsroman*, while *Don Segundo Sombra* represents the epitome of the gauchesque, the quintessentially Argentine subgenre.

The ascendancy of prose should not surprise us, for Liberal Argentina perhaps always esteemed fiction over poetry. After Hernández, only Lugones was able to sustain a reputation for greatness primarily on his poetic achievements. For the rest, the Generation of 1880 was one of novelists, and Lugones' most famous contemporaries achieved renown not in verse but prose: Gálvez, Gerchunoff, and Quiroga in fiction, Ricardo Rojas in the essay. Some poets, Rafael Obligado for example, are remembered for a particular work, but most of those prominent earlier in the century were already gathering dust by the 1920s. There is a lyric tradition in Argentina, but it has, for one hundred years, almost always played second fiddle to fiction, which is, of course, the modern genre. Fiction is the response to industrialization, mass literacy, urban agglomeration, and the incredible complexity and nuance of contemporary life. It is the genre of social interaction more than the individual consciousness. The Boedistas emphasized it almost from the first. Mariani and Barletta first published as poets but turned immediately to prose. Yunque steered a middle course, while César Tiempo varied his later output, producing criticism and screenplays. The most original and determined of Boedo's poets, Olivari, soon sought refuge in Florida. Even there the vogue of poetry was fleeting. Those members of the group who retained the most powerful literary presence after the end of the decade—Borges, Martínez Estrada, Marechal—did so with prose.[3]

From 1880 to 1920, the fictional tradition of Argentina was largely novelistic, whereas the writers of '22 heavily favored the short story. In the tens and the teens, only one writer, Quiroga, carved his niche in literary history with the story. The young writers' preference for it is a consequence of various factors. First, as González Lanuza points out as regards poetry, the short story was the logical form for young men in a hurry. These were writers out to change art at least and the world at most, and the story was undeniably a "faster" form—more quickly written, more quickly consumed, more quickly improved upon and superceded—than the novel. In the midst of developing an aesthetic vision or a world revolution, who had time to devote three or four years to the production of a long, unified artistic whole?

Güiraldes did, but he, of course, enjoyed both maturity and the leisure his status as oligarch afforded him. As we have seen, the vast majority of these authors were punching time clocks of one kind or another. The novel emerges most easily when one can count on consistent periods of uncluttered hours to ponder out the complexities of plot and character, but a story can emerge whole in an evening and certainly in the space of a few weeks. For individuals as busy as these were—polemicizing, reviewing, editing, publishing magazines, holding forth in literary klatches, all while earning their livelihoods somewhere else—the short story was both an ideal and an unsurprising choice.

For Boedo, there was as well the ideological reason noted earlier. Written for a mass audience, one with limited free time and likely to be intimidated by the girth of a novel, the story provided the perfect medium. Its affords the opportunity for the exposition of a single, ideologically informed message, which the novel discourages by the multiple developmental demands inherent in its length. Boedo's readership was one that wished to be instructed and whom the authors wished to instruct. Both the producers and consumers of this literature were largely first- or second-generation immigrants, in the majority descended either from peasants, mostly Spanish or Italian, or ghettoized Jews.[4] In the former case, their heritage was the oral tradition of largely illiterate people, that of folk tales and ballads which served purposes both of entertainment and enlightenment. The Jewish tradition of the moral parable, meanwhile, is well known and was surely almost as hearty in the Once district in the 1920s as in Odessa a generation before.

The short story's speed of composition and sale had yet other appeals for this generation. For the most part, their labors were badly paid for if paid for at all. Simply to finance their artistic trade, a rapid turnover of material was necessary. *La Vanguardia* or *Crítica* was unlikely to gamble on a serialized novel by a relatively untested author, but one who could deliver a short story a month, particularly someone willing to publish pseudonymously from time to time, was welcome. The 1920s themselves made demands of writers. A self-defined revolutionary age, one enchanted with speed and motion, one worshipping the new (the automobile, the phonograph, the movies), the era wanted new faces, new ideas, new stories. This was perhaps a doubly powerful force in Argentina, so full of bravado, so determinedly at the threshold of greatness, that "cultural meridian of the Hispanic world."

And it was here that young men like Arlt and Mariani, González Tuñón and González Lanuza might make their marks. Boys from the petit bourgeoisie and the proletariat, children of those immigrants who had come to make a better life for themselves and their children, they would of course favor a genre which kept them in the public eye, in print. Inevitably scourged by a terror of failure, powered by the twin engines of class and ethnicity, anxious to have a part in creating a new culture in a nation still enamored of Liberal progress—no wonder they should be concerned with the amount of time necessary to move a work from concept to manuscript to press. Just like their contemporaries laboring away in the medical and law schools, those hoping to advance from stockboy to cashier, from laborer to foreman, these were men out to *hacerse la América,* and often, over the fury of their polemics, one can hear the steady whir of personal ambitions.

The six works discussed hereafter constitute a representative sample of the prose of the young generation. González Lanuza's ultraist *Aquelarre* is perhaps Florida's purest vanguardist work, while Mallea's *Cuentos para una inglesa desesperada* well captures the tension within Florida between its cosmopolitan and nationalist tendencies. With Enrique González Tuñón's *Tangos* we move into that frontier between the two groups inhabited by such writers as Enrique's brother, Raúl, Santiago Ganduglia, and Nicolás Olivari.

Castelnuovo's *Tinieblas* provides a crash course in Boedo's strains of almost mystical anarchism and tremendism, while Yunque's *Ta-Te-Ti,* a text intended for adolescents, demonstrates the didactic element so strong in much of the leftist prose. Finally, Barletta's *Royal Circo* lights the way towards a committed fiction both more subtle and supple, providing entrance into the subsequent discussion of three transcendent works of the decade: *Cuentos de la oficina, El juguete rabioso,* and *Don Segundo Sombra.*

Eduardo González Lanuza, the Spanish-born brewery chemist, was one of the essential vanguardists of the twenties. He contributed freely of his time and talent to *Prisma, Proa,* and *Martín Fierro.* Outspoken, intensely dedicated to principle, he elicited respect from both friends and rivals. After a politicized youth, he embraced ultraism early on and took it to its poetic limits in *Prismas* in 1924. He occasionally ventured into prose in his career, mostly in the essay. However, in 1927, *Aquelarre* appeared, a collection of stories representing perhaps the most successful vanguardist attempt at fiction.

The book begins with a prologue fascinating both in its content and its rhetoric. González Lanuza describes his work as *"cuentos imajinados en imájines"* ("stories imagined in images"), presenting a world of the "unthought of," not of the "impossible" but the "apossible."[5] They place the reader in "another universe distinct from his own," connecting, by means of images, "each emotional point of the new world with a similar point in the quotidian one." The tales are magical. One involves the "Landscape Shepherd" who is worshipped by everything—chairs, puddles, lightpoles, trains; the "above" and the "below"—but is eventually destroyed by them for his failure to act the part of an assertive god. Another tells of a conspiracy against one individual, who finds that all mirrors and shop windows and lakes refuse to reflect him. In spite of such fantasy, all the stories are somehow tied with everyday reality. The most delightful and frightening aspect of González Lanuza's fiction is its determined use of the most mundane objects, which suddenly take on characteristics not properly their own.

After a spirited, predictable, and, from a contemporary vantage, rather silly insistence that while these are "fantasy stories," they do not represent a "sissified sensibility," González Lanuza asserts that "there is no sociologism in my stories."[6] The declaration's intent is clear: to separate the author from an "activist" aesthetic, specifically that of Boedo. Nonetheless, his determined denial that his work sustains "any philosophical or ethical idea, or any type of curiosity beyond the literary" smacks of a certain self-doubt or a certain awareness of self-delusion. The pieces, of course, do not betray any influence of a Jack London–like naturalism or Dostoyevskian psychological depth. Their overt connection to the society of González Lanuza is minimal, apparent only in their use of quotidian objects and events. On a deeper level, however, they are quite obviously linked with a particular historical moment in a way much more significant than their originality, their "newness."

González Lanuza's concern in all the tales is largely metaphysical.[7] Might not his interest in the breaking of the universal laws, in the creation of a world in which things do not behave as they are supposed to, arise from the postwar response to the collapse of the nineteenth-century worldview? If the supposedly immutable laws of human progress could be so seriously shaken by the carnage at Verdun and the Somme; if suddenly physics, that most orderly of sciences, was afflicted by relativity, then why should anything be accepted as "given"? Might not one of us wake up some fine day confronted with an image in the mirror not our own, or no image at all, simply because mirrors in general had taken it upon themselves not to do what they are supposed to do? Might not someone else, like the narrator of "El alba de Dios," meet a man tomorrow who claims his essence wanders from body to body and discover some months later that this wandering soul is inhabiting him?

González Lanuza's ontological panic—the confrontation with that most fundamental of questions: Am I, was I, will I be who I at this moment think I am—is one very central to the twenties, the beginning of this age we call modern. The implications of this issue were perhaps even more significant to Argentines of the time, most so recently arrived in their new land, and even more apparent to this author than to most of his contemporaries due to his personal memory of the immigratory experience. He was nine, after all, when he ceased to be Spanish and became Argentine. His identity changed. He had been one thing, then became something else. Such a childhood awareness of the possibility of change, intensified by a general consciousness of mutability as a consequence of the First World War, perhaps helps explain the tenor of *Aquelarre*, and puts in question its independence from philosophical, ethical, or social concerns.

In their metaphysical musings, the stories presage later works by such writers as Bioy-Casares and Borges, particularly such quasi-Berkeleyian meditations as "Las ruinas circulares." Less evidently, they speak of an element central to the fiction of the decade: the evocation of loneliness and isolation. In González Lanuza, characters rarely interact. They seem oddly *in vitro*, suddenly alone in a world that is still whole but frighteningly unpopulated—by humankind, at least. This focus upon the single man is altered only superficially in "El final," the last story. There, society is seen in terms of a great, gray mass, as a community robbed of individuals, forming instead a vast amoeba awaiting some sort of apocalypse. At the story's conclusion, González Lanuza's metaphysical obsession and preferred symbol are united in his rendition of the eschatological end:

> It was the definitive rupture. Hope's cohesion having failed, the multitude suddenly collapsed, dead, blown apart, shredding reality, that single reality of millions of contradictory and confused realities, its murmur crumbling in a million cries.
>   It was as if god's mirror had fallen from his hands, and he could never again contemplate the immensity of his face.

The name of Eduardo Mallea is usually not connected with the Generation of 1922. It was only in 1932 that his first major work, *Historia de una pasión argentina,* made its appearance. Nevertheless, Mallea associated with the circle around *Proa* and *Martín Fierro* in the mid-1920s and produced during that period an almost forgotten work, *Cuentos para una inglesa desesperada.* Written when the author was only twenty-three, the book well illustrates those contradictions which afflicted the *grupo de Florida,* emerging strikingly in something so basic as the counterpoint of the stories themselves. The first, third, and fifth transpire unmistakably in the oligarchical milieu of the 1920s, the world of the *cocktailería, estancias,* and trips to Europe. The second and fourth, on the other hand, share a mythic time and place, set in some undefined era in the vast Argentine outback bordering the sea.

This is somewhat to be anticipated in view of Mallea's own background. Though not a scion of the ruling class, his upbringing was a comfortable one. Mallea's father, an old Mitrista and successful surgeon, encouraged the intellectual and artistic ambitions of his son even when the boy was small. Mallea's childhood and youth, however, were spent not in the cosmopolitan capital but in Bahía Blanca, the burgeoning and still raw port city on the underbelly of Buenos Aires province. Only in 1916, when Eduardo was fourteen, did the family abandon the seacoast to set up housekeeping in the Federal District. Hence, he brought with him the memory of that "other Argentina" so often forgotten, overlooked, or ignored in Buenos Aires. After a brief and unsuccessful career in law school, Mallea joined the staff of *La Nación* (the Mitres' paper) and soon became acquainted with the *porteño* vanguardists.

The division of the short stories of his first collection into two such distinct categories reflects, of course, not only the dualism of Mallea's own background, but the schizophrenia of Florida itself. In their public pronouncements, these writers associated themselves with contemporary international culture, with bohemianism and its relaxed sexual morality and fascination with the new. A story like "Arabella y yo" well illustrates this aspect of Florida's vision. The text is laced with anglicisms, with the ennui which comes of wealth and position, and with a languid sensuality bespeaking the postwar moral liberation. The narrator, Virgilio, speaks of "courts de tennis," of ukeleles, of pennants from Yale and Oxford. The tearoom at Harrod's, the country house, and *Cosmopolitan* emerge in the same breath as the war, neurasthenics, and "five suicides dredged from the waters of the public bathing beach."[8] And then there is the object of Virgilio's affection—Arabella: "inconsistent, blonde, insufferable, proud, snobbish, minimally instructed in geography, not at all in history, and rather too much in French." Recently rejected by her lover, Axel, a poet and Virgilio's best friend, she has come to ask the latter to intercede for her. His obviously slavish attraction to her, however, convinces her that she just might see if "I can, by chance, fall in love with you."

The dominant impressions and metaphors of the three *porteño* stories are of exhaustion and loneliness. "I am tired, hollow," Virgilio tells us in the book's first line. "Sonata de soledad" ends with the narrator contemplative on the sofa, "on the edge of all the activity, his passions restrained, even those never loosed." "Cynthia" describes the desultory affairs of various men with a vivacious and madcap Danish woman. Mallea's aristocratic story-tellers are dreamers, constantly envisioning never-to-be undertaken journeys to Hawaii, Venice, the Great Wall of China. Through all of them and their tales runs a thread of luxurious desolation and the threat of some dark paralysis. They are sensitive men, filled with passionate desires which they know will remain unfulfilled. In their stasis and boredom they contrast sharply with the central characters of the two rural stories, "El capitán" and "Neel." The first evokes an almost bardic figure, a former mariner known to all in a small town who spins yarns each afternoon on the plaza. The second is a love story, that of an elopement aborted by Neel's unwillingness to abandon her home and father for life with the enamored Rabel. Both the captain and the lovers are vibrant and intense, and their stories reveal a strength obviously lacking in the europeanized aristocrats of the other tales.

This bipolarity casts into relief that central paradox of Florida—its nationalistic cultural cosmopolitanism: an allegiance to a "new sensibility" born in Europe, coupled with an increasingly powerful attraction to the ostensibly solid virtues of the *criollo*, of the noncosmopolitan world, of the *barbarie* emblemized by that literary character from whom their magazine took its name. In *Cuentos para una inglesa desesperada*, this tension is particularly apparent due to the obvious differences in the two types of stories presented. The dualism connects, of course, to the disjunctures within Argentina itself in the 1920s, disjunctures becoming increasingly serious as the decade progressed and visible in such phenomena as the split in the UCR and the vociferous traditionalism and xenophobia of Lugones, the proto-fascist *Liga Patriotica*, and others of their kind.

There is a sixth story. "Seís poemas a Georgia," with the epigraph "Al margen de Charlie Chaplin," retells the story of the 1925 film *The Gold Rush*. In so doing, it evokes perhaps most powerfully of all the tales that world of the twenties, employing one of its most durable symbols, Chaplin's Little Tramp. Quite significantly, however, Mallea closes the action not with Chaplin's final triumphal winning of Georgia's love, but at the point

> the little man, utterly outside himself . . . delivered over to "her," inhuman, dehumanized, begins the dance of the forks, the dance of the bread, that merry confession of the essense of love.
> Solitary confession.
> Georgia, uncapturable. Pitiless Georgia.
> Feminine Georgia.

While Chaplin dreams of the dinner he has set but not shared, we find outselves suddenly back in the bar where Georgia dances, captivating every man and woman, captivating the wind itself—beautiful, omnipotent, and very frightening.[9]

Mallea, even at twenty-three, was not a careless writer. His prose version of one of Chaplin's greatest films, a version consciously truncated, serves to reemphasize the spirit which, despite their differences, runs through all the tales. If the characters of the pampas seem stronger and more determined than the wealthy decadents of the city, they are vanquished just the same. The Captain ends mad; Rabel waits futilely for Neel to elope with him. Mallea's heroes emerge finally as impotent: prisoners of unattainable desires, confined to sickbeds, alone and asleep—all defeated. We may wonder if, on some level, this despairing vision arose not only from private concerns of the author but from the national reality itself, from a vague sense of some vast, impending failure. Perhaps 1925 is too early a date to postulate as one when Mallea felt his society in peril. Yet retrospectively it invites speculation. It must have been disquieting then, as it is disquieting now, to confront such elegantly written tales which echo themes of weakness, fear, and humiliation.

Enrique González Tuñón was not an easy man to classify.

> Lean, with loyal, searching eyes, longheaded and pale . . . he preferred to surround himself with con men and ragpickers, sleep in horrific hotels when he had a peso in his pocket for a bed, or if not on a bench in one of the plazas. He liked to sing *Tosca* in the most unlikely diners, visit the pawnshops where they trafficked in dead men's clothes, and mercilessly, to dream in the back of some dive— like some hermit possessed—of glory made woman or vice versa.[10]

Tubercular, uninhibited, a journalist for the often-sensationalist *Crítica*, he has been identified as a member of both Boedo and Florida, as one of those talents who seems to bridge the two groups or belongs in some category completely his own. Associated eventually with the Argentine Communist Party, his politics were nonetheless more those of a "romantic and messianic anarchist."[11] Stylistically, his works seem tied to Florida. They are full of experimentation—complex imagery, oblique narration, a difficult vocabulary. In their subjects, however, they are very much related to the realism of Boedo and that group's fascination with the seamier side of *porteño* life.[12] González Tuñón had little concern for sparing his readers' sensibilities, as a description of his work of 1932, *Camas desde un peso*, indicates: "Solitude, unemployment, prostitution, tuberculosis and even exhibitionistic masochism . . . do not prevent the stories' . . . achieving artistry on the strength of their humanitarianism and tenderness." [13]

This mixture of realism and profound compassion emerges from the very first in González Tuñón's canon, in his 1926 publication, *Tangos*. These twenty-two stories take their titles and much of their action from the popular song genre.[14] Betrayal in love, the code of honor of the

arrabales, murdered lovers and romantic rivals, the bleakness of proletarian life, the fate of the working girl turned prostitute—these are the
themes González Tuñón presents. Not surprisingly, the book suffers from
time to time from some of the same defects as the tango itself—a certain
repetitiousness, a tendency towards sentimentality. In general, however,
the author succeeded in producing a text that is simultaneously entertaining, experimental, nationalistic, universal in appeal, and peculiarly political.

The stories are oddly structured, divided into sections between
three and four pages in length, if that, a narrative technique based, it
seems, in the tango's stanzaic form. In prose, this stylistic idiosyncrasy
often saves material from becoming predictable or lachrymose. The reader
is always slightly off guard and somewhat distanced from the characters
and the action. We see the men and women of the stories come and go,
hear them speak, watch them get on the bus, all disjointedly, so that at
story's end we feel almost as if we have heard a fragment of gossip about
some vague acquaintance, seen some familiar face in passing, but the
details of the anecdote, the story behind the face, must be partially
provided by our own imaginings.

For the foreign reader as well as for many Argentines the book
presents definite linguistic difficulties. González Tuñón delighted in the
lunfardo, the *porteño* argot mixing native expressions, Spanish, and various European languages together with underworld slang. He also had a
good ear for the deformations of Spanish by the city's various immigrant
groups. Thus, the denizens of La Boca, of La Cortada, of Las Heras, speak
in *Tangos* in the dialect natural to them: "Naide lo sabía. Ni ella
mesma. . . . Aura vos sos el único."[15]

Such language, realistic and yet highly poetic, invites us to consider
the peculiar duality which characterizes the subject matter of *Tangos*. In
the stories, González Tuñón captures the exigencies and grim monotony
of proletarian life. The omnipresence of illness and death, the sameness of
the daily ride to and from work on the *colectivo*, the poor meals, the
endless children, the gray existence of the *arrabal* broken only by the
pleasures of liquor and love—these are central to the book. For most,
there is no escape. A few may dream over their Kropotkin of a paradise
free of exploitation; others may seek diversion in "a wake, a baptism or a
workers' picnic on the Isla Maciel." The young women, the beautiful
ones, may look for excitement and some material comforts in prostitution.
If lucky, they will find a wealthy lover on the Calle Maipú who will set
them up in a room with a telephone and a private bath. There are risks, of
course—the chance that no lover will appear or that his affection will

prove fickle. Perhaps the young girl will end up like "Rulitos," dying in a cocained dream. But perhaps not. There is Regina from La Cortada, after all, who finds "downtown was hers. She had conquered it with the proletarian beauty of her eighteen years." Given the choice of a laborer's life, grinding her youth and beauty away in a factory, or living instead "on the edge of the abyss," she has little trouble choosing the preferable course.

Coupled with the gloomy reality of the workers' existence, however, there is in González Tuñón a tendency toward idealization. The lives of many of his characters seem charged with a terrific intensity, filled with crises and passion and sudden violence which lend them an aura of romance. His whores and workers and barflies become interesting, pathetic, or tragic, closer to elemental experience than the petit bourgeois readers who formed the bulk of González Tuñón's audience. Hence, *Tangos* oddly presages certain later Argentine works, particularly the *historias de arrabal* of Borges, with their suggestion that in the urban ghettos life maintains a certain authenticity, that there the semifeudal ethic of the *culto de coraje* still holds sway.

Still, even with their "mythic" quality, González Tuñón's creations in many ways possess a greater realism than do those of certain writers of Boedo. Free of the need to uphold a particular political position, his stories do not suffer the problem of those of more overtly leftist authors, who create workers of otherworldly wit, insight, or virtue. Beyond this, it can be argued that the very inspiration of Gonzalez Tuñón's tales—the tango—predisposed him toward mythification. Set in the bar, the street, and the home rather than the factory, concentrating on those moments of most evident universality in the human experience, told obliquely in such evocative language, tied inextricably to a popular genre which throve on the transformation of incident into legend, *Tangos* inevitably represents an aesthetic distinct from that of other, more determinedly "proletarian" works.

Still, the choice of that aesthetic was, in large part, the author's. González Tuñón wrote what is ultimately a bohemian book, one of experience twice transformed, first by the creators of the tango, then by the artistic consciousness of a petit bourgeois journalist enamored of an urban folk form become national institution. The author well represents certain elements of his class, many of them intellectuals in the 1920s. Possessed of a political vision already oddly anachronistic, though progressive and utopian in doctrine, González Tuñón still felt comfortable spinning stories which affirm the life of the underclass according to the fantasies and ideals of the dominant ideology, and he made no attempt to indicate either the social and economic structures which created urban suffering nor how such conditions might be overcome. From our vantage, then, he stands with Florida rather than Boedo, a vanguardist rather than a "revolutionary," though, as will become apparent, a spoken allegiance to *un arte izquierdista* did not necessarily imply a more politically progressive result.

"The Argentine Gorky," Manuel Gálvez proclaimed him. Payró and Quiroga, along with the nation's leading socialist intellectual, José Ingenieros, did him homage. A Premio Municipal for fiction was conferred upon him in 1923, and the newspaper *La Internacional* called his book "the first serious attempt at proletarian literature that has come to light in South America."[16]

The object of these panegyrics was the thirty-year-old Elías Castelnuovo, a Uruguayan resettled in Buenos Aires. He wrote in the evenings and during any other free time away from a long series of jobs. He seemed the perfect representative of the new, leftist aesthetic—the son of immigrants, an autodidact raised in appalling poverty, a laborer who wrote of the disinherited in a language "rough and naked which initially seemed disconcerting, barbarous."[17] One of the founders of Boedo, he was influential in the 1920s in determining the course of the group. He tended to his own writing chores while acting as an editor at Claridad appraising manuscripts, among them that of an unknown *porteño* named Roberto Arlt.

By 1941, when Claridad reissued the book which had brought such fame to Castelnuovo, its star had faded considerably on the left. His editors took pains to point out that, in 1923, "there did not exist the ideological clarity which exists today." Argentina's first example of proletarian literature, it seems, had not proved particularly durable. Nonetheless, Claridad attempted to emphasize that "the emotional and aesthetic" merit of Castelnuovo's effort, the short stories of *Tinieblas*, could not be questioned.[18]

Tinieblas is an anarchist book, product of an ideological vision which has lost adherents and influence gradually but steadily over the last sixty years. Among leftists its greatest appeal was always to southern Europeans and Latin Americans, perhaps because in its doctrines of equality and justice, its almost mystical faith in the humble and dispossessed, its suspicion of organization and emphasis on a sometimes fanatical dedication, it appealed to that same awe and mystery which is the soul of the Catholic faith.

Castelnuovo's aesthetic is consistent with these observations. Christianity's role in *Tinieblas* is overt. Jesus speaks; characters evoke in their appearance and lives Lazarus and St. Francis of Assisi. The author's respect and love for the most oppressed of the oppressed expresses itself in "tremendist" terms. His characters suffer appallingly. The first five pages of the first tale are given over to the description of the beatings the narrator endures as a child, which leave him a hunchback. In other stories, a deformed baby drowns in the uterine blood of his dying mother; a desperate prostitute drinks poison while her lover languishes in jail. Castelnuovo, unlike González Tuñón, knows no glittering mistresses of Maipú-Pigalle, no workers aware of anything but the numbing brutality of their jobs. His book is one written in heat, unsparingly awful, a salvo fired into the smug middle-class worldview of Argentina in the 1920s.

Still, both *Tinieblas* and its author may ultimately suffer from the qualities which originally made them so noteworthy. Perhaps we have grown hardened to human misery in the years since the book's appearance; still, the technique of horror piled on horror eventually seems to lose effectiveness. The reader ends up second-guessing the author, imagining the most dreadful turn of events possible, only to find two pages later that he has guessed exactly right. Beyond this, the tremendism too frequently slips into a sort of grand guignol. The action is so ghastly it borders on the pornographic: the reader becomes a voyeur before circumstances so dreadful they seem unreal. This element of Castelnuovo's work, of which *Tinieblas* is exemplary, might be less disturbing if the characters themselves were more solidly human. Instead they are one-dimensional saints, the passive recipients of fate's cruelest turns. Their passivity is first remarkable, then frightening, then vaguely annoying. They undergo no epiphanies except those which cast them even more deeply into despair. They are truly lost souls, men and women whose hope must be not a revolution, but the Millennium itself.

This is perhaps the reason for the Left's eventual criticism of Castelnuovo. He cannot be easily dispensed with. Even at its worst, his prose has a raw power, and there are few writers in any language who can so skillfully evoke the hellishness of mechanized production—the clatter and heat and anxiety.[19] However, "committed literature," indeed all literature of modern life after the early twenties, developed a greater sophistication in its presentation and analysis of the individual and society. *Tinieblas*, however, and most of Castelnuovo's subsequent work, remain fixated upon stories of the horrible and pathetic which arise from the French naturalist tradition, though it must be borne in mind that certain specific elements of his fiction are based in Castelnuovo's own life as a child and adolescent.[20]

Still, the author has eloquently defended his creative methods:

> One must emphasize this: although we were revolutionaries, we did not pursue a type of writing which was "militant," cold, regimented, committed, dull and false. We sought clarity, simplicity, naturalness . . . because we would not separate ourselves from reality and from life . . . we did not take the "underclass" as laboratory rabbits or specimens for study of a theory of revolution, but rather as the living, boiling raw material which generates that phenomenon.[21]

Castelnuovo's concept of fomenting rebellion through pity and horror has found few champions on the contemporary left, and proved not to be a keystone of Boedo's aesthetics. Within the group, there were writers who began to explore more sophisticated and ideologically complex responses to the problem of a committed literature, and others who worked in accord with more traditional models. Among the latter, perhaps the most successful was Boedo's oldest major talent, one who often played the role in the group of the elder brother. His real name was Arístides Gandolfi Herrero, but he is much better known by his pseudonym: Alvaro Yunque.

Yunque, "The Forge," likely remains Boedo's best loved figure. If he lacks an amaneunsis in the way Castelnuovo and Barletta have enjoyed the attention of Lubrano Zas and Raúl Larra respectively, both of the younger men, from time to time, have sought from Yunque his balanced judgment of a particular incident which their more polemical mentors could not provide them.[22] Scion of a prominent family in decline, Yunque was trained as a mathematician and occasionally taught the subject, but for the most part made his living as a writer and journalist. His upbringing was likely the most intellectually stimulating of those of the writers of Boedo, there amid books, a household altar, and the good conversation of endless friends. The family, without rancor, watched its fortunes rise and fall as its sons—Arístides, Augusto, Alcides, and Angel—sought different destinies. The second, a noted doctor, also achieved some renown as the poet "Juan Guijarro," while Alcides made his mark as a boxer and the author of *K.O.*

lírico, a collection of *lunfardo* verses. Angel, as Angel Walk, became a successful actor in popular melodramas.[23]

Yunque, though he published reviews, essays, and poetry both in major dailies and such magazines as the renegade *Inicial* and *La campana de palo,* did not publish a book till he was thirty-four. *Versos de la calle,* the second offering of the "Colección Los Nuevos," brought him considerable attention as one of the new generation's champions of social verse. In 1926, two prose works appeared, *Barcos de papel* and *Zancadillas,* the latter of which received a Premio Municipal. The following year, in defining himself as a writer, Yunque placed emphasis on the primacy of content and communication in his work: "My destiny is to be a useful writer, one who presents sentiments and new ideas, thus collaborating in the evolution of humanity, in whose future I have faith."[24]

Ta-Te-Ti: Otros barcos de papel (Cuentos de niños) appeared in 1928, and well illustrates Yunque's aesthetic applied to fiction. If Castelnuovo's is a tremendist muse, Yunque's is a "simplist" *(sencillista).* The stories, if not solely intended for children, are all about children. The protagonists are boys between ten and fifteen years old, and each of the tales recounts an adventure which ultimately demonstrates some moral or social truth. The plots develop linearly, the vocabulary is straightforward, and there are no experiments in structure or narrative technique.

Even with these self-imposed restrictions, Yunque emerges as a canny and affecting writer. His thematic range is considerable: from the real emotional seriousness, both to a boy and his teacher, of an adolescent crush ("Cara de viejo") to a satire on the use of religion to justify oppression ("Cabeza raptada"); from an exposition of the absurdity of racial prejudice (the title story) to a touching illustration of a boy's Freudian "family romance" in "La ilusión." Each parable is introduced with a quotation from the work of a famous figure—Rousseau, Pasteur, Heine, Tagore—relative to the purity of a child's nature. The stories teach lessons which are surely progressive, though in the end, virtually anyone, regardless of political ideology, could subscribe to their philosophy.

Yunque's tales typically evoke the suffering of those on the bottom rungs of the class ladder. In "Nico y el abuelo," for example, a boy accompanies his grandfather to his "job" in the home of a bored and very wealthy bachelor. The old man's major function, it turns out, is to entertain the young man and his equally jaded friends. They force him to drink, then demand that he dance and sing, laughing at the spectacle. Nico, horrified, attacks the host, and both he and his grandfather are thrown out. The old man admires the boy's courage, but tries to explain to him why he had acceded for some time to such shameful treatment.

I've humiliated myself all my life. Suffered. For what? Now I'm old and I don't have hardly anything, just a little saved up in the bank. Why have I degraded myself? Why have I been such a coward? And now? . . . He gave me fifty pesos so he could enjoy having a slave. When he got drunk with his friends . . . they would make fun of me, of the old dago, and they'd throw little breadwads at me, glasses of wine in my face, and I let them. . . Because if I didn't, where were these old bones going to get fifty pesos? That was my job. Playing the clown, so you all could eat, so my five grandchildren and widowed daughter didn't freeze, so they didn't have to go begging in the streets."25

The story does end optimistically, as Nico proposes the old man again embrace his former occupation of vegetable vendor now that the boy is old and strong enough to help him pull the cart through the streets. Still, its lasting image is that of the old man's humiliation, an extreme representation of the working man's oppression, that necessity of accepting the boss's demands, whatever they may be, in order to maintain one's income, home, and family.

"Bola sin manija," a rather more tough-minded piece, deals with the same issues, but it provides no happy ending. The idealistic Claudio, tossed out of his father's home at twelve, cannot abide injustice. Consequently he has great trouble retaining a job, for he will not submit to the patently unfair demands or caprices of his employers. In one instance, the very worker to whose defense Claudio has come turns on him, helping the owner eject him from the business. He eventually falls in with a thief and lands in jail. A judge, however, takes pity on him, brings him home, and puts him to work. Soon after, however, Claudio defends the gardener's grandson against the false accusations of the judge's son, and for his impertinence is dismissed. The gardener, meanwhile, is ordered to beat his grandson in front of the master's family. As Claudio leaves:

> He moved slowly. Suddenly he stopped to listen.
> "I'm sorry, son. I won't do it anymore, son!"
> It was the gardener's voice . . .
> —"I'm sorry. I won't do it anymore."
> To escape it, Claudio began to run.

Perhaps the most powerful and interesting of these stories are those which deal with issues we shall see arising again in the works of such writers as Arlt and Mariani. The themes of humiliation, sadomasochism, and the introjection of injustice figure strongly in the leftist literature of the decade. Yunque's dedication to a "useful" art, often employing children as characters, allows him to confront these issues overtly. Though artistically less rich than Mariani's stories or Arlt's novels, Yunque's parables favorably represent the didactic strain in fiction. Within an activist aesthetic, it might be argued that Yunque's production falls closest to the traditional ideal of committed literature, stories of merit which nonetheless attempt to communicate ideologically with the largest possible audience.

Leónidas Barletta, of all the members of Boedo, most successfully combined the careers of writer and professional leftist. An untiring prologuist, critic, and polemicist, he kept the flame of Boedo alive until his death in 1975. With a talent for organization, he played a central role in establishing the Teatro del Pueblo in the 1930s, which provided not only a showcase for Argentine drama, but maintained the tradition of the literature of protest during a period now referred to as the "Década Infame." During the first five years of his career as a writer, he produced nine books—short stories, poems, novels, and essays. Even with his other activities, he remained a tremendously prolific writer in later life.[26]

Barletta's early works leave little doubt of his sincere commitment to an ideologically conscious literature: it is apparent in their very titles— *Cuentos realistas*, *Canciones agrias*, *Los pobres*, *Vidas perdidas*. His stories remain largely in a naturalist vein, though he avoids Castelnuovo's tremendist excesses. Barletta favors an anecdotal approach to his material, sometimes so abbreviated as to constitute little more than a vignette. The immigratory experience is central to many of the tales, which allows Barletta skillfully to interpolate some dialogue in foreign languages, particularly Italian. He has little use for Castelnuovian mysticism, as the first story of *Los pobres* makes clear. The protagonist, a blind woman long a beggar, maintains her faith in God throughout a life fraught with unspeakable misfortune. At story's end, however, when her adopted daughter is stolen from her by a pimp, "she bunched her fists, raised her dead eyes toward that leaden sky, and from her twisted mouth three words fell like stones: '*Dio! Dio maldetto!*'"[27]

In spite of the power and craftsmanship of some of his stories, Barletta's most lasting work of the 1920s is probably a novel somewhat lacking in polish, superficially divorced from social concerns, and finally published only in 1930. *Royal Circo* relates the short and none-too-happy

life of a tacky carnival troupe, founded by the greedy penny arcade owner
Sardinia and composed of an unlikely assortment of has-beens and never-
arriveds: Mingelgraum, the animal trainer; Estella Francis, the bareback
rider and occasional prostitute; John Geeps, the former sailor and good-
hearted clown, whose nickname is "Timón"—"the helm." The plot is
episodic, sometimes to the point of clumsiness, but it allows Barletta to
exhibit his impressive talent for characterization. Care is lavished on even
the most minor members of the company, such as the Chevalleries, the
circus musicians, whose bourgeois pretensions are satirized not cruelly,
but with an undercurrent of sadness which nonetheless never becomes
sentimental.

The novel's key figure is Salustiano, a melancholy little man constantly afflicted but never completely overwhelmed by misfortune. With
John Geeps, he forms the moral center of the story, demonstrating in his
quiet humanity a self-abnegation reminiscent of (but far more realistic
than) the saintliness of Castelnuovo's creations. Geeps's good humor, meanwhile, is coupled with a social and psychological awareness which makes
him better able to understand and combat the injustices of a materialistic
world. The circus, with its emphasis on illusion, provides an effective
symbol for the shallowness of the culture it serves. It also allows for an
oblique but interesting commentary on the function of art or entertainment in any society. After Sardinia absconds with Estella Francis and the
circus receipts, the troupe dissolves. Takeo Yamada, the father of the
Japanese gymnastic team in the company, argues with Geeps:

> "It's a dog's life," murmured Timón.
> "It's only just. That's the life of the artist. This isn't work. We're
> not workers. We don't produce anything."
> "We make people happy."
> "Who asked us to make them happy? We don't do anything.
> Washing, ironing, that's work . . ."
> "Man doesn't live by bread alone. Happiness is good . . ."
> "Happiness. Yes. People laugh. But us, what are we? Happy?
> It's our poverty that's funny to people."[28]

It is this issue of art and audience that forms one of the most
interesting themes of *Royal Circo*, for it questions the artist's function,
both within the dominant social structures and also, by implication,
relative to efforts to alter those structures. Can the artist be certain of his
value as he perceives it, or is he providing his audience with some sort of

pleasure antithetical to his aims? This, of course, represented a central question for Boedo itself. Did the stories of poverty and suffering really do anything to alleviate poverty and suffering, or did they simply provide a sort of sideshow of social anomalies? Did they radicalize their readership and encourage them on a revolutionary course? Or did they provide a voyeuristic glimpse into a violent and morbid world from which readers felt happily insulated, thus encouraging the maintainance of that insulation in the real world, regardless of the cost? That this concern was operative in Barletta's mind is apparent from the passage which follows the dialogue just quoted, a passage in which Geeps, enamored of Estella Francis, realizes that, "He felt now a certain hatred for the whole world. . . . he knew that if he had had money, Estella Francis would have loved him. . . . If he had had money, even if she didn't want to, Estella Francis would have rendered up to him her beauty, her love, her fidelity . . . and he understood vaguely that this was all somehow monstrous."

Money perverts even love. What hope is there then for art, the very usefulness of which is circumscribed by its profitability? This question, obscure though its expression may sometimes be in *Royal Circo*, emerges forcefully from time to time and helps explain some of the more peculiar turns in the plot. For example, Salustiano, assisted by his stepdaughter, Elena, finds work in chapter 24 as a magician in a small *porteño* theater. He performs before an initially inattentive and passive audience. His magic, however, is truly astonishing. The audience goes mad, pulling up chairs and almost rioting in the theater. Salustiano triumphs, then fails. The theater manager is horrified. He cannot afford real magic, real art. Its effects are too extreme and expensive. Perhaps this implies that truly revolutionary art, art which would move people to rebellion and destruction, is also too dangerous and volatile to be allowed in our "theater" of the world.

In any case, when we next see Elena, she forms part of an *orquesta de señoritas* in a cheap bar, partaking in a socially acceptable illusion, for the women do not really play their instruments. A real orchestra is hidden behind them, making the sounds they only mime. She attracts the attention of a middle-aged English sailor, who is, of course, John Geeps. *Royal Circo* ends sentimentally with Geeps's and Elena's marriage, though Barletta does attempt (a bit ineptly) to undercut the conclusion's predictability by intruding directly into the text:

Now you will all say: But this Barletta is one cheap novelist. Does he want us to believe that this fellow with the interested eyes that likes

Elena is good old John Geeps, that was a sailor for fourteen years and then the clown with the Royal Circo?

Hold your horses. There's no reason to lie. Timón was always a good boy and wouldn't deserve a nasty turn.

And there is no reason to get impatient. You'll see.

The device is rather too bald, but the finale does not by any means ruin Barletta's tale. *Royal Circo* is hardly a work of genius. Yet, it is both interesting and promising, dealing with issues central to leftist literature without exhibiting them front and center. Its political concerns occasionally become so obscure as to be completely lost, but in eschewing the naked naturalism of earlier efforts both of his own and of other members of Boedo, Barletta here indicated new roads which an artistic and ideologically valid literature might follow.

Escaping the naturalist mode presented a dilemma for writers of Boedo. The manifold horrors described in Castelnuovo's work and Barletta's early stories, while evocative, did not function particularly well either politically or artistically. They seemed to reinforce González Lanuza's opinion that "it seems absolutely inevitable that anything that calls itself politically left wing is aesthetically right wing."[29] Naturalism, after all, was an old movement in the twenties, one associated with late nineteenth-century bourgeois reformism. However, Boedo's artists were, to an extent, trapped by their self-imposed ideological function. They could not engage in excessive stylistic experimentation, for to do so might eliminate from their readership the very people they sought to reach: the petit bourgeoisie and the proletariat. *Royal Circo* represents a small attempt to deal with this dilemma, though it perhaps does so with only marginal success. A far more significant effort, one which may represent the finest single prose work to emerge from Boedo, will be the first work analyzed in depth in this study: Roberto Mariani's *Cuentos de la oficina*.

The texts considered hereafter—*Cuentos de la oficina*, *El juguete rabioso*, and *Don Segundo Sombra*—appeared within slightly more than a year of one another. Mariani's, the first, was published in the winter of 1925 and Arlt's, the last, in the spring of 1926. All, however, had been in process for the greater part of the decade. Arlt apparently wrote the first part of his novel as early as 1919, Mariani was publishing drafts of his stories in the early twenties, and Güiraldes had completed the major part of *Don Segundo Sombra* by 1923. That all three should finally appear just past mid-decade is perhaps more than a felicitous coincidence. The years 1925–26 represent not only the chronological watershed of the decade, but the psychological and cultural one as well. The economy was healthy, the Alvear presidency half over, the Prince of Wales well entertained. The Generation of 1922 had achieved legitimacy, and Boedo and Florida had staked out their aesthetic territories and were skirmishing briskly. *Martín Fierro* was in its glory days and *Los Pensadores* poised for its final transformation into *Claridad*.

In spite of such brightness, however, what remains most striking about the books produced during this period—representative of Boedo, Florida, and the ground in between—is their critical perspective on the nation in which they appeared. In analyzing them, one can feel the strains within that apparently flawless fabric of Radical Argentina. What these writers and their texts tell us about Argentina—its society, its mind and soul—provides a necessary basis for understanding that country both in the 1920s and in the turbulent decades which followed. The appearance of these three key texts in such a brief period of time indicates both the terrific intellectual and spiritual ferment and the cultural sophistication of Argentina in that age now sixty years past.

PART III

Fathers and Sons

CHAPTER 6

In the Heart of the Beast,
Of the Beast in the Heart

The Short Fiction of Roberto Mariani

NO ONE, it seems, knew Roberto Mariani very well. Anecdotes abound about Güiraldes and Arlt, about Borges and Barletta. But in interview after memoir after literary biography, as regards Mariani the same stories circulate endlessly. It is almost as if the colleagues of his youth—Castelnuovo, César Tiempo, Eduardo Suárez Danero—had conspired to provide those who knew him only in his later years—Raúl Larra, Juan Pinto—the identical, maddeningly oblique vision of this man they collaborated and argued with. Perhaps there were secrets better left unsaid; perhaps this apparently morose and acerbic man did maintain an almost pathological privacy. And perhaps, in both these speculations, there is a part of the truth.

Mariani was a complainer. His friends' recollections sometimes seem little more than a chronicle of Mariani's ill-tempered gloom. He was a man perpetually at odds with his conditions. He detested office work in the capital; he loathed office work in the country.[1] He disliked journalism, and apparently did not care for his short stint as a truckdriver in the 1930s.[2] All he loved was writing, and it brought him little money and less glory. His desired fame and security eluded him all his life, in many ways unjustly. Mariani's fiction always courted success and never really achieved it. His name was bandied around for various literary prizes, which in all but one instance ended up in the hands of others. Time and again, his books were lauded critically, sold briefly, and vanished from the bookstalls and the public mind.[3] He watched, discontented but powerless, as lesser talents of his own and succeeding generations achieved the public recognition he craved.

Yet there is more to the man than a deep sense of personal injury, a wounded vanity that cried out against a world which relegated him to relative obscurity while he lived, and has since made of him little more than a component in the list of writers of Boedo. His sense of injustice— not solely that of a particular political or social system, but that of life itself—raged within him from the time he was a prize colt in Antonio Zamora's stable of engaged writers until his death in 1946. In those repetitive memoirs of his cohorts, one thing they remember again and again is his fury at the world's brutality, its meanness. He respected children for their innocence, but the nasty realities of daily living in the twentieth century maddened him.[4] This could manifest itself in that rowdy aggression against the established powers so typical of the 1920s. The editors of *Claridad* delightedly recount Mariani's activities at the premiere of *Mundo al revés* ("Upside-down World"), a patriotic and moralizing drama by one Hermelindo Rocha:

> The most outstanding note was struck by our comrade, Roberto Mariani. When the "Doctor" [Rocha], without anybody having called for him, finally appeared on stage, smiling and prepared to unleash on the public a speech practiced that very afternoon, Mariani loudly called him down:
> "You mystifier! You come preaching morality and you have a usurer's bank, the Banco Comisionista Argentino, at Corrientes and Florida. You smother your employees there! . . ."
> The clown blushed, and amid the scandal produced by the arrival of the police and the shouting of his friends and our friends, he tried to defend himself.[5]

Yet, even in those early years, Mariani could tumble from public braggadocio into harsh and terrible fantasy:

> I'm ashamed of myself. I'm not fulfilling any mission here on earth, except to constitute a needless weight on it. I console myself by thinking that maybe God in his inscrutable designs is keeping me around for something, though I have no inkling what it might be. I'd like the R. S. [Revolución Social] to break out and to take part in it. Quite serenely, I would take on myself the historical and moral responsibility of a terror which delivered to the basket the heads of 99 percent of my fellow citizens.
> But really, is this human bazaar of swindlers, phonies, thieves, politicos and murderers worth taking such trouble and responsibility for?

One day, I thought about doing something which might explain the grotesque and ridiculous idea I have of life and life's creatures: locking myself in the bathroom and hanging myself with my suspenders.

I didn't do it, because I'm also a sensual man and a coward. I am, then, just like everybody. Cowardice on the one hand and, on the other, the suspicion that one more pleasure might be waiting is what kept me from bidding everyone adieu in that final role of tragic and obscene clown.[6]

Mariani's worldview bore considerable resemblance to that of his contemporary, Roberto Arlt, and indeed, according to César Tiempo, Mariani was the writer beside Güiraldes for whom Arlt reserved a special respect and affection.[7] But while Arlt tussled with life with manic intensity, Mariani faced it with grim hopelessness. Arlt's anger burns with a white heat; Mariani's is a cold, blue despair. The author of *El juguete rabioso* could at least momentarily enjoy the heady fantasy of nihilism: let us destroy what is now made, for whatever comes after must surely be better. He believed, in the end, that injustice was the invention of human beings. In Mariani, particularly as he aged, the suspicion grew that injustice was cosmic, that humanity was the victim not simply of capitalism and liberalism or a failing of soul, but of some eternally unfunny joke, of injustice created and ordained by some unknowable God. Arlt's vision is wildly absurd, pyrotechnic, rabid; Mariani's is mundane, understated, bleak.

Mariani differed from his fellows even in his literary tastes. For Arlt, for Castelnuovo and Barletta, for Boedo in general, the heroic figures to be emulated were mostly Russian: Tolstoi, Gorki, Andreviev, and most especially Dostoyevski. Mariani, meanwhile, was Argentina's great champion of Proust and one of its earliest appreciators of Joyce.[8] He certainly knew his political theory—socialist, communist, and anarchist—but was also an avid reader of Freud.[9] Unsurprisingly, he was also attracted to the great pessimist of Spain's Generation of 1898, Pío Baroja. One of the pieces which brought him recognition in that well-starred fiction competition sponsored by *La Montaña* was appropriately titled "Un personaje de Baroja."

Though extant accounts are limited, Mariani's intellectual life was apparently vast and varied. After he had completed secondary school, he studied briefly at the College of Engineering, likely under parental pressure, but he soon dropped out, telling his sisters he was determined to become a writer.[10] He then seems to have redoubled his efforts as an autodidact. Castelnuovo says: "Of all the boys of Boedo, he was the one with the most culture."[11] He read not only in Spanish, but in Italian and French, and was adept enough to help prepare translations from the foreign tongues for various magazines.[12] During the decade, he wrote and spoke on a number of writers—Alfonso Reyes, Proust, Pirandello.[13] He was the official instigator of the polemic between Boedo and Florida with his *"Martín Fierro y yo,"* and insofar as Boedo had an official aesthetician, he was probably the most distinguished candidate, setting forth the artistic philosophy of the left in such pieces as "Ellos y nosotros" in *Claridad* and his preface to César Tiempo and Juan Pedro Vignales' anthology *Exposición de la poesía argentina contemporánea.*[14]

Mariani's personal life is even less well documented. After leaving his parents' home in La Boca, he lived in a series of rented rooms in the capital, in Cuyo, in the suburbs, then in Esquel, before finally settling in the house of two spinster sisters on Boulogne Sur Mer near the Once Station.[15] In the early twenties, he seems to have gone whoring occasionally in La Plata with Suárez Danero and José Gabriel, registering in hotels as "Pío Baroja."[16] He apparently suffered a disappointment of the heart during his sojourn in Mendoza (1915–20?), if a number of early works, both poetry and prose, can be trusted as evidence.[17] According to Barletta, he maintained for some time a chaste affair with a married woman while employed in the late twenties as the clerk of a judge in Bernal.[18] There is evidence to indicate that Mariani suffered from severe sexual problems during the whole of his adult life, though the form and origin of those problems remain obscure. In any case, he never married, though he still has surviving nieces and nephews in Buenos Aires, including a namesake in Morón.[19]

The spottiness of information on Mariani's private life is distressing, for his work, the most successful engaged fiction of the age, seems intensely personal. Castelnuovo's efforts, though often autobiographically based, are infused with the author's didactic and sometimes almost religious intentions. His stories, with their tremendist horrors, impact like Goya's *Caprichos*, acid etchings of the most dreadful of life's brutalities. Barletta, likewise, is prone to extremity in his stories, while in such an autobiographical piece as *Royal Circo*, he employs atypical circumstances and characters for their symbolic usefulness. Arlt, meanwhile, in a work like *Los siete locos*, swings wildly from political attack to assaults on his private demons, and, in any case, the world which he brings to his fiction, though one his readers surely recognized, is suffused with that outrageousness which became his trademark as much in his life as his work.

The office workers who populate Mariani's canon, however, are very much of the sort he himself labored beside in his periods as an employee of the Banco de la Nación and the Dirección Nacional de Arquitectura; the sort one still sees north of Florida, in the commercial and financial district, hurrying here, hurrying there, bolting a sandwich and coffee at one of the cheap cafés along 25 de Mayo or Cangallo. Carefully suited, shoes shined, ink stains on their fingers, they are men of small salaries and little dreams—money for a movie, money for a dinner out, money to cover the rent without too much sacrifice. They hoard their pesos (or today, their australes) for enough of a nest egg to get married, to buy the daughter her schoolbooks *and* a new raincoat, to take the wife for a long weekend by the sea. The cramped and monotonous lives of the "white collar proletariat," those men who infuriated Mariani even as he loved them, have not changed much in sixty years. In spite of his attempts to deal with other social groups—professionals, urban laborers—Mariani always returned in his fiction to the office workers. It is not surprising then that the only work to survive his eclipse, the only one which, regardless of political regime and changes in public taste, continues to emerge in new editions, is the collection of his most finely honed sketches of that life he hated and knew so well: *Cuentos de la oficina,* "The Office Stories."

Characterizing Mariani's stories as sketches is perhaps unwise, though none of the eight pieces comprising the book runs more than ten thousand words or so. The term implies a certain slightness, a beguiling but shallow presentation of scenes of daily life, like a collection of snapshots. It is probably this apparent superficiality which has prevented *Cuentos de la oficina* from receiving the sort of commentary it merits. Critics tend to view the book as a sort of loose chronicle, something to be dealt with in passing if at all. Indeed, it *is* possible to see these small, sad stories as little more than slices of small, sad lives, admirable in their minute observation, touching in a pathetic sort of way, and nothing more. Such judgments, however, do not explain the book's resilience, and signal, perhaps, little more than the critic's own too hasty reading and failure to note what is occurring beneath the surface of the smoothly flowing text.[20]

Beyond this, there is in *Cuentos de la oficina* a unity which approaches the novelistic. Most of the stories occur in the same business establishment, and tangential characters in one piece later figure centrally in others or vice versa. More importantly, however, the stories manifest a certain thematic development and cohesion. Particular motifs, now dominant, now implied, recur throughout the book, lending it an air much more similar to that of an episodic novel than to that of a volume of unrelated stories.

Mariani was, if nothing else, a subtle and exacting writer. His admiration for Proust surely arose from a shared fascination with life's minutiae, the mundane and oblique ways in which tragedy manifests itself and takes it toll in the twentieth century. From his political readings and from Freud, he seems to have developed a sure sense of how the world in which we live affects us, how we internalize it and how that process can change us, without our realizing it, into what we most despise.

The tales of *Cuentos de la oficina,* published in 1925, began to appear as early as 1922, for the most part in *Nueva Era,* a publication which, born as a magazine in the late teens, grew to a weekly newspaper as the twenties dawned, and was transformed into a biweekly and then a shortlived daily before finally sliding into bankruptcy. Mariani was likely collaborating there as early as 1920, when several incidental pieces were printed authored by "Maximo Lagos," the name of a character later to appear in a number of Mariani's works. Of the eight stories of his first book of prose, one comprised part of his winning entry in the literary contest at *La Montaña* ("La ficción"), while three were first published in *Nueva Era* ("La balada de la oficina," "Rillo," and "Toulet"). In addition, several stories from Mariani's next collection, *El amor agresivo,* first saw light as primitive drafts in *Nueva Era.*[21] Comparative readings indicate the effort the author put into his work. Sometimes, the textual revisions amount to mere rewordings, occasional cuttings or expansions. More often, however, whole paragraphs are struck or inserted, and major secondary characters are eliminated and entirely new characters introduced.[22]

It is apparent, then, that Mariani worked on the *Cuentos de la oficina* for at least four years, though he could conceivably have spent much longer on it. During his five-year stay in Mendoza, he published locally and prepared his first book, *Las acequias y otros poemas,* which appeared under the imprimatur of *Nosotros* in 1922. At the same time he was almost surely developing the stories which would appear in *El amor agresivo* while producing two novellas, *El amor grotesco* and *Culpas ajenas.*[23] This was also the period of Boedo's formation, Mariani's contributions to *Los Pensadores* and other literary magazines, of the late-night discussions of art and life with his fellow young Turks of the new sensibility—all this, while he put in eight or nine or ten hours, five days a week with half days on Saturdays, at the office.

What the office signified to Mariani and to the Argentina of the 1920s, and continues to stand for in this late capitalist century, is at the heart of understanding this book.[24] *Cuentos de la oficina* is about repression: political, economic, social, sexual, and spiritual. In its minute observation of the seemingly trivial lives of its characters—employees of the department store "Olmos y Daniels"—the text encompasses a whole universe.[25] Beneath the quiet surface, Mariani as an artist employs his full reserves as symbolist, psychologist, witness, and political animal to expose the reality of a system which appalled him.

The book opens with the "Balada de la oficina," a short prose piece "spoken" by The Office itself, establishing the book's major symbolic motifs. It demonstrates from the very first word the care Mariani took with his prose. *"Entra,"* it begins.[26] The command implies the relationship of the institution to those who work there, to those outside, to the reader. *Entra* is the second person imperative, implying either intimacy or condescension. It is written without an accent, indicating that the understood pronoun here is *tú*, rather than the Argentine second person variant, *vos*.[27] The use of the Spanish familiar form, especially in speech, is an affectation of elements of the upper classes and those who wish to identify with them. It represents a self-conscious effort to appear cultivated, European.[28] Hence, the first word of the text identifies The Office with a particular social class, and further, establishes a vertical relationship between The Office and the reader, characterized as a "robust boy." The Office speaks from a position of power, familiarly and elegantly, like parent to child, exhorting, in what follows, maturity from this young potential employee. He ought to abandon the street, the "lazy and contemplative sun," the wind "playful as a lamb." All these are "phantoms," delightful for children and old men, but inappropriate, indeed embarrassing familiars for a healthy adult—almost as shameful as the rain: "Aren't you humiliated? Remember how the other day you spent three hours— three *hours*—watching it through the café window—falling, falling, falling monotonously, stupidly—a long, monotonous, stupid rain."

For him, instead, there is The Office, *La* Oficina, an older, wealthy woman who entices him from the juvenile and disorderly world, urging him to "enter; penetrate my womb . . ." She draws the youth to her like a lover, and yet she is more: "Penetrate my flesh and you'll be safe from the burning sun, the howling wind, the soaking rain, the sickening cold." Seduction by The Office means reabsorption into the womb, the abandonment of the physical mother for the greater institutional one. She offers certainty, a "breast" which provides the means to feed "those children of your flesh and blood, of your companion's flesh and blood." A wife, in this scheme, is only a *compañera*. The Office brooks no rivals.

There is, of course, a price. Working is also "your duty." "Work doesn't sully, it ennobles. Life is a duty. Man was born to work." In the second part of this prologue, the idea of obligation arises again and again, along with stress on work's certainty, which provides life with a "matrix," a structure "exact, precise, mathematical." Such security demands, in exchange, a disciplined man, one "serious, honest, without vices," from the moment he enters the office, "all through those twenty-five years, those 9,125 days" of his employment, right up to retirement. . . . Then, you'll enjoy the sun and the next day you'll die. But you will have done your Duty!"

In the "Ballad of the Office," three interlocking psychosexual and sociopolitical motifs establish themselves. The first of these is that of The Office as seductive, consuming mother, dominating and disciplining her employee sons. She provides a womb for them, of course, but a man returned to the womb, incapable of independent existence, is no man at all. The Office does not merely castrate the worker, she negates him utterly. He is, in the end, her parasite. She asks no thanks for her generosity ("Don't thank me! That's the way I am!"), but she demands obedience. The threat unspoken but implied in the concluding half of the prologue is that of abandonment, of expulsion from the sustaining mother. In practical terms, this translates into "termination": the branding of a worker as troublesome or lazy, a reputation which will deny him employment elsewhere, and reduce him, eventually, to penury.

Separation from The Office is tantamount to secular excommunication, indicative of another of the book's central images: the Church. The very word "office" evokes within Catholic and particularly Hispanic societies a unique and weighty ecclesiastical association: El Santo Oficio, The Holy Office. Mariani's Office, institution of the dominant, capitalist faith, possesses the inquisitional power to root out and destroy political and economic heresy. It demands acceptance of a particular dogma, of a particular morality, by those under its sway, and it can punish error by the imposition of penance (the denial of advancement, for example, or of an increase in salary) or, in extreme cases, by casting out the malefactor, perhaps, if his crime is sufficiently grave, into the arms of the "secular authorities."

The maternal Office, then, functions in contemporary society like the maternal Church in past centuries. She defines sin. She exacts orthodoxy. She determines the structure of daily life. In the minute exposition of tasks repeated day in and day out, year in and year out, the "Ballad of the Office" imbues white-collar duties with the aura of ritual. Capital must be propitiated. In serving Olmos y Daniels, the employees endure God's curse on Adam, affirmed in The Office's paraphrase: "Man was born to work."

The church is evoked not only in the repetitive tasks, but in the office's very structure, in its physical space and its organization. The bulk of the stories concern those who work in or near the cupola of the store, in a "chapel-like convexity" which the employees refer to disparagingly as "paradise." There they toil under the direction of Sr. Torre ("tower"), referred to as a "Jesuit." He is but a middling angel in this parody of heaven. At the lowest rung, at least among those workers we come to know, are the *cadetes*, the uniformed office boys, who are a step below the *auxiliares*, the common clerks, who among themselves are divided by seniority and salary. Sr. Torre is a supervisor, which places him below the managers, who are themselves presided over by the rarely glimpsed *gerentes*—directors. Finally, unseen, hardly mentioned, there is "Mister Daniels," perhaps resident in Buenos Aires, more likely in London or Paris, distant as some secular Pope, or as God himself.[29]

Throughout *Cuentos de la oficina*, there is a tremendous sense of this hierarchical organization. The office, a place where we meet only men, has that peculiar ambience of a monastic or military order, and is permeated with the cruelty which seems most specific to structures defined by rigid relations of power. Those in the upper echelons scold and punish the employees as if they were, indeed, mere children, and the latter seem to accept and play out their assigned role. There is in the masters a certain sadistic relish, in the underlings a masochistic resignation. However, none of the various disciplinary actions meted out, the demotions, fines, transfers, is nearly so horrifying as what the workers do to themselves. Mariani had a visceral understanding of The Office's power and its position in the larger social and economic sphere. The ideology of the workplace is that of the society. His characters are hopelessly trapped by the system in which they live; they carry within them a terrible capacity for self-denial and self-torment.

In the years that Mariani was writing *Cuentos de la oficina*, Freud had just formulated the concept of the superego as the introjected father.[30] It is impossible to tell, at this point, if Mariani was conversant with that theory, either through his reading or by hearsay.[31] What can be asserted is his intimate awareness of the actual process of introjection, here of the "father" in terms of a specific worldview. It is a process that seriously calls into question the capacity of the class which his characters represent ever to break free of their oppression.[32]

In order to see this, and to illustrate the expression of the other motifs previously discussed, it is necessary to turn to the stories themselves. In the interest of brevity, only five will be analyzed. The other two are certainly worthy of discussion (indeed, "Santana" may be the single most realized piece), but "Rillo," "Riverita," "Uno," "Toulet," and "La ficción" collectively offer sufficient opportunities to appreciate the various resonances of Mariani's complex vision.

In the first paragraphs of "Rillo," which immediately follows the "Balada de la oficina," Mariani plays heavily upon religious and hierarchical motifs in relation to the lives of the workers in the Supplies Department, located in "paradise." At the center of the story is Rillo, a long-time employee who is sent to the personnel manager for violating one of the cardinal rules of the new supply supervisor, Sr. Torre: no socializing during working hours. Torre explains his action to the other workers as follows:

> Sr. Rillo has repeatedly disobeyed my orders. I'm sorry, because I really do value every employee. I was an employee just like all of you, but I knew when it was time to talk and have fun, and when it was time to work and be serious. . . . In order to maintain discipline, Sr. Rillo may have to be punished. I hope none of you are headed down the same path as Sr. Rillo. I would like to think you all understand it's best that everybody just obey . . .

Rillo himself describes his interview with the manager to his fellows the very next time they are left alone in the office by Sr. Torre:

> "Sit down," Sr. Araldo told me. "Why is it you don't obey your supervisor's orders?" Me? What was I going to say? Was I going to say it was a stupid rule about not talking? So I clammed up. "You are incorrigible," he told me. Then he said, "But you are going to straighten up: we're going to pass you on to the Credit Department, and we're going to make you wait a bit for that promotion. You're down for a raise up to two hundred pesos. If you want it, all you have to do is straighten up . . ."

Torre's smug lecture, the manager's assumption of Rillo's culpability, the latter's contrite silence, and even the words employed ("orders," "punished," "discipline," "obey," "incorrigible," "straighten up"), Rillo's trip to Araldo's office recalls nothing so much as that of a schoolboy to the principal's. The military and religious resonances of the vocabulary are self-evident, and the power which these words carry is more than that of mere humiliation. The manager's sentence, the withholding of the raise, means Rillo cannot afford to proceed with his planned marriage.

The clerk does get his revenge. When Torre is absent from Supplies, an unexpected visit by one of the directors, anxious to economize on matériel, provides Rillo with an opportunity to shine. Torre, when he returns, is forced to rely on Rillo's familiarity with the useful life of ledgers and red pencils, which allows the latter to manuever his superior into an erroneous response to one of the director's questions. That single mistake is sufficient to condemn Torre to a transfer to Reception—a fall, as it were, from paradise, seven stories up, to the department located closest to the street, to the frontier of that frightening, natural world outside the precincts of The Office. Rillo, meanwhile, is promoted to Supply Supervisor, and gleefully proclaims a "republic," where the strangling regulations of The Office no longer apply.

The structure and functioning of relationships set forth in "Rillo" are grim enough. In the end, the employee's puerile vengence belongs as much to the ideology of The Office as Sr. Torre's schoolmasterly authoritarianism. Rillo, though a self-declared socialist, in a political debate with Romeu does little more than manipulate to his advantage the absurd hierarchical power which reigns in the workplace. The rules of the game, the fatality of a single error, remain in force in spite of any grand claims of the triumph of democracy. Mariani drives this ugly truth home in the story's brief, ironic coda: "But he never did get promoted [further up] to manager. Rillo too was one of the victims of the abortive strike. He worked for years afterward, at two hundred pesos, still a supervisor, and nothing more ..."

Rillo has a reputation as a troublemaker. He is allowed his little joke on Sr. Torre, partaking as it does of The Office's morality. Union activity is another matter, but when the labor action is crushed, Rillo is not fired. The Office has triumphed, and the employee is chained to her, on her terms, for the rest of his life. Another misstep, another error, the slightest violation of the model of a worker, and Rillo will certainly lose his job, terminated, marked as a revolutionary. The Office has broken him, and one can almost hear him, years later, in the untold story signed by that ellipsis: "I was an employee just like all of you. . . . Without discipline, it's impossible to get anything done. . . . I would like to think you all understand it's best that everybody just obey."

In "Rillo," the power of The Office—its chain of command and its impact on the employees' lives—is overt. A far more insidious manifestation is to be found in "Riverita," which again focuses on two workers in Supplies: Lagos, the narrator of "Rillo," and Julio Rivera ("Riverita"), the *cadete*.

The plot is simple enough. The two characters are assigned to inventory the office stock, working nights. They are given a month for the task, and Lagos discovers happily that, with only a couple hours of labor every evening, they can easily complete the task. Hence, they spend a great deal of time reading, daydreaming, and talking. One especially hot night, the conversation turns to sex. Lagos weaves the stories of his amorous adventures and ends up explaining to the fifteen-year-old Julito the facts of life. The boy extracts a promise from the older man to take him along the next time he goes whoring. Riverita brags of his good looks, his fine complexion, of how the prostitutes will like him. He invites Lagos to touch his hair, then his face:

> He smiled and looked me sweetly in the eyes, innocently, confidently. So I could touch his skin again, he had to bend toward me slightly.
> "The girls are going to like kissing me . . ." I don't know what lightening bolt struck me then. Possessed by I don't know what powerful and inexplicable force, I suddenly struck him a blow so violent and unexpected that Julito fell to the floor.
> "Your conceit is disgusting."
> He got up without a word.

They return to work. The next day, both ask separately that Julito be replaced on the inventory.

This is Mariani at his most Proustian. The evocation of the uniforms of the employees required to wear them, of Julio himself, of the oppressively hot night of the denouement are minute, langorous. Large swatches of dialogue appear, fraught with ambiguities and double entendres. The story develops slowly, and its point emerges only obliquely. The meticulously observed action implies much more than it speaks.

"Riverita" is, first of all, a tale of homosexual attraction. Lagos, as narrator, spends nearly the first third of the text describing Riverita: how he dresses, how he walks, what he reads. The fascination is subtle, but present. Julio seems curiously and appealingly androgenous. He is graceful; the uniform fits him well and he knows it; he is almost feminine in his care of his appearance. His office boy's shoes have high heels, similar to those of the salesgirls. His socks, like theirs, are silk. Yet he goads Rillo and jokes with Lagos and the others. He endlessly mimes cleaning his pen, so that under the noses of his superiors he can sneak readings of the latest mystery or adventure magazine lying in his half-open desk drawer.

When Riverita and Lagos begin their inventory, the sexual tension between them grows. Working outside normal office hours, during the evenings' sweltering heat, they roll up their sleeves and take off their jackets. The climax comes one humid and bug-ridden night, as their attraction simmers under the determinedly heterosexual banter. Lagos initially appears to be the instigator of the game, though as it develops, it is difficult to tell where Riverita's naiveté leaves off and a certain conquettishness begins. In both narration and dialogue the seduction builds. There are veiled allusions to venereal disease, to cunnilingus, to Riverita's femininity. Lagos describes himself "sitting, really relaxed, in the revolving chair, and to get even comfier, I put my feet up on the desk so I was in a really shameless position. Julito suddenly sat down on the corner of the desk, nearly touching my ankle. He pulled up his pants so they wouldn't bunch at the knees, showing off his fine, silk socks."

The conversation continues, through Lagos' tomcatting, through Riverita's single encounter with an older woman who attempted to seduce him, through the promise of a visit to the brothels.

> He asked me questions, completely illogical ones, others which revealed a subtle intuition or a childish ingenuousness. Suddenly, in one, there was a spark. Ingenuous, or malicious?
> "One of them's going to want me, because I'm not ugly, you know what I mean, right? Look: I've got a good body, you know what I mean? I'm one cute boy. I've got good skin. Look. Touch it. See? Touch it. Lagos!"

Then comes Lagos' initial amusement, followed by that "inexplicable" bolt and the blow. The moment is lost—the seduction aborted, the human connection missed. The next day, both Lagos and Riverita act to assure that no further opportunity for such a thing will arise.

That this private and carefully circumscribed tale possesses an ideological significance may seem, at first, improbable. While homosexuality was not all that exotic in the cosmopolitan Buenos Aires of the 1920s, and the type of adventure which Mariani describes may not have been particularly unusual, the author's decision to include it in his book has a certain radical significance.[33] If some office boys received their sexual initiations from older office mates; if *porteños* with specific tastes could as easily find the Cities of the Plain on the banks of the Río de la Plata as could the Baron Charlus on those of the Seine, discussion of such matters remained beyond the ken of polite conversation and polite literature. If, by chance, such activity were to be evoked, it would be anticipated in a story of the demimonde, that peculiar point of contact of the oligarchy, bohemia, and the lumpen, but certainly not in the world of office workers, "serious, honest, without vices." But it is precisely in that world that the sort of contact Lagos and Riverita reach for and fail to achieve is most threatening to the dominant culture. Official public morality may be safely violated only by society's greatest renegades and greatest beneficiaries, those whose power in either rebellion or security is so great that they have nothing to lose. Had Lagos, however, pursued his momentary impulse to its natural conclusion, he, as a worker, would have assaulted the contemporary idea of decency imposed upon him by the culture, and by association, the entire political and economic structure which that code represents and which it protects. In an oblique but profound way, he would have attacked The Office herself. The realization of the buried desire implies an outrageous and peculiarly revolutionary act, a reality it seems doubtful was lost on Mariani.[34]

Beyond the homosexual element, the idea of introjection, the unconscious control The Office exerts on those who serve her, is threaded throughout "Riverita." It expresses itself sexually, and indeed, counterweights in the story the overt expression of homosexual longing, providing an alternate avenue of sexual release. In the first paragraph, Lagos remarks that Sr. Torre, the former Supplies Supervisor, "felt an almost voluptuous sensuality in giving orders of every kind, and being obeyed, with love or without it." Power provides a nearly glandular thrill in the authoritarian structure. Lagos again and again reiterates to the office boy that the great advantage of working nights is that they are there *"sin jefes"*—without bosses. In the end, however, Lagos himself strikes out against the boy to whom he might have made love, the act a brute manifestation of the strength the word "jefe" possesses. The final night's failed seduction is actually bracketed by blows. The amorous dialogue begins when Lagos, unable to concentrate on his reading because of the insects drawn by the light, watches as Julito looks "persistently at his left arm, where perhaps the little green dot of an insect has lit; and with the palm of his right hand, he strikes himself on the arm to crush the enemy."[36] It closes, of course, with Lagos slapping Julito.[35]

"He strikes himself . . . to crush the enemy." The office boy, for Lagos, is the enemy in the end. That "powerful and inexplicable force" which moves him to violence is not, after all, that obscure. It is The Office within Lagos which lays Julito flat, the whole scheme of the world in which he lives and which lives in him that drives him to the assertion of power and the denial of love, an act in defense of the *jefes* he despises. But to crush the enemy, Lagos must also crush himself. For both him and for Riverita, the blow is the sign of their solitude and their enslavement.

From "Riverita's" intimacy, the text then moves to the most self-consciously universalized of the stories, "Uno." Here, the nameless characters—"the man" and "the woman"—suffer the consequences of the former's slapstick tumble on a fruit peel. In the fall in the street, he hurts his knee, though he is initially unaware of the seriousness of his injury. From this point, inexorably, the couple's lives and their life together slowly unmake themselves. The man uses up his vacation time convalescing. His employer—obviously Olmos y Daniels—puts him on leave without pay. His problems persist, and there are the costs of medication, of trips to the doctor and the doctor himself, of day-to-day living. Piece by piece, the couple pawns the furniture. Finally, there is nothing left to sell. Only then is the man admitted as a charity patient to the Hospital Rawson, in the Constitución district.

From this point on, "Uno" focuses on the woman. She abandons the couple's apartment, rents a room in a *conventillo*, begins to take in laundry. Still there is not enough money. She fights eviction, learning the ruses of the poor: she fails to appear for hearings; she makes promises of payment she knows she cannot keep; she borrows the nursing child of a neighbor to take with her to court. Meanwhile, she seeks assistance. The Radical ward captain suggests some people who might need their washing done. The supervisor at Olmos y Daniels insists that the company cannot give her any money, but that it will continue to hold her husband's position vacant. His fellow employees take up a collection.

Most of all, she works. Money runs even lower. She loses sleep washing at night. She uses cold water, as she can no longer afford coal to heat it. Winter comes. She develops a cough.

Then, one morning, she cannot get up. The neighbors file in and find her feverish. An ambulance is sent for, and she is taken to the Hospital Ramos-Mejía. The facility is located in the Once district.

Gálvez could have made a novel of this, Castelnuovo or Barletta a long and bombastic short story. But Mariani opts for a little tale six pages in length. In so doing, he dispenses with all opportunities for melodrama. The starkness, the impersonality, the flatness of the narration allow instead the unrefined exposition of the situation's implications. "Uno" resonates through the whole of Argentine (and most Western) society. It is a thumbnail sketch of the tenuousness of life, in any sense beyond mere existence, in the modern world.

"Uno" is the petit bourgeois and proletarian nightmare. The breadwinner suffers a silly accident, and two people's lives fall apart. A couple ceases to exist, its unity shattered as surely as the man's knee. Outside of that couple, there is no unity—no community—at all. Aside from the *oficinistas'* pathetic, one-time gesture, there is no charity shown by any sector; or better, what charity there is is too little, too late, or both. The story's enduring image is of waste and solitude. Both man and wife end alone. And as Mariani notes ironically immediately after the accident which initiates the chain of events:

> Do you think that before he started walking again, he [the man] might have kicked the peel—the origin, the cause of his fall—into the gutter?
> No.
> And there it is, in the middle of the sidewalk; cunning, vigilant, in ambush for some passerby, seeking a new victim. A fruit peel.

Rillo's petty vengence wins him a promotion; his attempt at collective action delivers him eternally to The Office's whims. Lagos will buy his sex anonymously in the whorehouses but will not surrender to his own body's wanting, and defends himself with the overt sign of his own repression. The man who ends alone in the Hospital Rawson so lacks concern for his fellow man that he does not take the trouble to save someone else from the fate he has suffered. Our chances for human intimacy, for generosity, for communion are few, often trivial, and precious. In Mariani's view, The Office—either outside us or within us—will assure that they are missed.

"Toulet," the next of the *Cuentos de la oficina,* falls midway between journalistic distance of "Uno" and the psychological delving of "Riverita." Here, social class, news events, the political convolutions of the Radical epoch provide grist for discussion and allusion. This story most overtly characterizes the office as microcosmic, as the symbol of an entire political and social system, though it concentrates primarily on two characters: the Toulet of the title and his co-worker, Juan Antonio Fernández Guerrero.

Toulet, "the Frenchman, Toulet," descended from a man fleeing the 1789 revolution, proudly flaunts his "old *criollo*" heritage at the same time he stresses his Old World antecedents. He is the personification of the dying Sarmiento's nightmare: two cultures in one body, hopelessly separated. Though his family has never achieved any prominence, Toulet is the office's most vociferous defender of the established order. Fascinated by title and wealth, scandalized by leftist "irreverence" toward social convention and hierarchy, a voracious newspaper reader who loves to talk economic policy and world events, Toulet emerges as that most pathetic and obnoxious social animal: the snob. He symbolizes the success of the dominant ideology: a man so profoundly repressed that he champions the very system which enslaves him. Still, Lagos, who plays a very minor role in the story, defends him:

> His is a relatively simplistic, elemental, gross psychology. But the funny thing is, I have faith in Toulet's honesty. He is honest, in his fashion. He's incapable of sacrificing anything for anybody. What I mean is, he's incapable of hitting somebody, or robbing him, or hurting him in any way, because doing that would mean sacrificing his very self, his feelings, his ideas . . . that are worth more, that he respects more, than the advantage doing something bad would bring him."

Both complement and contrast to Toulet is his fellow clerk, Fernández Guerrero. While others labor to put bread on the table, Guerrero, son of an old, wealthy, and distinguished family, works so as to have something to do. His mother pays his dues at the capital's elegant clubs; his sartorial needs are taken care of by the account at the tailor shop paid by his brothers. His wages go for ties and apéritifs and automobile excursions. In the office, he chatters with Borda Aguirre, remnant of a now-ruined oligarchical family, about the social notes in the dailies, about who is related to whom, about common friends from their days at the aristocratic Colegio Nacional or the Catholic University: "They always recalled that in the family and among friends, so-and-so was called . . . some diminutive: Cachito, Linito, Pirito."

Toulet and Guerrero, of course, have similar views on most political and social issues, but they do not care for each other. Toulet, in particular, finds his co-worker frivolous and insufficiently pugnacious in his defense of privilege, of "the aristocracy, capital, tradition," those things the Frenchman reveres. Even more, Toulet "reproached, silently, this tolerance of Guerrero's for extremists and syndicalists, whom he didn't even seem to hate; with whom, indeed, he sympathized."[37]

Fernández Guerrero is that paradoxical scion of a powerful, aristocratic family in decline, that youngest brother who recognizes, even with some delight, the shortcomings and absurdities of the extant social system, though he can or will do nothing to correct them. Living de luxe for no other reason than accident of birth, he understands the capriciousness of his good fortune, while Toulet, on the outside looking in, still desperately believes in some sort of hierarchy of virtue: those who wield power must do so as a consequence of some superior ability, some more profound intelligence, some greater spiritual worth. This is the root of the muted antipathy between the two. Guerrero, whose own guilt or simple ennui leads him to sympathize with his own class enemies, is a palpable negation of the ideological mythology Toulet embraces.

Their story reaches its climax one stifling summer day, as they labor beside their fellow auditors to complete their assigned quotas. Here, in a passage of nearly a thousand words, well past the midpoint of the book, Mariani torturously describes the heat of the office, and in so doing, drives home the true nature of this *paraíso*. The images here are infernal: sweat, molten lead, the impossibility of any relief. The metaphor emerges directly: "Sudden and subconscious association of ideas: that hot afternoon with a lithograph of an oil by Pinelli, which for all those childhood years remained over the head of the bed, showing souls in human form burning in the flames of Hell, beneath the delighted gaze of a devil with a tail and pitchfork." This what The Office truly offers, and it is to the street, that silly world they abandoned for the security of work, that the employees dream of returning, if only for the evening. As night falls, more and more escape to the cool outdoors. In the end, only Toulet, Guerrero, and Honorino Acuña remain.

The last, dapper and agreeable, is originally from the provinces, from San Juan. He suffers with some unnamed illness, for the sake of which, he says: "I don't climb stairs, . . . I can't play football . . . one fine day, I'll feel all dried out, breathless. I don't know, but on the day I least expect it . . ."

That fine day, though Acuña does not realize it, has arrived. He complains occasionally during the afternoon of faintness and nausea. By evening, his sickness has grown apparent enough to be noted by Guerrero, who urges him to quit for the day, promising, with Toulet's help, to finish up the necessary figuring. Suddenly, Acuña faints and starts to strangle. Guerrero, leaving Toulet supporting the sick man, rushes for water. In his search, he doubles back through the office. He freezes

because he sees the Frenchman holding their friend clumsily, and more important, because of a useless and inexplicable manuever by Toulet.

What's this?

Guerrero had just seen an object fall to the floor. A wallet. The leather billfold, Acuña's billfold, where Acuña kept his few pesos . . .

The scene stunned Guerrero. Was it possible . . . this? In an

insignificant fraction of time, the smallest fraction of a second, Guerrero accepted the reality; an abortive attempt of . . .
    "Guerrero . . . Honorino . . . Honorino . . . !"

Toulet's botched theft resonates on various levels. In the first place, there is the question of his responsibility for his friend's death. Did the manuevers to pick the sick man's pocket contribute to his suffocation? Indeed, if the loss of the money is to remain undetected, is it not to Toulet's benefit that Acuña die? That the possibility of murder should surface here is all the more appalling for the paltriness of the crime's possible rewards.

Guerrero's chance observation not only reveals Toulet for the wretch he is, it also exposes the naiveté of Lagos' judgment of the Frenchman and of the system he defends. Lagos errs in believing that, at least, those who embrace the dominant ideology practice its professed ideals. Toulet's act is the sign of both his moral bankruptcy and that of The Office herself.

Beyond this, it must not be forgotten that Guerrero is, in the end, at least as much a part of the system as Toulet and a much greater beneficiary of it. His symbolic complicity in the theft strikes out at the reader in the sentence fragments which conclude the passage just quoted: "an abortive attempt of . . . 'Guerrero . . ?'"

The robbery ghoulishly parodies the robbery that Acuña has suffered all his life at the hands of the oligarchy and the liberal state in the form of low wages, high prices and taxes, those payments into a system which ultimately allow Guerrero to live the life of a *señorito*. The Frenchman, pathetic champion of an order which offers him nothing, surrenders the last rag of his decency in a bid for a few extra pesos, unconsciously miming the victimization he himself endures. It is the story's final irony that the man who attains some sort of realization from this event is not Toulet, but Guerrero, the aristocrat.

In achieving epiphany, in having his entire sense of the world and his place in it thrown into question, Guerrero is oddly reminiscent of Gabriel, Joyce's smug protagonist, who recognizes, at the conclusion of "The Dead," that he will ever be haunted by the ghost of Michael Fury. Before Toulet, Guerrero now

felt a fear, definite and disquieting, that fear one feels before Divine Mystery . . . As if, suddenly in the night, a tree might uproot itself and start advancing toward him of its own volition . . .
    The recollection of Acuña's death was made up of the death of a

man—a perfectly normal, quotidian thing—, and an act incredible, mysterious, terrible . . . that scene with the billfold . . .

Guerrero's complacency is irrevocably shattered, but unlike Gabriel, he must deal not with the ghost of his wife's dead lover, but a ghost alive, the personfication of the corruption of a whole worldview and the act which destroyed it:

> At times, Guerrero was the prisoner of a psychological phe-
> nomenon. He thought that Toulet would suddenly cut off his ram-
> blings about the government's abuses of the Federal interventionary
> powers in the provinces, to say to him, his face transfigured:
> "He's dead, Guerrero! He died in my arms! Oh! . . ."

By this point, Mariani has exposed The Office and all it represents as a truly infernal machine. It is physically hellish, its hierarchy arbitrary, its human relations brutal, its ostensible virtues a sham. Toulet himself is the quintessence of introjection, the negated ego, the man absolutely alien-ated from the reality of his own self and his circumstances. Yet this savaging has occurred with remarkable subtlety. A more overt writer, a different, more optimistic consciousness, might finally have offered the reader some scrap of hope, an example of how this monstrous structure might be, if not thrown down, at least resisted. The penultimate narrative, "Lacarreguy," finally presents us a man who acts, stealing money from his cash register to pay his debts. But those debts have been accrued in his hopeless attempt to maintain a mistress in oligarchical style. In the end, he finds she has abandoned him. Her name is more than coincidental: Consuelo—consolation.

So we arrive at the finale of *Cuentos de la oficina,* "La ficción."

The "fiction" we see here is a playlet, but the title reflects back, of course, on all those fictions gone before, both the stories themselves and those "fictions" exposed in the lives of the office workers—the illusory promises of success and security; the false dreams of honor and freedom. All of these *Cuentos de la oficina* confront us with lost innocence, and this last story, appropriately, deals with innocents, with children still pos-sessed of that naive belief that the lives of everyone in the world are very

much like their own. Here a brother and sister play house in the hallway
of their apartment building, mimicking their parents, recreating events
with a complete unawareness of the forces which shape them. Their
audience, a boy whose mother is visiting next door, sits perplexed. He
cannot fathom these scenes of desperate decisions, the choices made
between paying the butcher or the greengrocer, between buying shoes for
the little girl or yogurt for her mother's anemia. He sees no resemblance
between the breakfasts he knows in his own home and the mime of a
hurried *maté* gulped down by a man who punches a time clock. He cannot
understand how payday can be a time not for gifts, but for argument and
sacrifice. From his vantage in a world of comforts, of physical closeness, of
nannies, a world which has dressed him stylishly (and with nasty irony) in
a miniature sailor suit, he is perhaps like many *porteño* readers of *Cuentos
de la oficina,* unwilling or unable to believe in that bleak world Mariani
insists exists behind the bronzed doors and elaborate façades of the
fortresses of commerce lining Florida and 25 de Mayo and rising splen-
didly on vacant lots along the new Diagonal Norte.

It is this boy, this child of the bourgeoisie, who in this story (like
Guerrero in "Toulet") achieves a new awareness as a result of his experience. In the siblings' game, there is a mention of how their imaginary
daughter is now wearing mismatched shoes. At the story's conclusion "the
little girl has sat down nearby and is using her fingers to get one of her
shoes back on. While they were playing, the heel of her little foot kept
slipping out, because the threads have broken which hold together the
back seam, torn and resewed again and again." The little sailor observes,
"She's wearing two different shoes!"

The office worker's children do not see. They do not understand
what is odd about shoes from broken pairs. They cannot comprehend the
meaning of what they imitate. As they grow older, perhaps their consciousness will grow, though Mariani provides no indication that their
power to alter their lot will do the same. Likely, the brother will eventually be seduced off the street by promises of security and exhortations to
duty. His sister, after marriage, will find herself reduced to a *compañera*
at her husband's side, displaced in importance by a more powrful and
significant woman. The workers of their generation, like their parents
before them, will suckle at the breast of The Office, be imprisoned in her
womb, and they will never escape her. Mariani has brought us full circle.
In the first words of his book, he presented us that awful mother. Now, in
the end, he shows us the children, playing at grown-up. They do not know
that, within the Argentine capitalist world, to mature is to change from

child to stepchild, to suffer, just as in a fairy tale, exploitation, pain, and neglect. Unlike a fairy story, however, an office story bears no promise of a happy ending.

The comparison of *Cuentos de la oficina* and fairy tales is more than a turn of phrase. As the latter, in their symbols and development, demonstrate to us the visceral concerns and obsessions of our primitive selves, so Mariani's reveal those of the culture in which they were produced. As noted before, these are tales of repression in both its overt and internalized forms: Rillo crushed for rebellion; Riverita slapped and Lagos traumatized for desire; the man and woman of "Uno" torn asunder when their usefulness as producing agents vanishes; Fernández Guerrero haunted and Toulet animalized. This is what the power of The Office does.

As the "Balada" tells us from the first, The Office is more than a mere commercial entity: she is the central institution around which men must organize their lives. One notable element in the lives of all Mariani's characters is their lack of (or the secondary and tenuous nature of) any ties outside the office. In "Toulet," there is a brief allusion to his family. In the stories "Santana" and "Lacarreguey," we glimpse briefly these employees away from their jobs. However, in both these instances, their lives are shown to be utterly dependent on events at Olmos y Daniels. The prospect of Santana's loss of work as a consequence of a bookkeeping mistake sends his wife into a panic; his self-humiliation in order to retain his position, nonetheless, compromises him in her eyes, perhaps forever. Lacarreguey's mistress, of course, abandons him when the debts he has accrued for her benefit threaten to destroy him.

The characters, almost to a man, lack any history. No one mentions parents or siblings, with the notable exception of Fernández Guerrero, the son of the oligarchy. We know of the distant past of Toulet's family, but hardly anything of its present. Where is Lagos' home? Does Riverita live with his parents? Is Acuña married? The only sustained portraits of family life in *Cuentos de la oficina* are in "Uno," in which we watch the obliteration of a relationship, and in "La ficción," in which the children unwittingly act out the unmitigated bleakness of their parents' existence.

This absence of fulfilling family relationships is not accidental. As the "Balada" makes clear, there is no place in the modern capitalist world for ties and allegiances to anything but the workplace. A man's role is not that of father, husband, or son. He is a producer. A woman may be mother, wife, or daughter, but her major function here is that of *com-*

pañera: companion, sacrificer, suer for help in times of trouble and, in the end, as "Uno" demonstrates, as producer herself. "Man is born to work," The Office tells us, but if his capacity fails, a woman will do just as well.

The Office, then, destroys the family, displaces it, offering instead a society which retains the worst elements of traditional patriarchy—hierarchy, fear, punishment—without affording any of its benefits—love, security, a sense of place, and the assurance of the younger generation's eventual temporal triumph over the preceding one. This reality likely held particular power for Mariani and others of his background. The immigrant sons and daughters, descendents of parents or grandparents who remembered partriarchal but highly unified agricultural or ghetto cultures, found themselves part of a new nation whose own social arbiters viewed these new children of Argentina with great ambivalence. Mariani himself, in his posthumous and not altogether successful novel, *La cruz nuestra de cada día,* paints an idealized but still not wholly inaccurate picture of the unity of immigrant life, both on the level of family and on that of the *conventillo* and barrio. In Once, in La Boca, in Boedo, there was an attempt to assert community, to affirm the interdependence and hence the ultimate equality of each of its members.[38] However, as *Cuentos de la oficina* demonstrates, The Office—modern capitalist production—militates against any such sense, works via repression and introjection to destroy any other systems of relationships which might challenge it. In so doing, The Office creates a world reminiscent of the primitive culture of absolute patriarchy speculatively sketched in Freud's *Totem and Taboo.*[39] All loyalty, all wealth, all privilege are claimed by the domineering father. In Freud's model, however, an alternative, renegade system of social organization emerged, which defies and ultimately destroys the patriarch. This group—the band of brothers, of exiled sons—kills and devours its oppressor. Just as a model of community existed in the Argentine consciousness via the remembered and idealized European world, so this other model—male, heavily charged with homoerotic energy and, likewise, idealized—presented itself in the rustic universe mythologized in the gauchesque.[40] *Cuentos de la oficina* makes clear, however, that any attempts to establish an alternative—broadly and socially in the form of a union, as "Rillo," or personally and sexually, as in "Riverita"—are doomed by either outright repression or the insidious power of the introjected father.

The problem with the application of Freudian terminology in this context is obvious. Freud writes of fathers. The Office Mariani creates is most definitely female, an odious and domineering mother. Such a symbol, however, is accurate for the contemporary Argentine circumstance.

The father in the national system of repression and reification was (and remains) largely absent, his power wielded by his "consort," The Office. In Mariani's book, the fathers are those who bear the unspeakable names Olmos and Daniels. The latter particularly—so English, so intrusive—is the sign of the final destination of all the wealth The Office produces, the real locus of power in Argentina, which is not the executive suites on the Calle Florida nor the palaces in Barrio Norte, but London. The father, he who controls The Office and demands the regimentation of those employee sons, is Europe, most especially England, those anonymous capitalists who own not only Harrods and the Bank of London and South America, but also the Anglo-Argentine which built the subway which takes the man home in "Uno," the presses which print Riverita's favorite magazine, the popular periodical *Tit-bitz*, and the textile mills whose products end up as tiny imitations of the uniforms of the Royal Navy.

Cuentos de la oficina explores with consummate subtlety how an economic system works. Its setting is the medium of production, and its action chronicles the multifarious ways that system enslaves those trapped within it. The dream of leftist revolution is the establishment of the *Gemeinschaft*, of the harmonious community of humankind united in labor for the common good. Surely, the ideological point Mariani, an intensely empathic but critical man, sought to make in this lapidary book is the difficulty inherent in achieving any such goals. His characters are prototypes of the symbolic Argentine the slightly younger writer, Raúl Scalabrini Ortiz, would immortalize eight years later when he presented *El hombre que está solo y espera:* "The Man Who Is Alone and Waits." Surely, Lagos, Rillo, Toulet might be that lonely figure, each hoping for a deliverance he cannot quite name, there on the corner of Corrientes and Esmeralda.[41]

"There are now, in his still limited work, characters sketched or fully drawn who are not unworthy in their life and truth of comparison with Gandissart, with César Biroteau or, if we think of merchants, with the unfortunate Goriot."[42] *Cuentos de la oficina*, at least according to Roberto Payró, placed Mariani in heady company. The reviews in *Nosotros* and *Martín Fierro* were highly laudatory.[43] Mariani seemed virtually assured of the Premio Municipal in fiction. It went to someone else, of course.[44] So it was down the years. Mariani wrote constantly and left a respectable body of work: one book of poems, three collections of stories, three novels, and two plays. In addition, scattered through the newspapers and magazines of the twenties, thirties, and early forties, there is enough uncollected material to fill a volume easily. Most of his unpublished manuscripts have been lost or destroyed, though Rosa Eresky of the Teatro del Pueblo possesses a typescript of Mariani's titled *Ventanas de la soledad: Antipoemas con asunto*.

But he could never live from the work he loved, and so moved from office to office, vending his skills as clerk and typist, filing and figuring his laboring life in a uniform shade of gray. With the years, his faith in politics faded. He flirted with nationalism, then returned to the Church, following, it seems, the route of many Argentine writers—Lugones, Gálvez, Güiraldes—from youthful rebellion to mysticism, religious or ideological.[45] Yet, in his metaphysical quest, Catholicism was not enough. He apparently believed, in the midst of impotence both sexual and political, that he might somehow understand his own spirit and that of the men he labored beside by the minute exposition of their quietly tragic lives.

According to Larra and Pinto, Mariani never lost his acerbic wit and his respect for children, nor, in the end, was his final allegiance to the humanitarian and egalitarian ideals of his leftist youth seriously in doubt.[46] Upon his death—a heart attack? suicide?—his old friends and antagonists joined together in La Chacarita at his graveside to do him homage: Barletta, Suárez Danero, Rafael de Diego. Even Borges was there.[47]

Years later, another unquiet and very different Argentine, a man of the left dead before his time, noted his envy of North American radicals, who live "in the heart of the beast." Che Guevara, of course, was speaking metaphorically of the power concentrated in the Colossus of the North, which had become an omnipresent giant. Roberto Mariani, too, had seen the Beast, but with an artist's insight rather than a revolutionary's necessary rhetoric, he recognized that it resided in no one place, that its heart beat everywhere, beat in The Office, in every office all over his own nation and all those other nations all over the world. And he realized that the Beast lived too inside the men he worked with and within himself, poisoning the hearts of all of them. Perhaps Mariani saw his mission as the exposure of that truth, and, if so, he enjoyed a rare success that has remained unheralded. But, if the bleakness of *Cuentos de la oficina* and Mariani's own life are anything to go by, the cost of that knowledge and its expression was terrible indeed.

CHAPTER 7

Treason and Transformation

Roberto Arlt's El juguete rabioso

ROBERTO ARLT'S was a violent muse. Words from the titles of his canon tell the tale: "Rabid," "Madmen," "Flamethrowers," "Terrible," "Cruel." The events recounted in his books and plays reaffirm the judgment: murder, suicide, humiliation and betrayal; insanity, physical deformity, moral depravity. There is little sordid or brutal that is not dealt with by Arlt. It had become a commonplace to compare him to Dostoyevski, to define him as a sort of "pre-existentialist," though the final nihilism of most of his work, his characters' inability to achieve redemption either through the spirit or the will, makes such identifications somewhat less than perfect.[1] Arlt's fictional world was a dark one indeed, saved from the tremendist excesses of Castelnuovo only, perhaps, by Arlt's savage irony. It seems apt and inevitable that the first and, as yet, only book-length biography of him, published in 1950, should christen him *Roberto Arlt: El torturado*.[2]

This said, it is important to assert that Arlt's life was really not much better or worse than those of most of the other members of the Generation of 1922. His father was undeniably the portrait of a German bully, the Sergeant King to his son's Prince Frederick, and Arlt's childhood was much more pleasant during the man's prolonged and happily frequent absences. The boy left home for good at sixteen, moved to Córdoba, and there lived a scrabbling late adolescence which saw him through various apprenticeships and military service. He was apparently deceived by his first wife, who failed to tell him she was consumptive, and their marriage was not a particularly happy one, filled with inconclusive separations.[3] He was poor for many years and worked a a journalist most of his adult life to support his family. Still and all, he eventually achieved considerable renown. He was spared separating from his first love to marry his second

when the former expired from her chronic illness. His books were popular, his plays well-attended, and his job a newspaperman's dream: a daily,
bylined column in *El Mundo* based on his peregrinations through Buenos
Aires, which made him famous even among those who never set foot in a
library or a legitimate theater.[4]

To risk a dangerous and uncritical generalization, there is something
"typically" Argentine about Arlt, more so than about most of his contemporaries. This may be one of the roots of his popularity. The ambitious
child of an immigrant petit bourgeois, he detested the class of his origins.
If his fiction is anything to go by, the proletariat interested him not a whit.
His characters are almost all marginals, either by birth, choice, or circumstance. He seems to have felt a simultaneous attraction and repulsion for
the lumpen, and a somewhat less ambiguous fascination for the very rich,
or at least their style of life. He possessed a voracious sexual appetite, or at
least talked a great deal about it, while retaining an almost adolescent
romantic belief in love. He adored polemic and long nights' discussions
over endless coffee and cigarettes, and was a great aficionado of pamphlet
literature as well as a dedicated reader of the classics, with an autodidact's
disdain for formal learning. He was prolific and mercurial, highly creative
not only in his writing but elsewhere. Indeed, his greatest unrealized
ambition was to invent some product that would leave him *podrido de
plata*, "rotten with money." At the time of his fatal heart attack in 1942, he
was hard at work on a "vulcanized" (and thus, "unrunnable") silk stock-
ing.[5]

In spite of his relatively happy albeit short life, Arlt in his work
stresses autobiographical and imaginary episodes of humiliation and betrayal: paternal beatings, women's infidelity, failed revolutions. His texts
brim with that adolescent (and Argentine) nightmare—appearing
ridiculous, being the *cornudo*, the *boludo*, the *gil*: the cuckold, the dope,
the sap. As David Viñas has noted, Arlt's famous admissions that he did,
indeed, "write badly" (in the grammatical and syntactical sense) smack of
a certain aggressive pride, a vanity in breaking the rules.[6] The anecdotes
Arlt's associates tell, which are innumerable, make much of his extremity.
He emerges "a real character." Yet, that zaniness, after so many tellings,
seems oddly conscious, intentional, that boistrous impulse of his generation carried to pugnaciousness, terribly serious "fun."

And under it all, one suspects, dwelt a consciousness tormented not
so much by the demonic characters it created as by a consuming insecur-
ity, manifesting itself as rebellious outrageousness. In Arlt's mind, perhaps, the father with the strap might be lurking anywhere; the wife might

be trysting with some anonymous delivery boy at the very moment he, Arlt, unbuttoned the dress of his latest enamorata. That sort of fear is no stranger to the Argentine consciousness. The chauvinism, the obsession with appearances, the ostentatiously worn sophistication which characterizes so many Argentines (to an even greater extent than it may be said to for other critizens of this hemisphere) probably arise from very much the same emotions. Father Europe is always there ready to slap down pretensions. And that women, the land, at any moment might be surrendering her treasures to another.

Arlt's relationship to and membership in either Boedo or Florida has always been a matter of debate. Despite attempts to ensconce him on "the street of luxury and good taste," Raúl Larra is probably correct in asserting that Arlt was more in sympathy with his colleagues on the left, though, on the other hand, he was deeply fond of Marechal, Córdova Iturburu, and Nalé Roxlo, and adored the most indisputably oligarchical member of the Generation of 1922, Ricardo Güiraldes.[7] The point is that, regardless of his political pronouncements, Arlt's allegiances were largely personal, based on intuition and not ideology.

That ideology, from what his fiction indicates, was far removed from any known leftist orthodoxy, and indeed from most leftist heresy. Castelnuovo always claimed he rejected *El juguete rabioso* for Claridad because the manuscript was unreadable.[8] That may or may not have been the case. Castelnuovo could have objected to Arlt's language, an eccentric argot composed of street language and cullings from his wide and uncritical reading. Still, one suspects that the problem ran much deeper than that. *El juguete rabioso*, like *Los siete locos* and *Las lanzallamas* after it, is possessed of a worldview much at odds with the puritanical anarchism which Castelnuovo espoused. It is not difficult to imagine the horror the older writer must have felt as he followed the misadventures of Silvio Astier through a manuscript which, at that time, possessed the daunting title *Vida puerca*.[9] Even Mariani's bleak despair could not have prepared Castelnuovo for Arlt, a writer utterly lacking the subtlety of the clerk from La Boca.

Arlt's text, and Arlt himself, encountered appreciation from a very different and unexpected quarter, the staff of *Proa*. It was in the magazine directed by Borges and Brandán Caraffa that two sections of *El juguete rabioso* first saw print, and via the highly respectable Editorial Latina that the novel, in process since 1919, first reached the public in its entirety. In both these instances, the good angel interceding for the fledgling author who spoke with hard, German "r's" was Güiraldes.

During the twenties, there were probably no two figures more distinct that Güiraldes and Arlt. Still, of all his literary friends, Arlt seems to have loved only one other, Mariani, with the devotion he felt for Güiraldes.[10] Exactly how the two first met and why they developed such an intense bond remains obscure. One may speculate that Güiraldes encountered in both Arlt and his work an intensity and lack of inhibition he himself had never enjoyed, and that Arlt found in the older man a profound talent who respected him and, nonetheless, lived in that rarefied, upper-class world he so admired.

Whatever the cause, 1925 found Arlt almost a fixture in the Güiraldes' home as he prepared the final draft of *El juguete rabioso*. Ancedotes describe Arlt reading from the work to Güiraldes, and sending Güraldes' wife, the thoroughly modern Adelina del Carril, out of the room when he reached some of the novel's more scandalous passages.[11] Güiraldes, the story goes, advised Arlt aesthetically, proofread and corrected the manuscript, and provided the book's eventual title, all while his own last and greatest work, *Don Segundo Sombra*, was also in process.

El juguete rabioso came off the presses in October of 1926, when Arlt was employed at the tabloid *Ultima Hora*. It was not his first published work. At fourteen, through the good offices of Juan José de Soiza-Reilly, the facile and enthusiastic writer associated with *Caras y Caretas*, Arlt published a story, "Jehová," in *La Revista Popular*, a not-inconsiderable feat for a boy who had left school after the third grade.[12] *El diario de un morfinómano*, a lost text which may be apocryphal, supposedly appeared in Córdoba during Arlt's sojourn there in the late teens.[13] Also in this period, he published in the pamphlet series *Tribuna Libre* a piece entitled "Las ciencias ocultas en la ciudad de Buenos Aires."[14] If Arlt's preface to the second edition of *El juguete rabioso* is accurate, he wrote the novel's first chapter "Los ladrones," at about the same time.[15]

El juguete rabioso established Arlt as a serious talent. Rejected at various houses in addition to Claridad, it came to the attention of the Editorial Latina (probably not accidently, Güiraldes' publisher) as an entry in a literary contest sponsored by the publisher. Though it failed to win, the book was praised by two prominent jury members, Julio Noé and Enrique Méndez Calzada, and appeared in a deluxe, softbound edition of a thousand copies.

The critics, preoccupied at the time by the appearance of one very good novel *(Don Segundo Sombra)* and two very bad ones (Gálvez' *La pampa y su pasión* and Enrique Larreta's *Zogoibí*), had little time to spare for an eccentric book by an unknown writer with an unpronounceable last name. In December, Barletta did review it in *Nosotros*, calling it "an indisputably good novel."[16] More typically, *Claridad*'s anonymous commentator, in November's "Notas Bibliográficas," gave most of his alloted space to Mariani's new collection, *El amor agresivo*, passing over Arlt in a summary half-dozen lines, concluding with what was likely an indirect snipe at Güiraldes: "The title is more than a bit capricious and 'modern,' and out of alignment with the spirit of the book."[17]

Still, *El juguete rabioso* sold respectably and created quite a stir among young writers. Of all the products of the new generation to that point, Arlt's was the most unsparing in its reflection of the typical *porteño* life of the epoch. Freely employing *lunfardo*, unembarrassed in the presentation of the anomie of the city's youth, overt in his assault on the society's much-touted opportunities, Arlt spoke the disillusionment which simmered beneath the surface of the smug age of Alvear. Silvio Astier's brushes with the law, his encounter with the homosexual in a cheap pension, his final betrayal of his accomplice, El Rengo, demanded recognition of an urban reality which had heretofore remained beyond the ken of literature. Certain other authors, Gálvez for example, had dealt with some of the grimmer aspects of contemporary Buenos Aires, but neither the romanticized *Nacha Regules* nor the sensationalist *Historia de arrabal* had prepared readers for the casual, lower-middle-class amorality of Silvio. Boedo had certainly chronicled more horrifying human suffering, but, with the exception of *Cuentos de la oficina*, that production dealt with characters not likely to be so intensely similar to the reading public. *El juguete rabioso*, conversely, centers on a boy ambitious for life's finer things. He is intelligent, inventive, and optimistic. Silvio was not the victim of brutal thugs or brutalizing parents. He was, conceivably, the boy next door, down the block, or dreamily passing the time reading Baudelaire there across the living room. Conceivably, too, he was the reader himself.

Modern criticism of *El juguete rabioso* has been neither extensive nor particularly profound.[18] *Los siete locos* and *Las lanzallamas*—longer, more apparently unified, brimming with bizarre incidents and characters—have perhaps appeared to offer a more fecund interpretive field. Arlt's first novel, meanwhile, presents those problems of most initial literary efforts, particularly autobiographical ones. It is crammed with experience, emotion, literary allusion, ideas and obsessions. Vivid and often contradictory, it is complicated even more by the eclecticism of the author's own improvisatory youth and education. Commentary tends toward the dismissive, or to focus on the supposedly self-evident: the novel's place within the picaresque tradition and its "pre-existentialist" denouement, in which the "gratuitous act" of betrayal is valorized as the medium of individuation.[19] There has been little critical attempt to deal with the text as a whole, to seek the relationships among the four seemingly independent chapters which cover the life of Silvio Astier from ages fourteen to seventeen. Yet, if the narrative is carefully scrutinized, major thematic threads appear which reveal the central concerns of Arlt's tangled vision, and in so doing, ground the novel in the age and its reality.

El juguete rabioso was written in a nation in transformation, or, at least, apparent transformation. The twenties was a decade in which the "Argentine dream" seemed to reach fruition. The Radicals (even if the more oligarchical ones) were in power; the national economy was expanding; art and literature flowered. Buenos Aires, with its dazzling avenues and elegant promenade for ordinary citizens at the Balneario Público, seemed well on its way to becoming an international capital. New arrivals still poured through the Hotel de Inmigrantes from that Old World so recently ravaged by strife, to seek political freedom and economic mobility in a nation whose very name meant "money."[20]

The book itself is a Bildungsroman, a novel of growing up, of the transformation of the child into the man, of youth in a youthful nation. As such, it might be expected to partake of the kind of optimism which had turned sour in Europe, and, to a lesser extent, in the United States as a result of the World War. Not ten years had elapsed since Güiraldes had created his autobiographical Raucho, the young aristocrat who had barely escaped Paris's decadent blandishments, finding health and solace back on the estancia, "asleep on his back, his arms open, crucified with serenity on the earth that was his forever."[21]

Silvio Astier, however, is a far different breed, a boy of the city with no country estate to escape to, one upon whom money does not magically devolve (or cease to devolve) from parents alternately generous or disapproving. He must scramble for the pesos which will allow his truncated family—him, his mother and sister—to maintain some minimal respectability among the other immigrant folk of Flores, Caballito, and Floresta. It is in these barrios—raw in the 1920s—that his story unfolds. He does his best to maintain his youthful self-confidence, but life's reality makes it more difficult than it has been, perhaps, for other heroes of the genre. In addition, his transformation signifies much more than mere maturation. Silvio is seeking, throughout the story, the transformation that America promised to that multitude of Latins ("Silvio"), of Germans, Jews and Poles ("Drodman"), of western Europeans ("Astier"). These immigrants,

after all, had come prepared, unconsciously if not consciously, to surrender their old identities and assume that new one of Argentine. *Hacerse
la américa* translates most accurately, perhaps, as "to make America one's
own," to take advantage of its opportunities. Yet, the phrase's literal
meaning is much more powerful: "To make one's self America."

Silvio, son of those foreign waves of the 1890s and early 1900s, is out
to grab his part of the national dream: making the grade, getting ahead,
becoming someone. As might be expected, he wants his rewards now, if
not yesterday. Few who come from the lower or middle classes wish to
remain there, and less so the children of immigrants, whose parents have
sacrificed home, language, and heritage for a better life—for themselves,
surely, but especially for their offspring, who must suffer the glory and
burden of firstborn in the promised land. In his bid to achieve, Silvio
does, of course, have open to him the possibility of hard work, and he is
alternately a shopboy, a soldier, and a salesman. But labor as a solution in
what his erstwhile friend, Lucio, insists on describing as the Darwinian
"struggle for life," Silvio recognizes as alienating and unrewarding, both
financially and spiritually.

It is other routes to success which exert a more powerful pull on
Silvio's imagination. He, like all those men of Corrientes and Esmeralda,
"has in his mind an idea, a project, an invention, a plan of action . . .
[which will] leave him rotten with money."[22] Throughout the novel, Arlt's
character entertains or experiments with a panoply of possible means of
transformation, things that will change him from an anonymous boy on
the streets into someone who might feel himself "truly fortunate." That
condition was, not surprisingly, what Arlt himself described as his own
goal in life in an interview in 1929.[23]

Flushed with optimism in his first days in the army, Silvio likens his
own destiny to that of four figures: Edison, Napoleon, Baudelaire, and the
pamphlet-fiction hero Rocambole. These—inventor, general, poet, and
criminal—represent the four possible routes he attempts to follow. The
least plausible and shortest-lived is the second. Silvio's military career
ends almost before it begins, and is, in any case, heavily predicated not on
his skills as a leader, but as an engineer. Still, if the vision of Napoleon is
amplified to include strategist and conqueror, the image well bespeaks
Silvio's ambitions if not his accomplishments. His is a dream which will
provide him access to the glittering, oligarchical world he glimpses only
fleetingly in the cafés filled with idlers on the Calle Lavalle, or in the
apartment of some nameless plutocrat to whose mistress he delivers a
book. It is the world which, at fourteen, he, Enrique, and Lucio spend
their ill-gotten gains to imitate, and the one about which he still fantasizes

with Rengo three years later. Wealth promises ease and luxury, the unbounded sexuality of the French courtesan, and the purity of adolescent love that Silvio imagines when he sees a young couple on a balcony in Barrio Norte. Throughout the story, he is obsessed with what he might do "to triumph, to have money, a lot of money."[24]

Silvio desires wealth and the power it implies, but Napoleonic ambitions are not to be achieved by selling paper or sweeping a bookshop. There are, of course, other means: Edison's, for example. We are constantly reminded of Silvio's capacities as an inventor. Among the boy thieves, he is the "official chemist," and he and Enrique first hit it off due to the former's reputation as the maker of a tiny cannon. His abilities sufficiently impress the junior officers at the army base that they open an extra space in the ranks to bring him into the military. But his talents are also what encourages senior officers to purge him: they need not intelligent boys but "beasts of burden." In his contact with Rengo, we find the two discuss inventions "to cop money off the next guy." The interest of the theosophist, Vicente Tomaso Sonza, in helping Silvio is obviously predicated on the possible commercial value of the boy's inventions.

Those machines Silvio claims either to have produced or designed are not, however, particularly likely to earn either him or anyone else a fortune. The technical obstacles to the projected dictograph he describes to the three young officers are immediately pointed out by Captain Bossi, and Captain Márquez later notes Silvio's plans for a new kind of mortar fail to take into account basic laws of ballistics. The boy has a letter from the physicist, Ricaldoni, praising his design for a meteor counter, but his only invention which actually seems to have achieved concrete form is the little cannon which so impressed the neighborhood boys in chapter one. This is to say that Silvio, like his creator, is perhaps less an inventor than a dreamer. Indeed, two of the machines described seem peculiarly oneiric: one allows the transformation of the spoken word immediately into a text; the other retains a record of shooting stars—the visible, celestial signs of desire.

"Inventing" has other powerful resonances. Silvio, after all, is in the process of "inventing himself," or so he would like to believe. All those attempts to change himself from "no one" to "someone" are the human equivalent of taking disparate wires and tubes, metal and electric current, and from those fashioning something unique. A fascination with invention should not surprise us in the 1920s, particularly in Argentina. Did not the Radicals themselves reject the old classifications of capital and labor because, in America, "new ideals of human solidarity" were being forged? Were not the immigrants engaged in the dual process of making new selves and also a new nation, "inventing Argentina," as it were, in the very moment they were becoming Argentines?

Beyond this, there is invention as art. The very story we read is the transformation of transcient experience into word and image, refined and made eternal on the page. This novel, as we know extratextually, is distilled autobiography, and more importantly from our present vantage, is presented as "true" autobiography—Silvio's first-person narrative of his own adventures. Writing, we discover at the beginning of chapter two, is one of Silvio's other interests, and, if we partake of the fiction, is the one he most obviously realizes. It is unsurprising, then, that the third member of Silvio's heroic quaternity should be that figure of the poet, Charles Baudelaire.

The presence of literature in this literary text is large and multiform. It begins with Silvio's initiation into the penny dreadfuls by the old Andalusian shoemaker, and ends with his promised departure for Neuquén, where, we may presume, this "autobiography" was penned. Throughout *El juguete rabioso,* art and life conflate, reinforce one another: street verses amplify the despair of the Astiers in chapter two; Silvio, fantasizing after he thinks he has destroyed don Gaetano's shop, imagines himself the subject of a genre painting. Poets themselves, for Silvio, inhabit that charmed circle he associates with the very wealthy. They attend glamorous parties and attract elegant women, the reward for capturing beauty on a page, something Silvio's own misery prevents him from doing.

As literature itself transforms observed beauty into an object, so those objects, books, possess transformatory power. Books seems almost talismanic in *El juguete rabioso*. The boy thieves' final and most extensive burglary is of a library; Silvio find employment in a bookstore. Chapters two and three both begin with Silvio reading. Characters of powerful influence possess fine personal libraries, for example, the man who ostensibly first corrupted the homosexual of chapter three, and the engineer to whom Silvio finally betrays Rengo. Books can help one get ahead: Captain Márquez tells Silvlio he must study. They can also be subversive. The boy's revelation of his tastes not only for scientific texts but literature—"Baudelaire, Dostoyevski, Baroja"—raises fears among the officers he may be an anarchist. Books have commodity value. Enrique and Silvio divide the library volumes into two categories, *vale* and *no vale;* Don Gaetano's business is not a "bookshop," but a "store for buying and selling used books."

More often, however, books are gnostic. They provide Silvio with his knowledge of science; they inspire his spirit; they even give form to his

sexual fantasies. When he masturbates after meeting the French courtesan, his images of desire are drawn from books of obscene photographs,
and his great frustration is that he cannot possess a woman as beautiful as
those who appear in the dirty pictures. At times, books are almost human.
Enrique, after all, is betrayed by one: the Geography he carries under his
arm in the predawn darkness draws the attention of the police. And from
books comes the last of that pantheon by which Silvio measures himself:
Rocambole.

Rocambole, Salgari's fictional Parisian criminal, intimate of thou-
sands of *porteños* via one of the most popular journals of the age, *Tit-bitz*,
represents the most radical mode of transformation: crime. If, on the one
hand, the law is never more than a threat to Silvio (he never falls into the
hands of the dreaded *cana*), it does offer a unique thrill in its violation. In
each of the four episodes, Silvio either plans or participates in an illegal
act: robbery, arson, suicide, and robbery again. He feels, in each instance,
that these will somehow transform him, or at least provide him with some
means to transform himself. With the funds accrued from pawning hardware stolen from vacant houses, Silvio, Enrique, and Lucio hire a car and
take tea in an expensive café, entering for a few moments that magical
world of ease to which they aspire. Later, and more profoundly, Silvio lies
in wait in the school library for an intruder upon the theft to show himself.
There, all his senses heightened, an iron bar raised over his head to brain
whoever has stumbled upon the crime, the fourteen-year-old reveals:
"Suddenly, my fear reached its peak and transfigured me. I ceased to be
the child on a lark. My nerves went numb. My body turned to a grim-
faced statue brimming with criminality, a statue erect on stiff members,
poised with the understanding of fear."

Silvio is, in that moment, a real burglar, no longer a child playing.
Simultaneously he becomes a man, an adult. The images of change are
insistently sexual. This fusion of crime and sexuality emerges again a year
later, after Silvio believes he has burned the bookstore where he works. In
his bed late that night, he realizes it is "the hour of the 'coquettes,' . . .
the hour of the little girls . . . and poets . . ." His crime has liberated him,
matured him: "In the darkness, I smiled, free . . . free . . . definitively free,
for the consciousness of manhood that what I had done gave me." It is the
illegal act, the violation, while makes the boy the man, which makes him
feel "life is beautiful."

Even as he spirals toward his attempt at self-destruction, the crime
against his own being promises a certain lubricious luxury: "Under different circumstances, the theatricality which heightens the mourning at

the catafalque of a suicide had already seduced me with its dignity. I envied those cadavers around whose caskets beautiful women wept; seeing them leaning over the coffin's edge stirred my masculinity."

In the concluding chapter, meanwhile, Silvio and Rengo imagine the Europe they will conquer with the engineer's ten thousand pesos, moving through great cities like *bacanes,* like oligarchs, pursued by women anxious to be possessed by a man for whom the tango is birthright.

Crime in *El juguete rabioso* represents mettle, acuity, and everything that is opposed to the false and mean ethic reigning in the working world:

> To sell, you have to bathe yourself in mercurial subtlety, choose your words and disguise the concepts, flatter circumspectly, talking about things you neither think about nor believe in, getting enthused over nothing. . . . be two-faced, flexible, and funny . . . and suffer, patiently suffer the time and those sour, ill-humored faces, the rude, annoying answers, suffer to earn a few cents because "that's the way life is."

In the thief, however, there is something glorious, and in money stolen, something magical: "Not the vile and hateful money loathed for having been earned by painful labor, but agile money, a silver sphere with legs of a gnome and a dwarf's beard . . . whose smell like a generous wine bore us toward divine revels." The old shoemaker puts forth the robber as the agent of economic justice—Robin Hood—and as always the gentleman. Of all criminals, for Silvio, Rocambole is the most magnificent. It is to this pamphlet fiction hero that Silvio compares the faces of the army officers. Rocambole's precedent comes to mind as justification when Silvio makes his final and appalling decision to betray Rengo.

As is apparent, Silvio's heroes and the modes of transformation they represent fold in upon one another. Rocambole, after all, is himself an "invention," the product of a "poet." As criminality involves deceit, so too does fiction; as it implies alteration (your property become mine; loathsome money become "agile"), so does invention, disparate elements made something else. As crime violates, so too does conquest, invention, art. Rules are broken; the old physics does not apply; the most private confidences and imaginings are made public. All transformation implies destruction and creation. From this derives the intense sexuality of all its modes. Crime makes Silvio "erect on stiff members." He refers to handling his newly made toy cannon as "fondling my little monster." Poets move through a world of desirable women, and that imperial wealth of which Silvio dreams guarantees both love and the realization of exotic lusts.

Transformation, however, assures something beyond mere earthly pleasure, something more important:

> "It doesn't matter if I have a suit, or money, or anything else"— and I confessed to myself, almost ashamed:
> "What I want is to be admired by other people, praised by them. What difference does it make if I'm foolhardy? That's all right . . . But this life of mediocrity . . . to be forgotten when I die, that's the horrible thing. Oh, if only my inventions would work out! Still and all, someday I will die, and the trains will keep running, and people will go to the theater just like always, and I'll be dead, good and dead . . . dead for the rest of my life." . . .
> Oh, if only I could discover something so that I'd never die, even just live five hundred years!

Fame is the final transformer. The glow of immortality more than money or sexual fulfillment fascinates Silvio. It is what, above any single factor, unites his four heroes. Yet, beyond the routes of conquest, invention, poetry, and crime, there are other ways to achieve it. As will later become apparent, these other roads can lead to a hellish kind of immortality indeed.

Silvio, in the course of his story, is indeed transformed. Those modes of change he identifies, however, those previously discussed, though they may influence his actions and certainly his imagination, truly affect him only by fueling his disillusionment. There are other factors at work, however, which do alter him. They are not the products of fantasy. They are the mean realities of the culture in which he lives.

El juguete rabioso's presentation of labor's alienating nature is one of its most striking and unsparing characteristics, even more so because, rather than the grinding routine of the factory or the office, Silvio is employed in the small commercial sector of the *porteño* economy, that is, the sector in which the depersonalization of the economic machine should be least. There, however, rather than the awful but faceless mechanization of workers à la *Modern Times*, we witness the petty nastiness of petit bourgeois capitalism. Arlt's sketches of the small merchant—his falseness, obsequiousness, miserliness, and gratuitous cruelty—are studies in savagery. Don Gaetano—slick, cunning, and impotent—and his horrific consort, María, seem escaped from a mordant satire; along with their servant, Miguel ("Dio Fetente"), they are true grotesques. Yet, even the less extreme figures, the butchers, pharmacists, and grocers we meet in chapter four, are possessed by an awful avarice and smallness of spirit. From them, Silvio learns one harsh and ugly lesson: "You have to learn to dominate yourself utterly to abide all the insolence of the petit bourgeoisie."

How does Silvio come to recognize the need for this self-control? The answer is simple and appropriately Arltian: humiliation. Particularly in the two middle chapters, Silvio is shamed again and again, made publicly and privately ridiculous by those around him. Dreams matter not a whit. They will not provide the money to maintain the shabby apartment of the Astiers, nor buy the schoolbooks for Silvio's sister, Lila, so she may someday become a teacher and provide the family a certain respectability. The laboring world soon dashes any transcendent illusions. In the employ of don Gaetano, Silvio enacts scenes simultaneously amusing and pathetic: manuevering the owner's oversized shopping basket, or later, María's possessions stacked on an upturned table through the elegant crowds of Calle Lavalle, one of the city's great centers of entertainment. By the chapter's final pages, however, any risible element in Silvio's situation has been burned away by the black fire of his own despair. He grows quiet, withdrawn. He does not think.

> They gave me a bell. A cowbell. And it must have been funny—
> Good God!—to see a ragamuffin my size doing something so base. I
> stood at the door of the bookstore during the hours of peak traffic on
> the street, jangling the bell to attract people, to make people turn
> their heads, so that people would know that we sold books, lovely
> books . . . and that these noble histories and things of beauty had to
> be bought from a crafty man or his fat, pale wife. And I rang that bell.
> Many were the eyes that slowly stripped me naked. I saw
> women's faces I will never forget. I saw smiles that still scream their
> jeers at me . . .

Even in circumstances not so overtly dreadful Silvio is humiliated. In the army, the apparent respect of the junior officers compensates for the brutish life of a recruit, but the reasons for that respect, of course, soon lead to Silvio's dismissal. His very talents, in that instance, condemn him. While working as a paper vendor, we witness in the text the dislocation in Silvio between body and mind, labor and spirit:

> Along those narrow, neighborhood streets, miserable and filthy, flooded with sunlight, trashcans in the doorways, with those women pot-bellied, disheveled and squalid, talking from the thresholds, calling dogs or children, beneath that limpid and diaphanous arch of sky. . . . That memory I maintain—fresh, grand and beautiful.
>
> My eyes drank deep of the infinite serenity, ecstatic before that blue infinity.
>
> Burning flames of hopes and dreams enfolded my spirit, and within me an inspiration so joyous budded that, honestly, I could not express it in words.
>
> That blue dome awed me more and more, no matter how vile the places I did business. I remember . . .
>
> Those markets, those neighborhood butcher shops!

There, he finds the dirt, the offal, the bloody ugliness of everyday living, together with the nasty dealings of those men and women desperate to hoard a few pesos more, ideally at his expense.

Throughout the story, Silvio meets very few characters who manage to remain authentic, to pursue their own desires while they also make a life. The homosexual at the end of chapter three, if pathetic, is proud, at least, of fulfilling his "destiny," though his fondest wish—to be a woman and loved as one—is obviously beyond his grasp. The boy thieves seem to be living their fantasies, though eventually Enrique ends in jail, while Lucio "regenerates" himself by becoming a private investigator. Only Rengo, perhaps, is true to himself, and he makes the disastrous error of trusting Silvio Astier.

For the most part, the novel's characters no longer dream. They have conformed, accepted the rules of the game, allowed themselves to be manipulated by the ideals and values of the culture in which they live. This, perhaps, explains the *juguetes* (toys) of the novel's title. They emerge as an image in the first chapter, in which the boys adopt as their clubhouse a storeroom filled with abandoned puppets and mutilated toy soldiers. The puppet then surfaces, overtly or implicitly, on various occasions throughout the book. Surely Silvio's gradually losing his hearing, speech, and thought as he becomes the barker for the store represent dehumanization in the most literal sense. The split of imagination and reality, the sky and the street, which occurs within him as a paperseller surely signs his increasing alienation from his own self. His plans for triumph are, in a sense, his attempt to create circumstances in which he can "pull his own strings," as opposed to becoming the mere puppet of the invisible powers of the world in which he lives.

Inevitably, the gulf between Silvio's ambitions and his possibilities, the promises of the world and its realities, the disappointments and cruelties he is forced to endure generate within him not solely despair and shame, but rage as well. His growing torpor in the employ of don Gaetano arises from this: "My capacity to understand things buried itself in a concave anger, a concavity which, day by day, made itself wider and deeper. Thus, my anger remained obscured." The night after he has been discharged from the army, after his homosexual encounter, he flees the diner where he has sought refuge upon realizing that everyone else there has a home, while he has none. On the streets, he passes comfortable, monied houses:

> Trembling with hatred, I lit a cigarette, and meanly tossed the burning match on top of a human sack which was sleeping curled on a stoop. A little flame flickered on the rags, when suddenly the wretch arose, formless as darkness itself, and I fled, threatened by his enormous fist.

His fury is that of the defrauded, of those for whom promises have been broken, dreams deferred. It is that emotion of the homeless to which the immigrant, who has gambled everything, or the son of the immigrant, who must live with that gamble's consequences, is particularly prone. "Furious" best translates, in some ways, that third word of Arlt's title, for *rabioso* is used colloquially in the same sense as that term in English. Nonetheless, its literal equivalent, "rabid," is probably more apt in the end. Silvio dreams of transformation into an immortal: a poet, conquerer, criminal, inventor. The world offers instead to change him into a "toy." In the process, it drives him mad. His assault on the anonymous beggar is a sign of his disease. It is with El Rengo, however, that it bursts forth in its true and terrible virulence.

In Dante's Hell, in that ninth circle where Satan dwells frozen in a lake of ice, his three mouths eternally grind three men: Brutus and Cassius, who plotted Caesar's murder, though he thought of them as sons, and the arch-traitor of the Western imagination, Judas Iscariot. There is about Judas a dark grandeur. Only Lucifer himself outstrips him as an object of fascinated revulsion, and even so, Judas—a man, not a fallen archangel—seems somehow closer, a human sign of black potentials locked deeply within each of us. That infinitely fatal kiss, those thirty pieces of silver, the immeasurable remorse—they are all part of our most primitive consciousness. *El juguete rabioso* tells us they are, as well, among the most profound components of modern life.

Silvio's adventures, if carefully considered, seem an endless chain of betrayals, either by circumstances or by individuals. Even in the amoral idyll of "Los ladrones" (in which, of course, the boys themselves are violating the trust of those they rob), the theme begins to emerge at the chapter's conclusion. After Enrique has been hailed by the police, he flees to Silvio's house, rapping three times on the door. Silvio, terrified, does not answer. Enrique knocks three times again. This time, Silvio does respond, avoiding, as it were, the third denial. The consequence of the evening's dangers, however, is the vote of Silvio and Lucio in favor of "paralyzing the activities" of the boy thieves. Enrique, however, decides to continue alone. In a sense, then, the two other boys "betray" their friend. Their decision does, of course, have logic on its side. However, Enrique's eventual fate, compared with Silvio's and particularly Lucio's, reinforces the sense of their abandonment of their friend.

The theme grows in import in chapter two. As Silvio waits to move into the Gaetano's house, a cock crows, another resonant New Testament image. The boy's experiences in the bookseller's employ surely represent the betrayal of his hopes. Silvio thinks he may escape that awful fate through the good offices of the theosophist, but the old charlatan simply pushes him away when the impracticality of his inventiveness becomes apparent. The boy finally, in his despair, "betrays" his master by trying to set fire to the store, only to have his attempt "betrayed" by a stray puddle of water left from Dio Fetente's washing up.

In chapter three, even as he prepares to go to El Palomar, Silvio senses in Rebeca Naidath, the neighbor who has brought the job opportunity to his attention, "the desire to see me fail in my attempt." He feels his sharpest disappointment yet when Captain Márquez, the very officer who has assumed the role of his patron, signs the order dismissing him from the service. His plans to escape to Europe after that humiliation, instead of returning home once again without work, are frustrated by the ships' masters who refuse to take him aboard. In the end, his own will fails him during his suicide attempt: he faints before he can aim the bullet true.

During his career as a paper vendor, Silvio's customers constantly act in bad faith, and when, in his peregrinations through the city, he encounters Lucio, Silvio suspects him of trying to trick him into an incriminating remark which will allow his old partner in crime to turn on him. It is worthwhile to enumerate these instances, for they indicate that the delivering over of Rengo is not quite that unique, existentialist, "gratuitous act" of which criticism has made so much. While Silvio's treason does have resonances which must be investigated, it should be recognized as a repellent but by no means original act in the text. Quite simply, in the novel, betrayal is the way of the world. Rengo's tragedy is that, in the nasty, petit bourgeois, *porteño* universe, in the realm of the *viveza criolla*, he is foolish enough to trust someone, particularly a man so wounded as Silvio Astier. Among buyers and sellers, it is he who confides who ends up the *gil*.

That treason should be shown to be among the most common of crimes should not surprise us in *El juguete rabioso*, which demonstrates almost systematically the inversion in concrete reality of those virtues abstractly cherished. Neighborliness is a sham; intelligence is dangerous; generosity always revocable. Everything in petit bourgeois culture militates in favor of betrayal as an acceptable, logical means of advancement. Indeed, what is distinctive in Silvio's turning on Rengo is that most quotidian treachery is carried out against one's anonymous fellows or vague acquaintances. He, however, has the chance to commit a truly monstrous act. The man he denounces is one whom he respects, even loves, one who, as González Lanuza points out, is almost a father to him.[25]

The father is, perhaps, the most resounding "present absence" in *El juguete rabioso*. We hear of Silvio's only once. When Captain Bossi asks if the boy's parents approve of his literary tastes, he replies: "My father killed himself when I was very small." Given Arlt's incendiary relation with his own father, one might dismiss this as nothing more than the author's own ironic wish: better that Karl Arlt had done away with himself than to have survived to terrorize his son's childhood. Yet, such a simple, biographical solution ignores the various resonances of "fatherlessness" within the text, obscure and inconsistent though they may sometimes be.

A father is more than merely a progenitor. In any patriarchal social system, he is the bearer of culture and the law, the "legitimator" in far more than the narrow, legalistic sense. He "takes" a wife who comes to live in his home, to give him children who will bear his name. Those children, like the wife, by social custom if not legal dictate, were as property to the man, his to do with as he pleased within broad guidelines until, in the case of a daughter, she was "given" to some other man, or, in the case of a son, he achieved some prescribed seniority which signified his manumission and allowed him, with time, to establish himself as a "father" and so repeat the historical pattern. It was the fathers who shaped the customs and practices of a particular community, so maintaining its continuity down the generations.

The father, then, is the fleshly manifestation of human history, as opposed to the woman, associated in patriarchy with the natural—the seasons, the moon, the earth. In the families of *El juguete rabioso*, the father is peculiarly "gone." Only in the interpolated anecdote about the Naidath, with its self-consciously Biblical overtones, is the male parent present. He, interestingly, loathes his own heritage, which perhaps not accidentally is Jewish, that is, of a culture in which, though patriarchal, racial legitimacy devolves matrilineally.

Throughout the novel, Silvio seems to be groping for some sort of father, someone to fill the place of the one who killed himself. There is a level where, even if that father were present physically, he would still be a suicide. The immigrant himself, in leaving his native land, commits a kind of symbolic suicide. He erases himself from the community which has nurtured and known him, bursting full blown into the midst of another. He, however, always maintains the memory of his other self, of the world of his fathers. His offspring have no such recollections, having been born into a culture in which they have no roots, one with its own traditions and values—its own "patrimony"—which the immigrant's children must somehow make their own.

Silvio, in chapter one, first moves to steal a part of the national heritage. The boys rob a school library, a concrete symbol of the Sarmentine liberal plan which encouraged both mass literacy and mass immigration. Silvio, the Italian Lucio, and the *gallego*, Enrique, hope to make off with books, expunge the seal of the Consejo Escolar (thus making them "theirs") and, while selling some, keep others. The also fatherless Enrique insists on stealing as well a multivolume geography, a book, one might say, to help him and his cohorts locate themselves.

The upshot, of course, is the boys' near capture by the police, the official guardians of the culture's customs and the representatives of the authority of the "father" which is the nation. One apparently cannot steal one's way into Argentine identity, so Silvio, rather more reluctantly, tries to work his way in. He takes the job at the bookstore and moves in with the Gaetanos. The error of his choice is apparent from the first. Gaetano is, of course, an immigrant himself and a representative of the class in which immigrants were preponderant in that era. Beyond this, his unfitness as a symbolic father is reaffirmed by his literal impotence. "They don't have children," Dio Fetente tells Silvio. "He can't do it."

In the military officers and the army itself, however, Silvio seems to have found the means to graft himself onto larger history. The army, though it may itself be composed of newcomers, is an institution inextricably intertwined with the national being. Too, the relation between officer and soldier of domination and obedience mimics the traditional interaction of father and son. Captain Márquez, on a personal level, treats Silvio with paternal indulgence, encouraging his ambitions while spurring him on to further and more serious study. Yet, this "family" which created a place for him soon casts him out. The adoptive father Silvio craves will not have him.

There follows one of the most peculiar scenes in the novel, and indeed, in any work of the Generation of 1922: Silvio's conversation with the homosexual in the pension. This boy, if his own account can be trusted, is the only true representative of the upper classes with whom Silvio converses. Ostensibly corrupted by his tutor (the ironically named Próspero), the boy's function in the story is obscure. Within the present schema, his impossible transformitory wish, to be a woman, perhaps symbolizes the unattainability of any transformation, the impossibility of Silvio's ever integrating himself with the "Argentine father." The only way he might do so were if he were a woman, and thus might be "possessed" by a man of the community and hence become part of it. But Silvio is no more a woman than the boy in silk stockings across that dismal room who attempts to seduce him.[26]

Silvio then goes to the port to undertake his "anti-immigration," a return to the place from whence his father came, where there was history. In this too, he fails. He has run out of options. He cannot steal a heritage; he cannot work his way into one. He cannot be a woman and literally "take in" the father and create native life. He cannot erase the symbolic suicide which was his father's emigration from his own land. The only path he sees as remaining open is literal imitation. He will kill himself, just as his father did before him. At that moment, he is struck by what he himself calls "an absurd idea": "I don't have to die ... but I have to kill myself." This, perhaps, grimly encapsulates the act of immigration, for he who leaves is as good as dead for those left behind, and, in his new home, may feel as far removed from that world of his birth as he would having known it in some previous life.

Silvio botches his attempt to shoot himself through the heart, but it would seem the symbolic heart, that place where his capacity to love others and himself resides, is maimed nonetheless. Flashing forward in the moments before he tries to commit suicide, he tells us that the "absurd idea" of death in life has since "guided everything I have done." How this is so, what that undead state is like, and why, for Silvio, it seems the only option is revealed to us in that last chapter, "Judas Iscarote."

"Beware," Silvio recalls his mother telling him as he opens his story, "those marked by God." The words come to him in relation to the lame Andalusian shoemaker who introduces him to the heroes of pamphlet literature and the tales of romantic bandits of Spain, those first figures, as far as we know, to fire the boy's yearning for transformation. The old man has "one foot, round like a mule's, with the heel turned out." One of the few unmitigatedly kind characters in the book, he disappears from the text almost immediately. More than one hundred pages later, however, another man "marked by God," according to the Señora de Astier's definition, appears. He is El Rengo, "the cripple."

Rengo, lamed in a riding accident, watches the wagons at the market in Flores. Crooked, good-hearted, a gross wit and fine storyteller, Rengo is popular with the butchers and greengrocers. He wanders his suburban domain dressed as a horseman, whip looped at his waist, weaving his stories and singing his songs, enjoying his role. As González Lanuza points out, he personifies what has become of the gaucho and his way of life.[27] His cunning is courage in decadence; his tales of *compadritos*, the urban diminution of the oral tradition of the pampas. In this context, his handicap does good service symbolically—the nation's traditional self, in the twentieth century, has been lamed.

Thus, when Silvio denounces Rengo and the burglary of the engineer's house they have planned together, he not only turns on his friend but on a whole history. Rengo represents that Argentina which existed before the Liberal plan, a world imperfect surely, one in decline, but also one where human loyalty was indeed a most deeply valued possession, one where, at least in this text, there was love. Perhaps the most moving scene in the novel, and its only instance of dedication and sacrifice in a heterosexual context, is that in which Gabriela, the the engineer's servant girl and Rengo's lover, is apprehended and told of his capture:

> She trembled terribly, but when she was convinced that Rengo
> was in custody and would suffer if she did not cooperate, she began to

cry softly, with a grief so delicate that it softened even the hard faces
of her interrogators ... Suddenly, she raised her arms; her fingers lit
upon the knot in her hair; she untangled the comb and her hair
cascaded down her back. Folding her hands, she looked at them all as
if mad and said:

"Yes, of course ... of course ... Let's go ... Let's go to Antonio.
They put her in the wagon and took her to the precinct house.

Rengo, this older man so beloved of Gabriela, such a generous
friend, offers to the fatherless Silvio the same sorts of dreams and the
same moral code as did the pamphlet-bearing shoemaker so long before.
Silvio has changed since then, however. He has learned dreams end in
bitterness, and that the ethic which Rengo represents has no relevence in
the modern world. Just as the European father is irrecoverable, the
Argentine one offers no hope. Indeed, he himself plans to abandon the
nation after the robbery is done. So Silvio rejects Rengo, apparently
adhering instead to the law he has always abhorred, to that world of the
immigrant and the professional, of the engineer Arsenio Vitri.

Vitri's role in *El juguete rabioso* has never been much discussed,
perhaps because he seems so minor. Yet in many ways he personifies the
"anti-Rengo." The cripple is the heroic figure in decline; the engineer, the
petit bourgeois ideal in ascent. Through the story, Silvio has modeled
himself on inventive, nonconforming individualists—Napoleon, Edison,
Baudelaire, and Rocambole. His betrayal of Rengo is his accommodation
of those ideals with the prevailing reality, the new and apparently invincible order which he has always despised. Were this chapter written dif-
ferently, we might even applaud Silvio's choice, his "regeneration," as
Lucio would have it. Rengo is too lovingly drawn, however, and Silvio's
fate too obviously bleak to allow for such approbation.

Vitri himself, in spite of his rather perfunctory treatment in the text,
personifies the inevitability and fatality of Silvio's choice. A number of
characteristics make him the appropriate and more powerful opposite
number of a man "touched by God." He is oddly ageless: "young in spite
of his white hair." He seems precognitive: Silvio's revelation of the
planned robbery does not surprise him. He is merciful, arranging for
Rengo's detention before the theft, so as to ameliorate the seriousness of
his crime. He remains peculiarly superior to Silvio, interrogating him
gently after the denunciation, offering to assist him in his project to go to
the South.

In Vitri, there is something godlike. Indeed, who in the petit
bourgeois universe is more admired than the engineer—the man who

builds things, who makes things run? However, to see Vitri as a bene-
ficent figure, or even a neutral one, ignores the sinister echoes of his very
name. Arsenio Vitri—*arsénico y vitriolo*. Arsenic and vitriol: a cumulative
poison and a corrosive one. The order Silvio has embraced is one he
himself recognizes as venomous. He insists that life is beautiful, but says
as well: "I am peaceful now. I will go through life as if I were dead. That's
how I see life, like a huge, yellow desert."

Silvio has found the way to kill himself and not die. He has dis-
covered, after all those attempts to integrate himself with Argentina, with
the humanity around him, that there is nothing there. There is no history,
no community. The only transformation which can be attained must be
achieved within. It is secret, not public. It is not heroic, but horrible.
Silvio's act of betrayal will pursue him his whole life; his own knowledge of
it will separate him inevitably from the rest of humanity. He has established his own, infinite solitude, the only possible course, it seems, for
this man who would be inventor, conquerer, poet, thief. "Anguish will
open my eyes to new spiritual horizons," Silvio tell us. He has indeed
made an "existential leap," but unlike Sartre's characters is *Huis Clos*,
Silvio finds hell finally not in other people, but in himself.

The corrosive knowledge of our own treasons is what tells us we are
alive in this world, even though their commission may cause our spiritual
death. In an American, petit bourgeois universe, this is our only path to
transcendence. No father will legitimate us. We will suffer, but re-
demptive suffering, that of Christ, cannot exist. The only possible kind,
then, is the soul-grinding agony of Judas Iscariot. We can thus do whatever is necessary to continue in the modern world, sure in the knowledge
of our own damnation. After Rengo is betrayed, no act is unthinkable. If
we must be "toys" in a heartless world with no past, we ought at least, Arlt
seems to tell us, be rabid ones, striking out furiously, meaninglessly, at
the faceless order which has made us so, quite conceivably destroying, of
course, what we love, or what we might once have wished to love.

Explicating a text of Roberto Arlt is like entering a labyrinth more complex than any Borgean puzzle. The foregoing reading only begins to deal
with the multiple resonances of *El juguete rabioso,* many of which seem to
drown each other out. The novel is alive with the paradoxes of an imagination on the verge of riot. As Stasys Gostautas points out, it is a "human"
rather than an "artistic" novel, primarily concerned with the discovery of
what constitutes "humanness," and as such it lacks the kind of rigorous

development one anticipates in works of Mann or Joyce.[28] Many of the issues we have here discussed, however, those that flash and flicker through this intense and pyrotechnic novel, also arise in what is perhaps the most accomplished example of the "artistic" novel in Argentina during the 1920s. That, of course, is the work of the man to whom *El juguete rabioso* was dedicated: *Don Segundo Sombra*.[29]

CHAPTER 8

The Failure of Myth

Ricardo Güiraldes and Don Segundo Sombra

RICARDO GÜIRALDES was born in a house on Calle Corrientes, one with parquet floors and oriental rugs, and portraits and idyllic landscapes on wainscotted walls.[1] He first drew breath in that rare and overstuffed world the ruling class of the nineteenth century built for itself, whether on the Thames, the Seine, the Hudson, or the Río de la Plata. His place there—in the elegant, privileged society of the oligarchy—is something which must never be forgotten in a study of his work.

Don Segundo Sombra, with its cattle drives, rustic tales and rude gauchos, would seem the negation of that background. It was not that Güiraldes was a stranger to the world of the pampas. In spite of trips to the continent and private tutors and his success not only in *porteño* but Parisian society, his fondest moments from his boyhood to his death were spent on the family *estancia,* La Porteña, near San Antonio de Areco. Don Segundo, after all, owed his name to Segundo Ramírez, a gaucho Güiraldes knew from his youth, one who accompanied the author and his new bride, Adelina del Carril, to the *estancia* when they came to honeymoon there in 1913.[2] *Don Segundo Sombra* evidences its creator's familiarity with the finer points of horsebreaking, with those essential trivialities of life on the trail, with the nuances of the language of the men of the pampas. And yet Güiraldes was among them but not of them, and could not be simply because of the circumstances of his birth. Consequently, even before he sat down in 1920 to transform that gaucho experience into art, that experience had inevitably come to signify to him something other than what it represented to those who lived it, something more than the picturesque images it summoned forth for the contemporary urban dweller. Rather, it had become the vision of an ideal world, one

119

which would not be seen again and which perhaps never really existed in the first place.

The inclusion of Güiraldes among the members of the Generation of 1922 is fraught with problems. A good twenty years older than the youngest members of Boedo and Florida, he had published his first poetry and short stories in 1915, his first novel in 1917. He needed no Borges to expose him to the vanguardist ideas current in Europe. As a friend of the Franco-Uruguayan poet, Jules Supervielle, he came to know Larbaud, Claudel, Gide, St. John Perse, Jules Romain, and Paul Valery. His acquaintance with the vagaries and internecine squabbles of postwar art was firsthand. By the time he came in contact with the young *porteños* at work on manifestos to shock the bourgeoisie and Lugones, his youthful experiments were passed, and he was an established figure on the local literary scene.[3]

Yet, his relation to the young poets and novelists of the age was not a paternal but a fraternal one, and we may wonder, had it not been for his contact with the literary ferment of Buenos Aires in the twenties, if *Don Segundo Sombra* would have been the novel that it is. Might not Güiraldes have felt less intensely the need for the definition of a national character through a national literature had he not been surrounded by the young men of Florida?[4] It would be a mistake to see Güiraldes' relationship with Borges, Brandán Caraffa, and the others as purely one-sided, simply a case of an older and wiser writer doing a good turn for rising talents. Without *Don Segundo Sombra*, without the novel completed while he helped direct *Martín Fierro*, found *Proa*, and put *El juguete rabioso* through publication, Güiraldes would be remembered as a minor talent of the teens, an oligarch who dabbled in literature, a cattle-king from Argentina who knew some important French writers.

He *was* different, nonetheless: older, less impetuous and combative. The course of his life (though less of his work, perhaps in part because he began to publish so late) traces a path followed artistically if not actually by many of the *vanguardistas* in their later years. During the Centenario, that orgy of national puffery partially overseen by his own father (then *intendente municipal* of Buenos Aires), Güiraldes absented himself from the country, undertaking a tour which eventually took him completely around the Eurasian landmass. While they sang paeans to San Martín in Buenos Aires, he gambled in Monte Carlo, smoked hashish in Ceylon, realized the vastness of Russia in a rail carriage on the Trans-Siberian Railroad. When he returned to Argentina in 1912, to parents irate at his vagabondage and lack of profession, he associated himself with a circle of young, wealthy francophiles.[5] Yet, between 1913 and 1917, he appears to have realized, as generations of Argentines have realized after him, that the purported "true homes" of the Old World were not really that at all, that his definition both as a writer and a man had to be found in Argentina. The novelistic expression of this is *Raucho*, titled in manuscript "Los comentarios de Ricardito," a book based on Güiraldes' own European impressions which ends with the protagonist on his family's estate, recovering from overseas misadventures which have almost cost him his life, certain now that the key to self-discovery lies not in foreign places but in his own country.

The assertion in *Raucho* of the inapplicability of European ideals and values to the Argentine circumstance represents the first manifestation in Güiraldes' canon of an idea which achieves final and positive form in *Don Segundo Sombra*. Through his next two novels—the slight and sentimental *Rosaura* (originally "Un idilio de estación") and *Xaimaca*—this concern remains hidden, though the latter novel, in its oblique confrontation with the cosmopolitanism of the oligarchy and its presentation of the journey as not only physical but spiritual perhaps indicates Güiraldes' awareness that the issue raised in *Raucho* remained unrevolved, that the hero's return home was merely a first step in the development of alternatives to the European models he rejected. However, in his poetry of the period (unpublished in his lifetime), Güiraldes moved toward the postulation of that alternative, toward what David Viñas has dubbed *transtelurismo*. In such poems as "Pierrot" and "Aconcagua," Viñas claims, the journey into the Argentine hinterland is valorized as the means by which the individual is spiritually revived. Europe is rejected in favor of the true national essence, which resides in the Argentine earth itself: "in the pampa, beneath the surface of the pampa, lies the key to that anti-Europe which, through aesthetic passion, becomes real. It is that vision of a malignant Europe which implies as its counterweight the American *bonissima tellus*."[6]

National redemption, true *argentinidad*, individual salvation lies then not in the Babel of the capital, where life is but a caricature of the corruption of the Old World, but rather in the countryside, in what remains of indigenous Argentina, of what existed before the transformation of the country over the preceding fifty years. An awareness of this element in the text, of course, indicates the limitation of the critical tendency to define *Don Segundo Sombra* as a kind of nostalgic consecration of a disappearing stage of civilization. That it surely was, and not of a civilization disappearing but disappeared. But its function as a dirge for the gaucho life does little to explain its tremendous impact in 1926. *Don Segundo Sombra* became an "instant classic." Lugones rhapsodized over it in *La Nación;* Borges and the other members of Florida were wildly excited by it; even the left grudgingly proclaimed its value.[7] Güiraldes' novel spoke very strongly some element of the *Zeitgeist* of the 1920s, something much more profound than a sentimentality for a lost lifestyle. It represents, rather, a real confrontation with the historical moment, with the crisis of identity which had afflicted Argentina from its beginnings and had grown increasingly problematic during the Liberal era. To understand the form and significance of the novel's impact, we will consider first certain moments in the text which very apparently critique the prevailing Liberal-cum-Radical reality. After this, we shall turn to more obscure elements, which provide the key to understanding the novel's response to its age, to the ideology of *Don Segundo Sombra* and its resonances.

Güiraldes' novel, one of the education and maturation of an adolescent, partakes heavily of the idyll, ignoring the repressive and brutalizing aspects of gaucho life or presenting them so that they seem part and parcel of an "authentic" existence. His book is a vindication of the indigenously *criollo,* for the gaucho, in spite of his presence in Uruguay and Rio Grande do Sul, was and has remained the quintessence of *argentinidad,* the human emblem of the nation. Of course, the gaucho since Caseros and particularly since the Roca administration had become less and less significant in the everyday life of Argentina. Thus, Güiraldes' very choice of the gaucho as the focus of his novel represents an implied rejection of modern Argentina, of that anti-*criollo* system which had forced the old folkloric hero into a more and more marginal position.

The author's attack is not all that subtle. The text leaves little doubt as to Güiraldes' vision of the Liberal reality. In the first place, *Don Segundo Sombra* evidences considerable xenophobia. Characters of non-*criollo* origins are introduced, it seems, primarily to be denigrated. As early as the first chapter, we hear of "the half-breed Burgos' fight with Sinforiano Herrera, or the foulness of the dago Culasso, who had sold his twelve-year-old daughter for twenty pesos to old Salomovich, owner of the brothel."[8] Half-breed, Italian, Jew: belligerent, shameless, immoral. Such unpleasant characterizations, it might be argued, are somewhat balanced by the inclusion in chapter three of Don Jeremiah, "un inglés acriollado," who assents in Fabio Cáceres' joining the trail crew. Such may be the case, though the *patrón* enjoys the dispensation of that magical adjective, "creolized," and further may be spared attack due to his class position. He is, after all, an *estanciero*. Regardless, we never again encounter in the text an attractive character of foreign origins. The immigrants Fabio sees in a café in Navarro may be considered exemplary: an Irishman with "fish eyes" and a face "full of bulging veins, like the stomach of a newly skinned ewe"; his wife freckled "like a turkey's egg." A young and equally ugly man, who appears to be a grain agent, intervenes in a discussion with "thick German r's." Three Spaniards with "faces like stockboys'" talk with such volume and energy as to draw attention to themselves, discussing the suicide of a friend. This distasteful crew contrasts markedly with the natives in the café: one fat fellow who eats silently, with relish, and pats the waiter on the back when asking for more wine; the "team of *criollos*" across the café, scarred and tanned, who "ate hurriedly. During dessert, they laughed silently, their mouths covered with their napkins."

The deprecation of the immigrant is an occasional element in the text. The effects of the foreign invasion, however—urbanization and the rise of the petit bourgeoisie—are certainly central. The town in *Don Segundo Sombra* is the realm of the other, the antithesis of the freedom offered by the pampa. Its character is established from the very first chapter: predictable, monotonous, rectilinear; filled with corruption, obsessed by petty rules, impressed by empty victories. The house of Fabio's aunts is referred to constantly as a "prison," "calaboose," "cage." And it is not only Fabio's hometown that is confining, it is all of them: "all the towns were the same, all the people more or less of the same stripe, and the memories I had of those places, busy and useless, repelled me." This is where one is forced to attend school, to learn, as Fabio remarks, "the alphabet, figuring, history, none of which was any use to me." They are the seats of the police, the civil administration, petty and stupid, like those who briefly arrest Don Segundo in chapter thirteen. Finally, and most importantly, here lies the world of money, of buying and selling, of the insincere relations of exchange. If Don Pedro at La Blanqueada is portrayed as a kind and proud man, "the most gaucho shopkeeper in the world," he stands alone as the one admirable character from the commercial class. The *pulpero* of chapter twenty-three is a drunk and a bully; that of chapter fourteen leans forward to take Don Segundo's order "like a dog at the mouth of a vizcacha's burrow." When the police enter to harass Don Segundo, he is nonplussed, but the storekeeper trembles with intimidation: "Afraid of a fight, he fumbled with the merchandise, completely forgetting our order." After Fabio's inheritance, the barber, the jeweler, and the saloon keepers of his native town fawn over him, and he swears to shun them ever after. Men of commerce, the book demonstrates again and again, have been corrupted by their trade. They are avaricious, unctuous, and cowardly. They seem, like the briefly mentioned Festal—himself "the son of a shopkeeper"—"conceited and sissy," the antithesis of the quiet pride and manliness of the gaucho.

In reality, of course, the gauchos of Güiraldes' time were themselves (even if unwittingly) agents of commerce, the base of the primary export chain created by the oligarchy. While this status of rural peon is sometimes alluded to in the text, it is for the most part suppressed. Never do we witness payday for the gauchos. The sole mention of payment for labor on the trail is the advance Fabio receives in chapter five in order to buy a pony from Cuevas. Otherwise, gauchos appear to exist on the margin of normal exchange relations. Among them, of course, money does change hands, but most commonly as a result of gambling, an activity apparently less exploitative, involving chance and skill, acceptable even to Don Segundo himself. Even when the circumstances arise when a horse must be sold (as in chapter twenty-eight), it is done in response to the exigencies of the moment, with great concern over the new owner and with never a thought of profit.

In the course of the story, the central characters have little contact with the urban professional class. In chapter twenty-three, a doctor appears, one who remarks when examining the fatal wound inflicted on a unnamed older man by Antenor Barragán: "What a slice! When I was an intern, and I wasn't weak, I'd sweat a half an hour to open up a thorax like that." The doctor's self-deprecation places his mastery of his skills, and those skills themselves, in doubt. His clinical "thorax" and off-handed manner contrast markedly with the warmth and humanity of folk healers who have appeared earlier in the story—the old woman of Don Candelario's ranch and Don Segundo himself.

Doctors and their professional brethren appear in an even less neutral light in the second interpolated story (chapter twenty-one). In Don Segundo's explanation of why human suffering is always with us, the wily blacksmith Miseria traps all the legions of Hell inside his tobacco pouch, which he thrashes roundly every day on his anvil. As a consequence, all evil disappears from the world. There is no murder, no illness, no pain, no misunderstanding. "Lawyers, bureaucrats, justices of the peace, quacks, doctors and all those people who have power and live off the misery and vices of other people, were hollow down to their toes and beginning to die off." The professional classes, made up of those who thrive on misfortune, demand that the equally corrupt government force Miseria to release the devils. It is so ordered, and Miseria complies. The world must suffer for the livelihood of the professionals.

The gauchos, for Güiraldes, are unsullied by the materialism and greed of contemporary Argentina. They partake neither in the commerce dominated in the 1920s by the immigrants, nor in the parasitic relations between the populace and the emergent upper middle class which provided the bulk of the Radical leadership. That these groups did indeed control the nation in any ultimate sense was, of course, a fantasy of which they and any others who believed it were disabused in 1930. The greatest beneficiaries of Argentine development had been the oligarchs, who perhaps manifested less blatantly the vulgarity of the system because they had no need to sully their hands either with the grubby realities of trade or the inevitable complexities—the disputes, disease, and poverty—arising from modern urban living. The ruling class, after all, maintained its stranglehold on the land, on the trade in beef, mutton, and grain which was Argentina's economic life's blood. It was they, as a consequence, who had the capital to invest in whatever national industries had arisen, who collected the interest on the innumerable small loans which set up the small businesses run by Italians and *gallegos* and Ashkenazim in the small towns and urban barrios. This reality, however, has no place in Güiraldes' novel. The landholding class is rather part of the book's organic world. Don Leandro and Don Candelario are steeped in rural virtues, worthy associates of Don Segundo Sombra. Don Jeremiah and Don Juan, if rather less finely drawn, nonetheless evidence a respect for the life of the pampas which places them above reproach. The *estanciero* who sponsors the dance in chapter eleven presides genially over the festivities, a pacific and paternal figure at home with his "boys," an integral part of the community of the plains. Even Fabio Cáceres the elder, attacked by his son as an exploiter of innocent country girls, merits defense by Don Segundo himself: "Your father was a rich man like all rich men, and that was the only evil in him." This somewhat equivocal judgment is immediately rephrased by Fabio as narrator into: "Where my father was concerned, his only evil had been being rich. What kind of evil was that?"[9] Further, Don Segundo opposes Fabio's initial impulse on learning of his inheritance: the parceling up of the estate and its distribution among the poor. Fabio does not wish to abandon the gaucho existence, but he is "fated" to be a rich man, has no choice but to accept his destiny. Don Segundo's approval of old Cáceres' bequest at least partially absolves Fabio, and by association the entire landowning class, from any guilt for their fortunes. Despite certain ambiguities, *estancieros* are ultimately of the world of the gaucho, of the *criollo*, not of the other.

The most striking and sustained criticism of the Liberal social structure may be found in the highly symbolic episodes of chapters fifteen and seventeen. There, Don Segundo and Fabio have taken part in a drive down to an *estancia* near the Atlantic, and are passing the night with an old friend of the former's, Don Sixto Gaitán. This is, in Fabio's words, "an ugly land, ... rust-colored, sparse, as if ravaged by a fever. I remembered a night passed by the side of my Aunt Mercedes." The metaphorical connection with Fabio's detested aunt emphasizes the symbolic import of his experiences here. Though there are no towns, no schools, no gringos mentioned in these chapters, the action transpires on the edge of the beloved pampas, where the earth is sickly, as ugly and unpleasant as Aunt Mercedes. It borders the ocean, "that blue pampa," the other pampa, or, perhaps, the pampa of the "other." This unfamiliar world, the coastline, is that part of Argentina most favored by those who crossed the sea, turned Liberal plan into Liberal reality. If these people and their institutions do not appear overtly, they are embodied as the crabs who inhabit the surrounding bogs. Fabio visits the crab beds twice, the first time alone, when he almost loses a horse in the swamp. Afterwards, he recalls them:

> I couldn't stop thinking about the crab beds. The pampa must suffer for them and ... God help those skeletons! One day later they're white. What a moment, feeling the ground give way! Being swallowed up little by little. And how that mud must press against your ribs. To die drowned in earth! Knowing that those little creatures are going to tear the meat off you bit by bit ... Feeling them touch bone, reach your stomach, your privates, turning it all into a mash of blood and waste. Thousands of shells inside you, pulling out the pain in a voracious, nauseous whirl. ...

"The pampa must suffer for them." Argentina must suffer for the existence of such places—quagmires of voraciousness. If the imagistic connection of the crab beds to modern society is insufficiently strong, it is reenforced even more powerfully when Fabio visits them with his new friend, Patrocinio Salvatierra. They go to watch the crabs "pray."

> [Patrocinio] got off his horse on the banks of a gully with black, muddy banks, peppered as if by shots with holes of various sizes. Of various sizes too were some crabs, flat and clumsy, swaggering sideways, almost comic. He waited until, nearby, one of the creatures came out of its cave and then, quickly, he cracked its shell with a rap of his knife. With it still kicking, he threw it a few feet away on the mud. A hundred sideways runners, quick as shadows, converged on

the spot. There was a whirpool of black circles, claws raised, all of them, ridiculously, dancing a six-footed malambo over the remains of their dead companion.

What remains! In a moment, they withdrew, and no sign remained of the victim. They, on the other hand, frenzied by the appetizer, turned on one another, those in front clashing with those arriving late, battling face to face with arms raised and pinchers fully opened. Remaining motionless, we could watch some very close to us. Many were horribly mutilated. . . .

"Good Christians. Look how they love each other."

"Christian!" Patrocinio added. "Ha! . . . Now you will get to see them pray."

We moved along a bit, stopping at a huge, flat mudbank.

Patrocinio was right. The sun was setting. From every cave came one of those loathsome hard spiders, but even bigger, rounder than those at the gully. . . . They walked slowly, oblivious to one another, all of them turning toward the slowly vanishing fireball. And then they froze, their little hands folded before them, red as if dipped in blood.

That struck me hard! Were they praying? Would they always have, as a curse, those bloodstained hands? What were they asking for? Surely that some steer or, better, a horse and rider, might slip on that jellied earth they mined.

I looked up, and thought that, for league upon league, the world was covered with such repulsive vermin.

Perhaps this was solely Güiraldes' comment on the human condition in general, but these "vermin" inhabit only the coast, not the pampa. These creatures feed on each other; show no mercy; pray not to be delivered from their condition, but only to have it enriched by the cattle, horses, and gauchos who come from the heartland. There can be no mistaking the symbols here. These are indeed "Christians," men of bloodstained hands, and theirs is the world of greed and brutality which exists alongside the sea in Argentina. This, on the level of the mass, is the repetition of the amusing but bestial image of the merchant waiting ravenously for a sale. This is what the Liberal dream has become.

Don Segundo Sombra is an almost obstreperously masculine book. The pampa is a realm of men, and the occupation of gaucho "the most macho of callings." With this in mind, the reader perhaps accepts unthinkingly the scarcity of women in the novel, and their characterization, when they do appear, as convenient, troublesome, or dangerous. One need not be a feminist, however, to recognize the story as deeply misogynistic from the very first. Women have little place in the organic world of the pampa. Fabio's estimation of them in chapter four goes unchallenged throughout the novel: "What're women good for? For a man to have a little fun. And the ones that spit and nag? We'd boil them down to lard if we didn't feel so sorry for them."

In *Don Segundo Sombra*, women are "other," hopelessly entwined with the town, the school, with the Liberal scheme. They are agents of domestication, of the anti-*criollo* which opposes the freedom of gaucho life. Some at the dance in chapter eleven "made faces when they played folk dances," preferring mazurkas and polkas, the imported steps of the cities. Aunts Mercerdes and Asunción are, for Fabio, like "two jailers." Paula, whom he loves, wants to have him "tied to her life like a ribbon in her hair." His softening at her blandishments conjures in his dreams the image of burial alive: "I dreamt they dropped me in a hole, like a ironwood post, and stamped down the earth till my ribs cracked and I couldn't breathe." The idea has been evoked before in the novel, in relation to those sucked into the crab beds. The love of a woman implies a grim fate: entrapment in the Liberal world, a kind of suffocation which means death to the gaucho.

One woman who seems free of such gloomy associations is the aptly named "Aurora." Ingenuous and generous, she functions as a vessel of initiation, a means by which Fabio enters into the realm of men. Her symbolic role, however, reenforces the devaluation of women as individuals. Fabio certainly does not love her. He does little more than rape her. If she does eventually acquiesce in intercourse, it is largely in the false hope of gaining a sweetheart:

> . . . That afternoon, she did not fight me, and when we parted, it wasn't me who said, "I'll wait for you tomorrow."
> Poor baby. That morning had been our last meeting. . . . I felt like a really lucky man, a man who had within him the will and the necessary ability of a good gaucho, and even an adoring little wench to cry about his leaving.

Aurora, or rather, the taking of her virginity, is but an accoutrement of manhood. After Fabio's departure, there is no mention of his *chinita querendona* until after his inheritance. Then, he asks Raucho if the Cuevas family still lives nearby and is told they have long since left. The vague allusion is all that remains, and the memory is never again resuscitated. Fabio recalls Aurora only fleetingly, and only after he has already surrendered his freedom, has been forced to abandon the gaucho life. His inquiry is but another sign of his loss.

Aurora is an innocent. Most women in the novel, however, are flirtatious, difficult, and often the source of rancor and violence. The young women at the dance are willing to trade double entendres but little more. Paula plays Fabio against the farmhand, Numa. She toys with them from "pure meanness," while the lovestruck Fabio drinks the "venom" of romantic entanglement as if it were "holy water." The rivalry of the two men eventually engenders a duel, after which Paula, instead of praising Fabio's defense of her, rejects him coldly. The grimmest reminder of women's destructiveness is found in another duel, that between Antenor Barragán and an older man. In the affair of honor, the latter ends dead and Antenor a fugitive, all, as one witness asserts, "for women . . . for a woman I had once, and she was a bitch, like the kid said."

This woman's promiscuity, however, reflected primarily upon her lover, husband, father or brother, was a stain on *his* honor, one which had to be avenged. This theme in *Don Segundo Sombra* results, of course, from the Argentine social vision, not only the rural but the urban one. Women are not people with wills and personalities independent of their male protectors, but rather possessions, though still always potentially treacherous.[10] Such an idea, of course, is not unique to Argentina. It is rather a fixture in Western culture. Nonetheless, its significance is increased by the cult of *machismo* of the Mediterranean and Hispanic worlds which is manifested in new forms in the Argentine context. Julio Mafud notes that, on the pampa, the woman was always "distant," left behind, operating outside the world of men and labor. This allowed the *machismo* already inherent in the culture to develop into an ever stronger form of male bonding, through the *culto de coraje* and the *culto de la amistad*.[11] Women were valuable for the satisfaction of sexual needs and little more. Consequently, the institution of marriage, and indeed courtship and romance, were stunted. "In some statistics from those years [the first half of the nineteenth century], it was established that seventy-five percent of the households were based upon free love, or rather worse, on passing love."[12] This situation was replicated and exacerbated in Argentine cities during the alluvial era by a large preponderance of male immigrants. Argentina, through the period of great national development, was not only male dominated but populated by an inordinately large number of men relative to women.[13] Beyond this, the society's puritanical heritage "did not permit in most of its structures any contact or ties with the other sex. The man found himself surroundly solely by his own gender. . . . Living with no linkages [to women], the man was anchored by one passion: friendship. Friendship has remained the most significant Argentine social force."[14]

This sole passion functions in various ways in Güiraldes' novel. First of all, it reemphasizes the book's idyllic character. Fabio Cáceres, fourteen years old at the story's beginning, lives out a typical male fantasy of early adolescence—the partaking of a profoundly masculine experience removed from the disruptive and restrictive presence of women, in which the boy, after a series of trials, is accepted into the community of men. This, of course, raises a number of issues beyond the most apparent one: the yearning for the simplicity and the joy of boyhood. The lack of women in Don Segundo Sombra, the deprecation of those who do appear, the novel's obsessive "maleness," the intense validation of friendship among a group of sexually mature men obviously invites consideration of the novel's homoerotic strain. The only relationships here affirmed are those between men: Fabio and Don Segundo, Fabio and Patrocinio, Fabio and Antenor, Fabio and Raucho. These characters cooperate in labor which, in its intense physicality, its demand for strength, is by its very nature strongly libidinal. Riding, horse breaking, cattle roping all carry the charge of symbolic sexual activity.[15] Beyond this, of course, there is the hardware of gaucho life: lassos, the whip, and the omnipresent knife—the phallic surrogates in a world in which passion manifests itself in violence against other men. Surely, the much-idealized duel is overtly eroticized, the "conquest" of a male opponent implying a sexual as well as a merely physical victory. Fabio's battle with Numa illustrates the point. The gaucho slashes the farmhand across the forehead. "Numa dropped his knife to the floor and stood there, his legs spread and his head low, frozen with fear." Numa's weapon falls; he stands bent over—the image is certainly graphic enough. Its resonances grow even louder when Fabio remarks that, on his way to apologize to Don Candelario for spilling blood in his house, "I saw all the women gathered around. The wounded man must have been there." The vanquished Numa is now among the women, beaten by a better man—indeed, within the scheme of the novel, now effeminized himself, for the cut on the head and the posture of Numa when wounded certainly imply not only intercourse but castration.

The homosexual element of the novel functions not only on the plane of violent interaction. The friendships of the gauchos possess an intense if occluded sexual energy. Their teasing, their mutual admiration, their horseplay and exhibitionism have to them a certain innocent flirtatiousness.[16] Sometimes, the expression is more overt, as in the mock duel of Goyo and Horacio in chapter four. The two seek to mark each other on the face with sooty fingers. At contest's end, Goyo remarks: "You're hard to take." Horacio replies: "What? Did your sister tell you?" While the images on the one hand redirect attention toward a heterosexual context, they also draw a parallel between such activity and the battle just presented. Even more obvious is the narrator's characterization of the bond between Fabio and Patrocinio as they prepare to kill the bull which has gored Fabio's horse: "Out of the will to murder that we shared was born a strong sentiment of friendship. Two men enduring danger together come out of it intimates, like a couple after an embrace."

Obviously, the book's most significant friendship is that between Don Segundo and Fabio. The older man plays an extremely complicated role in the novel, the most central aspects of which will be discussed later. As regards the present issue, however, it can be said that his relationship with Fabio is uniquely presented in terms of the boy's humility, defer-ence, and passivity, and relies heavily on images of domination. Fabio's remark at the very outset of his adventures reveals the nature less of his involvement with all gauchos than with that one who to him is "my man": "The roughness of the quiet men mastered me." Don Segundo's control of Fabio emerges again and again in his overt or threatened physical abuse of him. "If this one doesn't quiet down," he says at the end of chapter seven "we're gonna have to to ship him back to his aunts' cage." Even at this early point, the warning implies a severe punishment: Fabio's subjugation once again to the unmanning influence of the town. More obvious is the conclusion of the following chapter:

> I threw my things into the zinc shed and fell on top of them like a mudclod off a wagon wheel.
> A whip-stroke I could barely feel fell across my shoulders.
> "Toughen up, boy!"
> And I thought I recognized the voice as Don Segundo Sombra's.

The situation is a paradoxical one. Don Segundo orders Fabio to "harden himself," to become a man, and yet, in any lasting sense, this is impossible as long as Fabio is under the sway of the man who has become his mentor. He can imitate, of course, this gaucho of gauchos, but there is a very real question if Fabio is or ever could be anything but a pale reflection of Don Segundo: the older man's power over him, both phys-ically and psychologically, is simply too great. Even after more than five years on the trail, at the age of nineteen, Fabio can be intimidated into abandoning his most profound desires. Attempting to deny his inheritance, Fabio in the process insults the gaucho Pedro, and a duel appears imminent. However, Don Segundo intervenes:

> I found myself facing my godfather, who took me by the arm, saying: "If you've fallen, I'll help you up again."
> I realized any resistence on my part would be met with a blow, and that pleased me in a way that perhaps other people wouldn't understand. For Don Segundo, I was still that little *guacho*.

The threat of a beating evokes joy in Fabio, one arising surely from various factors. To remain the *guachito*—the orphan—maintains the relationship of the pampas idyll, if not its reality. The boy, even at this age, remains a boy, continues to live in the "eternal morning" of the plain. This is the optimistic reading. Fabio's masochistic response possesses less pleasant resonances: the validation of the relationship of domination which exists between him and Don Segundo; a joy in mental and physical submission to another man; an assertion of a desire for security which, despite its idealization, implies both an obvious form of servitude and an unwillingness to confront the responsibilities of adulthood. These issues connect with what is perhaps the novel's most distinctive and significant strain, that which explains most fully its appeal in its own historical moment. Before proceeding, however, it seems wise to consider the major elements confronted thus far in a literary context, in order too understand how *Don Segundo Sombra* represents the continuation and closure of a particular tradition in Argentine culture, and how the final issue—that of the family and history—makes this book unique in its genre and so meaningful in its time.

The elements discussed thus far in relation to Güiraldes' novel—xenophobia, anti-Liberalism, anti-urbanism, misogyny, and homoeroticism—are by no means peculiar to this one book. Indeed, to a greater or lesser extent, they are present in most all works of the gauchesque. *El gaucho Martín Fierro* arose, at least in part, as a protest against Sarmentine Liberalism, and foreigners fare little better in Hernández or Gutiérrez' works than in Güiraldes'.[17] The relationships of Martín Fierro and Cruz, of Juan Moreira and Julián, obviously carry a homoerotic charge.[18] This is not to deny that one can find these same issues in some urban novels: the anti-Semitism of *La Bolsa* or the confrontations with homosexuality in Mariani and Arlt stand as evidence. However, the combination of these elements may be said to be more typical of the gauchesque than of any other genre.

A precise definition of the gauchesque is difficult. In the first place, it is formally distinguished from "gaucho" literature, which is folkloric—oral, colloquial, and primitive. The gauchesque is undeniably "literary," a product of the cities and most particularly of the capital. Its earliest roots may be found, ironically, in the works of the great Liberals Echeverría and Sarmiento. In both *La cautiva* and *Facundo,* the poetic characterization of the pampa, of its awesome and terrifying vastness, establishes a motif repeated over and over in the genre. Beyond this, Sarmiento's portrait of his detested *caudillo,* though it presents Quiroga in all his brutality and megalomania, still endows him with a certain primeval nobility, lends both to him and to his followers a sort of mythic grandeur Sarmiento surely would have consciously rejected. This literary stream converges with that followed by such poets as Bartolomé Mitre, the great champion of *porteño* hegemony, who attempted to maintain the thematic elements of gaucho verse, including those five here isolated.[19] Of course, his work was not sung spontaneously, but polished, edited, and printed. This step—commiting poetry to the page—marks the step from a popular to a literary genre.

Though the folk culture gradually declined after the battle of Caseros, the gauchesque throve. Some works, such as Estanislao del Campo's *Fausto,* rather capitalized on the gaucho as yokel, an object of fun for the "civilized" urban population. Generally, however, the early works of the genre, most all poetic, tended to lionize the gaucho. Mitre's products are exemplary of this, along with both Ascasubi's and Obligado's treatments of the Santos Vega theme. The genre finally comes of age, though, only with Hernández' *El gaucho Martín Fierro.* Born of reaction to Sarmiento's presidential policies, it is the point at which the anti-Liberalism of the rural population becomes an overt and central factor in the gauchesque. Ripped from his pastoral life by the incursions of the Ejército Federal, fleeing the press gangs into the Indian territories of the South, separated from wife and family, Hernandez' hero sets the standard by which all subsequent gauchos of literature are judged.[20] However, the anger and power of the first part of Hernández' epic are already fading in its sequel. Written seven years later, *La vuelta de Martín Fierro,* if sometimes more finely wrought than the original, rather dissipates its pathos and righteousness. Martín Fierro, the anarchic spirit of rebellion and exile, ends urging his sons to obey authority, to accept what comes. This move toward accommodation arose perhaps not only from the poet's own reintegration into the political mainstream. Surely, if bitterly, Hernández recognized the inevitable truth of the Devil's song in Rafael Obligado's *Santos Vega,* the one employed to defeat the old gaucho in a rhyming contest, a *payada:*

> It was the powerful thunder
> of Progress, thrown to the wind,
> the solemn clarion call
> to that most glorious battle.
> Breaking forever the quiet
> of the pampa, yesterday sleeping,
> the ennobling vision of labor
> until now, never respected:
> The promise of the plow
> Exposing the living furrow.[21]

The history of the gauchesque from this point up to *Don Segundo Sombra* is largely one of continued compromise. Indeed, there are those who refuse to recognize any works subsequent to *Martín Fierro* as truly belonging to the genre.[22] With the disappearance of the gaucho, whose final moment of glory was the War of the Desert, the impetus in the gauchesque toward *costumbrismo* grew ever stronger, along with a prejudice in favor of prose fiction instead of verse. Both impulses are manifest in certain works of Hugo Wast. Further, an emphasis on romantic interest, completely foreign to the folkloric antecedents of the genre, began to intrude around the turn of the century, and is perhaps best illustrated in the canon of the determinedly urban playwright, Florencio Sánchez. In *La gringa,* the marriage of gaucho and immigrant represents the fulfillment of the Liberal dream, the union of *criollo* and European.[23] The gauchesque novels of Roberto J. Payró, meanwhile, are more an assault upon "barbarie" from within the dominant ideology than part of the gauchesque tradition. They are descended from *Facundo,* not *Martín Fierro.*

The transformation of the gauchesque in the thirty years following Hernández' poem is perhaps best demonstrated in two works of the early 1900s, one of poetry and the other prose. Lugones' *La guerra gaucha* drew its rural heroes from the early years of the republic. But rather than presenting· them in the popular language as Hernández had done, Lugones opted for a diction so arcane as to make the work almost unreadable for the general audience. This is particularly ironic in view of the poet's leadership, along with Ricardo Rojas, in the sanctification of *Martín Fierro* as the national epic.

If Lugones' effort seemed distant from the gauchesque tradition in language, Alberto Gerchunoff's work was at least as far removed in content. Surely the very title, *Los gauchos judíos*, would have been incomprehensible to the author of *Martín Fierro*, the juxtaposition simply absurd. Yet, Gerchunoff was doubtless completely sincere, asserting in his novel the possibility of the union of the native and immigrant cultures.

This projected conjunction did take place, after a fashion, though less with Jews and other Eastern Europeans than with Spanish and Italian elements, who were more easily assimilated. Overtly, this emerged in the barbecues, the gaucho newspapers, the *payadas* and clubs which appeared in Buenos Aires in this century, most of them the projects of immigrants anxious to identify with their new homeland.[24] More subtly but significantly, the gaucho and his ethos survived in the urban barrios in the form of the *culto de coraje* and *culto de la amistad* which flourished especially among the second-generation foreigners. The world of *guapos* and *compadritos* became a sort of parody of the gaucho culture which had died, a transmogrification certainly understood by Borges, Enrique González Tuñon, and many lyricists of the tango.[25]

Perhaps the purest continuation of the gauchesque tradition of *Martín Fierro*, ironically, was also its most vulgar: the endless avatars of the folkloric hero, Juan Moreira. From Eduardo Gutiérrez' series of *folletines* in 1881, the heroic outlaw found his way through circus pantomimes onto the stage and into the Argentine imagination. All the gauchesque elements were present: the encroaching power of "civilization," persecution, greedy foreigners, a treacherous woman, a true and faithful friend. The popularity of *Juan Moreira* has always proved a bit of an embarrassment for those scholars anxious to assert a sophisticated national canon. Yet, it is perhaps the very blatancy with which the central issues of the most Argentine of genres are handled in the work that lends it its exceptional appeal. They are, in any case, the same elements which emerge in *Don Segundo Sombra*, the last major work which merits the definition gauchesque. In Güiraldes' novel, however, one other factor distinguishes the book from others of the genre while simultaneously asserting the relevance of the gauchesque at a time when the gaucho had finally become what Rubén Darío described just when the century turned:

> Who are you, lonely traveler in the night?
> I am the poetry who once reigned here,
> that old gaucho now leaving forever,
> bearing with me our old nation's heart.[26]

Güiraldes' tale is one of the transformation of "guacho" to "gaucho," a spiritual journey which implies far more than a simple shifting of vowels. His protagonist is an orphan, a child without history beyond that which he makes for himself. The boy's mentor is the quintessence of gauchos, "not a man but an idea." He too is free of history, appearing like a shadow and vanishing into the setting sun, "an anarchic and solitary spirit." He leads his protégé into a very special world in which time is peculiarly suspended, in which a man thinks "like one in a fight, with eyes wide open to danger and all energy ready to be used right there, without waste or hesitation."

However, within that "eternity" exists a complicated matrix of relationships, almost endless literal or symbolic links among the characters, some overt and some occluded, but all undeniably present. Don Segundo is Fabio's "godfather"; Patrocinio, Antenor, and Raucho, his "brothers,"; the old healer at Don Candelario's is as kind "as if she had borne me." Thus, a novel ostensibly the chronicle of two orphaned souls emerges ironically as one profoundly concerned with familial and intergenerational ties, with the problems of inheritance and history, for surely the family is the medium by which history becomes real, linking all individuals with the continuity of time.

Initially, of course, the nameless *guacho* who is Fabio Cáceres lacks any such connection. In the opening chapters, the skein of his memories is a gnarled one indeed, and his flight with Don Segundo functions, in a certain sense, to impose some sort of order on the chaos of his life in the streets. Thus, his very lack of parents, at least of whom he is aware, provides him with a peculiar freedom. He does, of course, have a shadowy recollection of his mother: "How old was I exactly when they took me from the one I always called 'mama' to bring me here and shut me up in the town? . . . [Recollecting,] I see the place where I grew up and the figure of 'mama,' always busy with some chore, while I played in the kitchen or splashed in a puddle."

This characterization is revealing, for "mama" is surely distinct from the other women presented in the novel: the sluttish lover of Antenor Barragán; the scheming and flirtatious ranch girls anxious to trap a gaucho husband; most especially from the shrewish, gloomy, head-rapping aunts Mercedes and Asunción. Indeed, these last and Fabio's real mother constitute the thesis and antithesis of motherhood. The spinsters embody a sterile and false maternity—capricious, humorless and stiflingly restrictive. The remembered mother, on the other hand, allowed her son to play freely while she went about her work. The idyllic world of Fabio's infancy seems, quite significantly, a rural one, removed from other human habitation. His mother, then, existed on the borders of the Liberal reality; was an ally not of the town, but of the land, which lends her a specialness approaching the sacred. Don Segundo himself calls her a "blessed soul."

Superficially, the beneficient mother is almost wholly absent from *Don Segundo Sombra*. Aside from Fabio's brief and tender recollection and a short allusion in chapter fifteen, Fabio's real mother remains unmentioned in the text. The principle she represents, however, does function at least twice in the form of the two *viejitas:* the kind witch of the first interpolated folktale in chapter twelve, and the nurse at Don Candelario's ranch. Both succor young men, Dolores and Fabio, assisting them in the face of strongly masculine threats, Mandinga and the rogue bull. Freed by their age of any sexuality, they present no menace to the unfettered, adolescent existence of the gaucho; are rather allied with him against possible domestication. Both practice a sort of "white magic," invoking the name of God to insure the success of their ministrations. These shamanistic figures possess some primordial wisdom associated with folk traditions and with the Argentine plains where, we must recall, time is oddly absent. They have about them the scent of immortality, and, along with Fabio's real mother, constitute the physical representations of the ultimate maternal figure in Güiraldes' novel: the pampa. It is Viñas' *bonissima tellus*, after all, which is the only possible female element of the triune parentage Fabio Cáceres claims for himself: "son of God, of the countryside, of one's self."

The equation of Earth and Mother is reinforced strongly in the text by recurring images of rebirth. The pampa is the medium by which Fabio becomes an individual distinct from the man he was before. Beyond this, the land's maternal nature heightens the significance of the affectionate "*hermano*" with which the gauchos address one another. They metaphorically constitute a "band of brothers," wandering free with the blessing of the pampa, united by her, unrestrained by time, the law, the Liberal scheme. These factors point up the developing psychological resonances of the text. The gauchos are autocthonous, sons of the Earth, and the novel constantly affirms their benignant mother and her representatives as it denigrates the urban world and her embodiments. This strategy resolves, on a psychoanalytic plane, the problem of the son's ambivalence before the mother, his simultaneous desire for and resentment of her. Still, this element operates only fitfully here in relation to the female parent. It is much more overtly functional where the male one is concerned. A son, after all, is rather more of two minds about the father than the mother, confronting him with both respect and fear, love and dread. The resolution in *Don Segundo Sombra* of this ambivalence provides the key to understanding the novel's attitude toward history.[27]

As with Fabio's mother, his father constitutes a "present absence" in the text. We do, however, find out much more about him. In his character, he seems almost like a fugitive from the Cambaceres canon, the quintessence of a jaded aristocrat: begetting a son on a peasant girl, first ignoring the child, then, as if on a lark, swooping down and removing the boy to the custody of maiden aunts. Fabio's recollections of his "protector" are, in the first chapter, happy if somewhat mystified. Initially, Don Fabio indulges the boy from time to time: "He showed me the chicken house, he gave me a cake, he presented me with a peach and took me out for a ride in his sulky to look at the cows and the horses."

The novelty of fatherhood, however, soon seems to cloy, and Fabio is left with a few gifts and some memories. Apparently, the *estanciero* has found more pleasing ways to pass the time away from the "pompous house" of his estate. There is, in any case, no indication in the text that Fabio ever encounters his father again.

Paternal neglect would probably be sufficient to brand Don Fabio an unsympathetic character. Within the universe of the novel, however, his actions are far more insidious. In taking the boy from his mother and placing him under the tutelage of the aunts, Cáceres attempts a sort of symbolic castration of his son. He removes him from the realm of good into that of evil; from the natural and maternal pampa to the false and effeminizing influence of the town; takes him out of eternity into time. Imprisoned in the Liberal city, Fabio can do little but embrace its corrupt values: materialism and roguery.

Don Fabio's subsequent neglect does impart, however, one invaluable gift to his son. Since he is unaware of his parentage, Fabio is free to indulge literally ·in the "family romance," the postulation of whatever heritage he chooses.[28] Thus, when he fantasizes that Don Segundo might replace Don Fabio as his "protector," Fabio the orphan is in a unique position to realize his dream. History here is turned on its head, for in chapter three the boy undertakes to select his own father. In so doing, the child becomes peculiarly father to the man.[29]

The break with Don Fabio and what he represents is symbolized in certain incidents in chapters three and nine. The boy, gathering his belongings together to escape into the night, recounts: "I threw on my cherished poncho, a gift from Don Fabio." Unwittingly, he treasures this token of his real father, and yet, almost at the beginning of his adventures, the talisman's value proves bogus. Facing his first real test on the pampa, in the cloudburst on the trail, "I realized that my little poncho was short, which deeply disillusioned me." His "little poncho," the remnant of his city life and real parentage, is too small, as opposed to those of the other gauchos, who are indifferent to the discomfort of the storm, who "did not seem any more affected that the countryside itself."[30] These are the true sons of the pampa, and it surely is not accidental that, as soon as the rain ends, Fabio finds that "I felt new, fresh, able to overcome whatever misfortunes luck imposed on me." As a consequence of a symbolic baptism, the emblem of Fabio's heritage has lost its worth, and he has been reborn. He has now entered that timeless pampa, fallen into its "willful, self-contained rhythm" which will draw him further and further into the world of the gaucho, and further away from the Liberal, urban realm to which his father's whim condemned him.

As Fabio rejects his real father, he embraces another. As with the maternal, the paternal nature bifurcates, with Cáceres in the role of the "bad" father and Don Segundo Sombra as the "good" one. As *padrino,* he becomes Fabio's guardian, surrogate for his anonymous male parent. However, as noted before, it is the child who has chosen the father, who decides "that my existence was tied to that of Don Segundo Sombra." As a consequence of this act of will on the part of the son and of Don Segundo's role solely as the "good" father, the tension inherent in the relation of father and son is negated. A critical word is never spoken about Don Segundo throughout Fabio's narration. He is an absolute ideal. Thus, psychologically, a very basic conflict is eliminated within the "personality" of Fabio himself: the clash between the self and the introjected father.[31] This may be a central factor in the idyllic character of Fabio's adolescent experience, in that he is spared that experience's most volatile component: the rebellion of the child against the parent. However, the boy's identification with his *padrino* achieves such a pitch that it threatens to obliterate Fabio's own individuality entirely:

> I was almost an instrument in the hands of my godfather, who guided my every action. . . .
> Fixed ideas pursued me like commands, and I heard them in my godfather's voice. Imperatives about little things, that I obeyed as if that voice were mine. Even when I was asleep, the lessons buzzed in my head, . . . I recognized my passivity and it might have bothered me, if my own desire for independence hadn't been saying to me: "Stop worrying. With time, all this will be yours."

It is Fabio's own ego which calms his fears about his self-admitted passivity, calms them with a promise of inheritance straight from a melodrama. The age-old paternal pledge, however, here has an extra twist. Because the gaucho bequest is abstract, the passing on of qualities and skills rather than anything material, and due to the lack of any friction whatsoever between father and son, it seems that Fabio is not so much heir to Don Segundo as destined to *become* Don Segundo. He is so much the passive recipient of the older man's wisdom, so much his slavish emulator and servant, so constantly by his side, that he, who is after all a nameless *guacho* up to within three chapters of the novel's end, seems anxious to be done with his independent existence, wishes his own history lost so he may identify completely with his hero.

This impulse quite obviously possesses a religious resonance, implies the union of man and Maker which lies at the root of so much spiritual longing. This should not surprise us, given that Don Segundo, as noted, becomes in the novel an almost divine figure, "not a man but an idea," apparently immortal and invincible. He evokes wonder and respect in all who come in contact with him, so much so that, though he has often fought, he has never had to kill a man. This aspect of his character, of course, is in no way contradictory to his role as "good father." Indeed, it enhances it, particularly if viewed in light of Freud's speculative anthropology in *Totem and Taboo*. Freud asserts that the sons who perpetrated the primal crime subsequently felt guilt due to their original ambivalence toward the father. They admired and envied his power and strength as much as they feared and hated them. Hence, they entered into totemism and eventually postulated a god or gods who represented the "good father," offering protection, aid, and wisdom. This, of course, is precisely what Don Segundo Sombra provides, particularly to Fabio. In his role as *padrino*, he offers Fabio "the things of life," instructs him in the gnosis of the gaucho world as a real godparent catechizes a child in the faith. Indeed, Don Segundo is so unswervingly worshipped by his protégé, stalks the pampa so much larger than life, is so universally held in awe that he seems eventually to transcend his role as "godfather" (the English word is particularly apt) to become "God the Father." His very name amplifies the resonance: he is not the shadowy figure of the father dogging his son's steps, but a supernatural "second shadow." As with Fabio's mother, who is identified with the eternal Earth, Don Segundo threatens to merge finally with God himself, providing the immortal mate to engender the eternal son, Fabio, "son of God, of the countryside, of one's self."

Though Don Segundo represents the "good" father, he remains too one of the "brothers," one of the gauchos. In the Freudian scheme, this is quite significant, for his role as first among equals in the brother clan allows all to share the favors of the symbolic mother, the pampa. Because he is also a brother, Don Segundo does not taboo the Earth, as the "bad" father does by fencing in the plains and subduing the gaucho. Don

Segundo's dual role also enhances the sense of eternity in the countryside. If he is both father and brother, then there is no time on the pampa, nor any history. Generations do not succeed one another. They simply coexist, conflate, remain.

While Don Segundo is affirmed and mythologized in the action, the rejection of Don Fabio Cáceres proceeds apace through a series of symbolic incidents and analogues. The first of these, if rather obscurely, is the psychomachy of the first interpolated story. Retrospectively, the reader can see how Dolores and Mandinga represent a bipolarity similar to that of the "good" and "bad" fathers. They are, in a sense, "good" and "bad" sons. Both are, as far as we know, orphans. Dolores' heritage is never mentioned, but Mandinga is of unquestionably evil antecedents. His father was the Devil himself, his mother a witch. From them, he inherits various powers and qualities. Among these are a terrific lust and a yen for accumulation, both represented by the collection of virgins he captures and keeps on his enchanted island. These same traits, of course, are much later revealed as typical of one of the central characters, Don Fabio Cáceres.

The opposite of Mandinga is Dolores, the country boy who desires only the beautiful Consuelo. Possessed of gaucho virtues, he obtains the aid of two symbolic parents, the *viejita* and God, in his battle with Mandinga, who has in his arsenal the spells of his wicked mother and hellish father. In their struggle, it is Dolores who is victorious.

The tale is obviously one of good and evil, but why characterize it as a psychomachy? The reason is simple: Fabio is potentially both Dolores and Mandinga. The latter is, in the novel, the only other son who inherits. Further, his characteristics are exaggerations of those associated with Fabio's real father. In counterpoint to this demonic figure, the representative of the decadent Liberal world, is Dolores, who symbolizes Fabio as the gaucho *guachito* of most of the novel. The tale's coda, which relates that Dolores and Consuelo have taken possession of the demon's island and transformed it into a fine *estancia*, asserts the possibility of inheritance without corruption, which is the unrealizable wish of the novel's conclusion.

Before that is entertained, however, another element of the interpolated story must be pursued through the text. Mandinga is a "bad" son, standing stead ultimately for the "bad" father. His castration and death is a mediated presentation of the real impulse in the book, which is patricide, the murder of the "bad" father. This desire becomes increasingly less occluded as the novel progresses. It next appears at the conclusion of chapter seventeen, after Fabio's second trip to the crab beds. Accompanied by Patrocinio Salvatierra, he encounters the rogue bull which previously gored one of his horses. Fabio first ropes the bull, breaking its back. Injured himself in the attack, he nonetheless drags himself beside the bull and cuts its throat. Then, "the hot gush bathed my arm and crotch. The bull made his last effort to straighten up. I fell over him. My head, like a child's, rested on his shoulder. Before I completely lost consciousness, I felt the two of us, motionless, there in the huge silence of countryside and sky."

Immediately afterwards, the delirious Fabio, now safe at Don Candelario's farm, has a clairvoyant vision of his inheritance. There is no mention of Don Fabio here, nor of his bequest of the property, only of Don Leandro, telling Fabio, "your *estancia* is waiting for you." The young man's response is ambivalent: "I was happy, very happy, but sad. . . . Extraordinary things had happened to me, and I felt almost as if I were someone else ... someone who had achieved something undefined and great, but had within him as well a sense of death."

This peculiar sequence of events, it seems, makes most sense if interpreted oedipally. The bull—the powerful, horned, masculine animal—is the "bad" father. He has phallically assaulted the horse, the animal of the pampa which "carries" the gaucho, the son. Though the bay is clearly identified as male ("el pingo"), his name—Weasel, "Comadreja"—contains the word "comadre," the term used by godparents in addressing the mother of their godchild. Hence, on a symbolic plane, Fabio has seen his mother possessed by his father. He has witnessed the primal scene.

Fabio then enlists the assistance of another son, Patrocinio Salvatierra ("the patron of the Earth's salvation"), who is, of course, also his brother with whom he is associated homosexually ("like a couple after an embrace"). Together, they confront the father, castrate him ("break his back" so he cannot "stand" and also "cut his throat") and kill him. However, Fabio, the murderous son, here suffers symbolically the same fate. He is castrated, first by the loss of a member ("I felt my right arm completely limp"), and also (by implication) in the fact that it is *his* groin that is bloodied. Then he faints across the corpse of the bull, his head resting on its shoulder "like a child's." His unconsciousness represents death. Thus, father and son die together on the bosom of the earth.

The pyschoanalytic interpretation of this scene is reinforced by the subsequent action. The novel's sole flash forward now occurs, carrying Fabio to a moment *after* the death of his real (and here still anonymous) parent. At that point, he feels himself "someone else," somehow dead, and so he is, doubly. In the context of the flash forward (though it is unrevealed in the vision), Fabio has been told of his heritage and hence lost his gaucho identity. He is not who he was before, a nameless *guacho*. In terms of the symbolic patricide, he has also died, in accord with Freud's speculation, making the blood sacrifice necessary to atone for the murder of the father.

Fabio then regains consciousness and is informed of what has happened. The mythic interlude closes with the revelation that Don Segundo Sombra is the one who has ministered to Fabio. He has trussed the boy's broken member, restoring both literally and figuratively his potency, and thus allowed him to return to a gaucho life. The imagery is pat: Though the son has to die to atone for the destruction of the "bad" father, the "good" father then resurrects him. The parallel with the Christian and other oedipally influenced myths is overt.[32]

Patricide figures yet again in the text in chapter twenty-three, where the act becomes even less mediated than in the previous incidents. Antenor Barragán, a man "like a brother" to Fabio, is challenged to a duel by a mysterious older man who appears one day in the local *pulpería*. Antenor, it seems, has at one time had intercourse with a woman somehow attached to the stranger, though the exact nature of their connection is left undefined. The oedipal overtones here are obvious. The youth (the son) has possessed the woman (the mother), and the man (the father) has come to extract the phallic revenge (the subjugation, castration, and murder). However, in the battle itself, it is the son who is victorious, lifting the father into the air on the end of his knife, an assertion of his superior potency and also, perhaps, an indication of the sort of rape implicit in Fabio's duel with Numa. Here, as in the previous two instances, there is reference to the bloodiness of the wounds, though, as distinct from the description of the gelding of Mandinga and the stabbing of the bull, a direct reference to the *verija* is supressed. However, castration may be inferred from the mention of the blood-soaked belly and thighs, which physically frame the groin.

The experience of Antenor is an ill omen for Fabio, one of a series which precede chapter twenty-five. The Liberal world, always lurking throughout the action, asserts itself more and more strongly as the "discovery scene" approaches. The gambling losses at the fair, the interpolated story of Miseria, the offer of a job at Don Juan's, the murder finally climax in the hellish night drive, a sort of anti-baptism in which Nature, before Fabio's ally, turns brutally against him. The descent into the ditch, the panic of the cattle, the exhaustion of the gauchos symbolize the end of the idyll, its transformation into a nightmare. All is preparation for the moment of the death of the nameless orphan and his rebirth as someone "other."

It is Goyo, who accompanied Fabio on his first drive and then vanished from the action, who brings the news of his inheritance. There on the pampa, the boy confronts his two fathers: one embodied in a piece of paper, the other potent in flesh and blood. Throughout the novel, one has been constantly denigrated, the other continually affirmed. They stand for diametrical opposites. Don Fabio Cáceres represents *civiliza-ción*. His is the Liberal scheme, the material world, adult heterosexuality, history, and death. He is the physical, phallic, threatening father. Don Segundo Sombra, conversely, represents *barbarie*. In him reside the rural virtues, the quest for the insubstantial "things of life," adolescent homo-eroticism, eternity, and immortality. He is the spiritual father, domineering surely, but one who offers the promise of union rather than conflict. For Fabio, there is no question of the choice. He turns toward Don Segundo, calling him "Tata." That declaration—"Papa"—toward which the action has been building throughout the novel, is the final, futile patricide.

This is the story's central moment, the key to explaining its significance in its time. It here manifests the effort of a particular class and of those who embraced its ideology to deny history, to escape what seemed to be a death warrant issued by progress. Previously, there has been mention of the peculiar "marginalization" of the oligarchy which apparently occurred during the Radical interregnum of 1916–30—"apparently" in that the victory of Yrigoyenism did not in fact profoundly alter Argentine social and economic reality. It did, however, *seem* to do so by bringing the middle sectors in some way into the political process.[33] Over the course of the twenties, the perceived threat to the basic social structure grew greater rather than less with the secession of the Anti-Personalists and the spectre of an inevitable second term for Yrigoyen in 1928, one in which he could advance his reforms free of the intraparty checks provided previously by Alvear and other oligarchical Radicals. It appeared, then, that the traditional ruling elite and the system it represented were doomed.

A realization of this, surely not a completely conscious one, prompted reaction not only within the ruling class itself, but also among all Argentines with an ideological investment in the dominant system. The age of the hegemony of the "foreigner" had arrived. Hence, among the more conservative, nativist sectors, the tendency arose to view with distaste the European culture which had for so long provided a model for

Argentina, to define it as decadent and materialistic and to assert in its place the lost *criollismo,* a way of life which had existed not in some mythic Arcadia in some Golden Age, but on the Argentine pampa before its subjugation to the modern world economic system—before Liberalism, before immigration, before, in fine, Caseros.[34]

Embracing such a myth implied a psychological crisis for the oligarchy and its supporters, for who, after all, had wrought the Liberal world? The oligarchs themselves. It was they who had supported the doctrines of Sarmiento and centralization under Roca, who had welcomed immigration and transformed Buenos Aires into the Paris of the Americas. Their *estancias* and town houses stood as monuments to the rewards of the primary export economy, and their conspicuous consumption had prodded the underclasses to set for themselves goals of material achievement. Theirs was the impulse that created the educational system, the first bureaucracies, the telegraph lines, railroads, and barbed-wire fences.

And yet, for the *criollos* of the 1920s, did the blame for the massive modernization of the country lie with them? The loss of the native culture, the importation of foreigners and foreign ideas, the domestication of the gaucho—were these the fault of the rising generations, or were they rather the fault of their fathers?

Here lies the appeal of the patricidal impulse so potent in *Don Segundo Sombra.* It was the generations of the nineteenth and early twentieth centuries who had pawned the national patrimony. It was they who had imposed bogus, foreign values upon a gaucho people and thus brought the nation to its present state. Their ideals, consequently, had to be rejected. These men, these "fathers," had to be killed. To accept their bequest was to accept its consequences: the inevitability of change, the expunging of the national identity, the certainty of class death—the usurpation and destruction of the oligarchy and the hierarchical structure of Argentine society by the underclasses. To avoid the horrors of the leftist "isms," the organic community which Liberalism destroyed demanded restoration. The actual, physical fathers of the Argentine nation had to be denied, symbolically "murdered." The true Argentina, trapped by the modern system in the *subsuelo* of the pampa, could be freed only by the adoption of the nation's spiritual progenitors, its "good" fathers: the gauchos, Don Segundo Sombra.

This is the political and psychological message of Güiraldes' novel up to this point in the text, one with considerable appeal to various sectors, but most especially to the Right. In its overt validation of xenophobia, anti-capitalism, anti-urbanism and tradition; in its subconscious validation of adolescence, idealized friendship, immortality and patricide, *Don*

Segundo Sombra's popularity with the likes of Leopoldo Lugones is unsurprising. Indeed, his enthusiastic embrace of the novel was perhaps less predicated upon his admiration of its artistry than upon its epitomization of the reactionary doctrines he so ardently espoused. For the Left, the book might serve as a memento mori of the fate of an idealized rural proletariat. The young clerk might find in it his dreams of a romantic, rural existence. The aesthete might delight in the lapidary polish of Güiraldes' prose. But for the Liga Patriótica Argentina, for the growing number of philofascists of the age, for all those who felt the nation had somehow lost her way, *Don Segundo Sombra* provided a compendium of Liberal sins, of the sins of the father, and in its title character provided these readers with the alternative parent they had always desired.

This is not to say, surely, that such an analysis plays fair with Güiraldes' intentions, or with his personal politics or relationships. He was unquestionably a conservative, a man who defined himself as "anti-Radical and anti-Yrigoyen."[35] Nevertheless, his political pronouncements were few and his activities even fewer. Psychologically, there is no evidence to indicate that his relation with his own father was particularly troubled. What is certain, however, is his increasing interest during the last decade of his life in spiritualism of one kind or another. Indeed, his final journey overseas, cut short by his death in Paris, was intended to take him to India.[36] It seems likely that, on a conscious level at least, it was this metaphysical impulse which encouraged Güiraldes to posit that "transtelluristic" realm of his novel; to create the character of Don Segundo, half man and half spirit; to entertain the possibility of a world outside time. It seems doubtful, however, that he recognized the profound political implications of his work. It is not our purpose here to explore the complex and highly mediated connections between mysticism and fascism, but it does seem safe to contend that, at the time he penned his novel, Güiraldes was unaware of them.[37] Ultimately, he was little interested in the terrestrial applications of spiritual growth, surely not on any mass scale. The dedication of *Don Segundo Sombra* lends credence to this, with its reference to the gaucho borne inside the author as a wafer in a monstrance. Even more convincing, however, is the evidence of the novel's concluding chapters, which seriously put in question the possibility of opposition to the current of history.

Don Segundo, who so often throughout the text has come to the aid of Fabio, cannot rescue the boy from his inheritance. The assertion of the tie of blood, the entrance into the story of Fabio's own mortality, is something the old gaucho, powerful and spiritual though he may be, cannot alter. Hence, he demands that his protégé accept the bequest and rejects his plans for a "communist" solution, the parceling of the land among the poor. Rather, he accompanies Fabio back into civilization, back into time, back into the Liberal reality, and oversees his reentry into the world. If, on the one hand, this validates the inheritance and, by association, unifies the nature of the father at last, it also represents the acceptance of the inevitability of the loss of youth, of freedom, of community. The price for the final patricide, the futile denial of the father, has been the "death" of the gaucho Fabio Cáceres. No platitudes from Don Segundo can negate this.

Throughout the final chapters, there is irony and gloom. At first, there is a brief ray of hope in the person of Raucho, some promise of the possible synthesis of two discrete worlds. Of all of Fabio's asserted brothers—Dolores/Mandinga, Patrocinio, Antenor—Raucho is perhaps closest to him, his mirror image, the "gauchified dandy" to Fabio's "dandified gaucho." Their lives on the *estancia*, however, become almost immediately an embarrassing parody of Fabio's experience on the trail. Sleeping with the gauchos in the barn, they are two *señoritos* playing cowboys. Gradually, with Raucho's aid, Fabio acquires more and more of the trappings of a modern man. He visits the capital, improves his reading, undertakes a bit of writing.

In the final chapter, Fabio's desperate assertions of the authenticity of his life as a gaucho offer little indication that he has successfully bridged the chasm separating the two worlds he has known, and leave little doubt that he is planted for better or worse in that one of the towns, merchants, his father, and his aunts. The discovery of his real parents has placed Fabio firmly in the power of time, so in the end he stands rooted at that deadly hour, "five in the afternoon," as the still-free Don Segundo Sombra disappears into the setting sun. He muses on the profundity of his loss, obliquely on the national loss, then turns his horse toward home.

Some readers, many critics, and perhaps Güiraldes himself wished some optimism into the novel's conclusion.[38] The text allows for no such emotion. "Me fuí," it concludes, "como quien se desangra." Fabio has no choices left. His is the inheritance of Cáceres, of Caseros, a similarity it is hard to believe is unintentional. History is the father's fatal bequest. Time is the agent of his vengeance. Both are inescapable. Like the demon, the bull, the old man, like the father, the son ends castrated, mortal, bleeding to death.

PART IV

Afterwards

CHAPTER 9

The Last Happy Men

Today it's the same being
A traitor as upstanding;
Ignorant, wise; thieving,
Generous, conniving. . . .

The twentieth century's a pawnshop
Full of problems, full of heat.
If you can't whine, you don't eat;
If you don't steal, you'll get beat.
    Go to it! Have at it! In Hell,
We'll finally get a chance to meet.

                Enrique Santos Discépolo,
                    "Cambalache," 1935

THOUGH they did not know it at the time, the world of the last happy men collapsed on September 6, 1930.[1] Political events had moved with incredible speed since Yrigoyen's second term began, and especially since the onset of the worldwide Depression. With the disruption of trade patterns and the tightening of credit, the ruling class moved from passive to overt opposition to the Radical administration. Rising unemployment made the workers restive. However, it was Yrigoyen's loss of the support of the middle sectors that doomed his government. The economic crisis derailed the Radical patronage machine, and with the party no longer able to deliver security to its central constituency, the constituency simply faded away. In a futile attempt to preserve the constitutional order, Yrigoyen resigned on September fifth in favor of his vice-president, but the government was already toppling. Troops under the command of General José F. Uriburu occupied the capital the following morning, and the Argentine experiment with liberal democracy, initiated legally in 1912 and practically in 1916, came to an end.[2]

Uriburu was a corporatist, an admirer of Mussolini, and, at the time of the coup d'etat, the sort of leader who fulfilled the fondest of Lugones' hopes. Fascism on the European model, however, was not to be the lot of Argentina. Uriburu's hopes for the abolition of the Saénz Peña Law and the restructuring of the state along Italian lines were scotched by the navy. Politically, he was outmaneuvered by his fellow officer, Agustín P. Justo, a former Anti-Personalist gone over to the Conservatives. As the reactionary essence of Uriburu's rule became more and more apparent, his revolution lost the popular support it had initially attracted. Just seven months after the ouster of Yrigoyen, in an election honest only due to Conservative overconfidence, the Radicals and Socialists captured a majority of the votes. The results were disallowed but proved fatal to the Uriburu regime. In the 1932 balloting for president, it was Justo who led the Conservatives, and through the manipulation and fraud characteristic of Argentine politics before Saénz Peña, headed the new "constitutional" government.[3]

The next ten years, known in Argentine history as the Década Infame, validated Marx's gloss of Hegel in *The Eighteenth Brumaire of Louis Napoleon*. Though one might quarrel with the characterization of the oligarchy's quandary before Radicalism as tragedy, the regime of Justo was surely farcical. Corruption in the bureaucracy was as rampant as under Yrigoyen. Elections were such shams that the Radicals once again adopted intransigency. The regime was intensely puritanical, shutting down the brothels and making arrests for lewd language on the public stage.[41] It also was likely the most systematically repressive government in terms of dissent the nation had yet seen.[5] Even more disturbingly, Justo and his ministers seemed not only willing but anxious to pawn a greater and greater share of the national patrimony to foreign capital. If the bad bargain of the Roca-Runiman Pact with Britain was, on some level, dictated by the exigencies of the Depression, the same cannot be said for the generous and unnecessary renegotiation of the contract with a French consortium for the port of Rosario.[6]

Such activity, however, may not be all that surprising in view of Justo's constituency. The Conservative government of the thirties functioned in favor of the great landowners, which meant the protection of the cattle industry and in turn maintaining the primary export economy regardless of the cost. Such interests had always formed the bedrock of

Argentine oligarchical politics. However, the policy was by this time anachronistic, obsolete in the era of capitalism's greatest crisis to date and an impending world war. Even within the nation itself, the locus of wealth was shifting. A greater and greater number of the nation's fortunes were founded not on land, but on milling, textiles, banking, and urban real estate. Many of the *dueños de la tierra*, in the years since the century's turn, had lost all or part of their wealth in bad investments or misreadings of the market. Ironically, though perhaps not unpredictably, those in the thirties who most assiduously defended the interests of the rapidly collapsing ruling class were themselves not even parvenus, like Otto Bemberg or Jorge Oster, but members of the middle class, among them Justo himself.[7]

Thus, for a decade, the power of Liberalism, that ideology of the fathers, was reestablished. What had been viable in 1910, however, had no relevance to circumstances in the thirties. This new *concordancia* was not the *unicato*. Nineteenth-century economics and the politics of fraud and coercion were signifiers of a now senile system. The shuffling onto the historical stage of a *Weltanschauung* a quarter of a century out of date proved alternately disastrous, embarrassing, or baldly silly.

In the literature of the period, the existential concerns operating fitfully within much of the work of the Generation of 1922 became central. Mallea's characters confront a lonely, silent, and solitary life. Mariani's production manifests a growing mystical bent, evident not only in his long novel finally published in 1943, *Regreso a Dios*, but also in short, quirky prose pieces which appeared frequently in leftist publications of the period.[8] Arlt abandoned the novel in 1932, concentrating his energies on short fiction and particularly on the theater. His dramas possess a power distinct from that of *El juguete rabioso*. They are heavily influenced by his growing interest in surrealism and develop those aspects of his talent stirred by what might best be called "tragic farce." Castelnuovo and Barletta remained closer, perhaps, to their youthful ideals, though the former's anarchism and tremendism seemed less and less in tune with the times. Barletta, meanwhile, produced no major work in the 1930s, his energies largely absorbed by the highly successful Teatro del Pueblo.

Among those of Florida, Enrique González Tuñón slowly expired of tuberculosis, while his brother Raúl became ever more involved with Communist politics. González Lanuza continued working, along with fellow *martinfierrista* Horacio Rega Molina, experimenting with drama and seeing their work produced by their old adversary, Barletta.[9] The most lasting prose works of the era were produced by two up to that point minor members of the Generation of 1922, Raúl Scalabrini Ortíz and

Ezequiel Martínez Estrada. *El hombre que está solo y espera* and *Radiografía de la pampa*, essays written early in decade, scalded the Argentine consciousness with their acid commentary on a nation in search of itself. And, of course, this was the era of Borges' first efforts in fiction: the manifold ironies of *Historia universal de la infamia* and the literary gamesmanship of "Pierre Menard, autor del Quijote," both emblematic of a withdrawal from a world, from an age, so obviously and infamously out of synch with reality.

The literature of the thirties saw the emergence of certain new talents—Bernardo Verbistky, Arturo Cambours Ocampo—but was for the most part dominated by the former vanguardists and revolutionaries of the twenties. It represents in many ways a distillation of certain elements typical of the writings of the entire Generation of 1922. Theirs always was and largely remained a literature of what Marcuse has called "The Great Refusal—the protest against what is."[10] None of the major constituents of either group wrote affirmatively of the prevailing reality. Among the *boedistas,* with their philosophically molded vision of the dominant ideology as a mechanism of reification, repression, and torment, this is perhaps unsurprising. Arlt the renegade's dark imaginings are also in some ways predictable. However, even among the *vanguardia,* the *grupo de Florida,* that most elegant and oligarchical of thoroughfares, there was dissatisfaction, repugnance, refusal. This manifests itself in Mallea's *porteño* stories, those renditions of a chic and eviscerated life of privilege. For an authentic existence, real passion and real pain, Mallea must look to Bahía Blanca, to the past, to the provinces, as González Tuñón and various poets turned to the *arrabales,* seeking among the downtrodden a "real life" that had somehow disappeared among the other sectors of society. Even Güiraldes, an oligarch himself, emerges not as a defender of his class but as its enemy, indulging in a nostalgia which, as Fredric Jameson remarked of Walter Benjamin's, is "conscious of itself, [representing] a lucid and remorseless dissatisfaction with the present on the grounds of some remembered plentitude."[11]

Still, it was the vanguardists who presented some sort of alternative reality, who from a recollected and idealized past asserted the possibility of a world qualitatively different, of an organic community. Even if drawn from an "outdated and surpassed culture," there is nonetheless the sense that their vision "in some of its decisive elements, [is] also a *post*-technological one. Its most advanced images and positions seem to survive their absorption into administered comforts and stimuli; they continue to haunt the consciousness with the possibility of their rebirth in the consummation of technical progress."[12]

The Left presented no such alternatives. In the writings of Boedo, in spite of their assault on the dominant culture, there is little or no indication that anything can be done to alter it. In Barletta, fists are shaken; in Castelnuovo, prayers uttered; in Mariani, abortive strikes mentioned in passing. Yet, there never emerges anything even so radical or optimistic as *The Jungle*'s concluding declaration, "Chicago will be ours!" The reader has little sense that Buenos Aires will even be inherited by the workers, much less taken. On the other hand, this perhaps represents a greater hard-headedness on the part of the *boedistas*. American socialists, after all, and in spite of Upton Sinclair's fervent exhortations, never did rule Chicago. Still, this reticence, the lack of the assertion of collectivity, of the provision to the reader of options, adds credence to the claims that Boedo did not represent a truly engaged literature.[13] The alternatives that readers of the 1920s *did* confront, in addition to those of Güiraldes and Mallea (visions unfortunately co-optable into fascistic worldviews), were thus not socialist or anarchist utopias, but the bleak cycle implied in Mariani's "La ficción" or the accidental apocalypse of González Lanuza's "Final."

The Left failed, then, both to present any models of social alternatives or to suggest any tactics the adoption of which might facilitate such postulations. Meanwhile, among the vanguardists, while there was the assertion of an alternate world, *Don Segundo Sombra* or a story like "El capitán" make it apparent that these schemes are ultimately doomed. This gloomy picture is oddly reinforced in the psychosexual dynamics of the works here under study. They are almost universally concerned with male bonding, whether among Güiraldes gauchos, in Mariani's office, or throughout the various misadventures of Silvio Astier. Women have little or no place in the work of either revolutionaries or vanguardists, except as representatives of treachery, failure, or impossible hopes. However, except in *Don Segundo Sombra*, homoeroticism seems to offer little comfort, providing only limited social solidarity and a consummation which is either impossible (as with Lagos) or destructively traumatic (as with Silvio Astier). The homoerotic element is, of course, heavily determined by social and demographic circumstances, and, in any case, given the era's prevailing mores, the presentation of a mature and consummated homosexual relationship would have been impossible. This strain in so many works may further be the consequence of a young literature and a young nation. Still, the fact that, whether in Güiraldes or Castelnuovo, González Tuñón or Mariani, Mallea or Arlt, heterosexual relations are *always* unsuccessful seems to represent a fixation upon the adolescent moment, the arresting of the characters at the crisis of identity, the solution of which is central to the acceptance of the role of adult and that of progenitor.[14] The negativity associated with such a role is apparent in *Don Segundo Sombra*, in which to embrace responsibility and heterosexuality is to accept the inevitability of death. The lack of sexual commitment, with the concomitant assumption of marriage and family, seems evidence of a fear of history itself, an unwillingness to enter into the process of generation and aging, as if to do so is to surrender any possibility of altering or escaping the present reality.[15] This is fatally linked to the inability to establish community, to assert a real brotherhood of men as Güiraldes asserts a brotherhood of gauchos.

These observations lead to what is perhaps the key link between the texts of Boedo and Florida—the overwhelming sense of the isolation and loneliness of the characters in the products of both groups. There is, with the exception once again of Güiraldes' gauchos, an almost palpable alienation separating these individuals not only from their labor, not only from their society in the abstract, but from their fellows. Mariani's clerks, time and again, make gestures toward communication and camaraderie, perhaps even toward love, only to be halted by the object of the gesture, by the system, or by themselves. "The man" leaves the treacherous fruit peel on the sidewalk; Guerrero observes Toulet's despicable theft and does nothing; Lagos rejects Riverita's advance with a blow. González Lanuza's characters are always solitary and González Tuñón's prostitutes, self-admitted commodities treading the edge of the abyss, while Castelnuovo's marginals are defeated even when they seek the companionship not of men but of animals. The world which the creations of the Generation of 1922 confront is one dominated by deception, injustice, violence, impotence, and betrayal. Even for Boedo, the answer to Lenin's "What is to be done?" appears to have been "Nothing, except try to survive." Lagos, Toulet, and Guerrero are so hopelessly enmeshed in modern production, in the dream and the ethic of the *oficina*, that they lie to and betray not only one another but themselves. In the world of *Aquelarre*, even mirrors and one's own soul cannot be trusted. Fabio Cáceres, whenever in touch with the Liberal reality, sees exploitation, deceit, and corruption. Bleakest of all is Arlt, whose Silvio Astier turns Judas, becomes himself a "rabid toy" of an ideology which offers him nothing, striking out against all around him, driven by his existential disease into a betrayal which is one not only of his friend but of himself. In all the writers of this generation, there is that anger, that horror at being manipulated, cheated, lied to, which Mafud asserts as a constant in Argentine literature throughout the Liberal era: "From Martín Fierro to Don Segundo Sombra, everyone refuses to collaborate [with society]. The hatred, in some cases, becomes so violent that characters think of destroying it. . . . The reason the

Argentine has for his social renunciation is always the same. He feels violently defrauded by his society. He does not feel it is his nor does he make it his."[16]

If this is, indeed, the repetend of modern Argentine culture, it would seem it achieved new heights in the work of the Generation of 1922. Previous generations produced writers whose affirmative tone somehow balanced the rejection voiced by their contemporaries; Obligado's optimism offsets Hernández' gloom; Cane's, Cambaceres'; Gerchunoff's, Gálvez'. The sense of "violent fraud," however, had apparently reached too great a pitch in the twenties to permit such balances, though it was not yet so intense as it was to become in the Década Infame, when even rage and pity were insufficient, replaced by escape and despair. Indeed, Mafud's analysis seems a bit flawed where the members of Boedo and Florida are concerned, in that their characters, though possessed of a sense of their deception, do not refuse cooperation with their society. Rather, they integrate themselves into it, or attempt to, though the very collaboration represents a sort of moral and spiritual self-slaughter. Though perhaps too broadly, Juan Carlos Portantiero sees this element as a reflection of contemporary class circumstances: Boedo and Florida "are united by one sociocultural constant: with a few personal exceptions, the literature of both groups is an expression of the failure and loneliness of the urban middle sectors."[17]

The "failure" and "spiritual solitude" of these strata would certainly seem an odd theme in an age when they had, apparently, triumphed through Radicalism. In that historical moment, however, there was perhaps a half-conscious recognition that the ultimate promises of nineteenth-century liberal politics, the secret ballot and universal suffrage, did not necessarily imply a new age, and themselves represented yet another deception. The oppression of the urban and rural masses continued as before, as Barletta, Castelnuovo, and González Tuñón documented and as the Semana Trágica and the repression in the Chaco and Patagonia proved concretely. A steady job and the good graces of the ward captain were no guarantee of security, as Mariani demonstrated, and the price for both was the loss of self. Arlt saw no hope for the present scheme in any form, while Güiraldes sought release from the horror of the modern world by the recasting and mythification of the past. None of the writers here studied was comfortable with the historical moment, or with much of the nation's history of the previous half century. This unease emerges in their characters, who are curiously disconnected from any kind of historical continuity. A family, that unit which grounds the individual within history, only occasionally appears in these stories, and when one does, it seems always to be truncated, repressive, inorganic, or doomed. Parents, particularly fathers, when they do enter the scene, tend to be a malevolent force, and there are no filial rebellions which meet with any ultimate success. Further, there seems little possibility of a connection with historical continuity through the formation of new families. For the Generation of 1922, there was no dialectic of life or history, no possibility of positive, dynamic change on either a personal or national level. There was only the eternal system—mind-numbing, alienating, soul-crushing—which was the bequest of the Liberal fathers.

Arlt's Balder, then, must have been correct about that age of "mangy avariciousness." How, with such a sense of hopeless manipulation or endless, futile rebellion characterizing his generation, could Mastronardi have ever asserted that he belonged in the company of the last happy men? What possible source of happiness existed? What slight, positive shimmer might distinguish the grim vision of the Generation of 1922 from that of succeeding generations? First of all, we must recall the philosophical and historical circumstances under which this particular generation, mostly born around 1900, came of age. Many were the sons of immigrants, the offspring of those come to *hacerse la América,* whose allegiance to an idealized vision of Argentina arose not from some abstract patriotism but from a profound investment of effort and emotion. These newcomers believed in the myths of the nineteenth-century propagandists of progress because they had to, because to reject them was to invalidate the very real and painful sacrifices of pulling up roots in Italy, Spain, or Russia to sink new ones half a world away. And indeed, for most, their conditions on the banks of the Río de la Plata were no worse, and usually rather better, than those left behind. Their children, however, confronted an anomalous historical situation. On the one hand, their Old World inheritance was abstract, tied to lands six or nine thousand miles away. On the other, in the land of their birth, they remained to an extent outsiders. However, most especially for those of Spanish or Italian extraction, who were thus more familiar with dominant Argentine values, both the pressure and the opportunity to adapt, to conform, was considerable.[18] All certainly remembered, from the impressionable age of ten or so, the affirmation of *argentinidad* of the Centenario, and most were as well products of the Sarmentine educational system. Thus, they were imbued with both the patriotism and positivism which formed the ideological basis of all courses of study. They were prepared to embrace their new homeland enthusiastically, perhaps more so than their *criollo* contemporaries, who were presumably more secure in their identity and traditions.

Further, in that most of the constituents of the Generation of 1922 arose from the various sectors of the middle class, the impact of Radicalism on the formation of their consciousnesses must not be overlooked. Yrigoyen's messianic promise of a New Jerusalem simply by means of free elections must have made a profound impression upon these young men whose entire lifetimes, up to the age of thirty, were spent in a world in which the Radical *caudillo* was a central, if not *the* central, political figure.

What occurred after 1920, the years in which these writers and their contemporaries matured, was their gradual disenchantment with the worldview of their fathers—natural, national, or both—and of their own childhood, a disenchantment shaped both by international and internal events. World War I shattered the complacency not only of the belligerents but of neutral nations as well. The fall of the House of Romanov and the rise of the workers' and soldiers' soviets indicated a shift of power of truly earth-shaking proportions. The effect of these events involving European youth, as we have seen, was felt by their contemporaries elsewhere as well. However, though by all rights the world of the fathers should have been washed away in the torrent of filial blood at the Somme and Verdun, such was not the case even in England or Germany, much less in uninvolved Argentina. There, however, the Semana Trágica indicated that the organic state of Radical rhetoric might not be quite the community it had promised. Yrigoyen's reforms, modest though they were, were mired in legalistic wrangling. Surely, even in the early twenties, a vague unease arose among certain elements of the young. These young men truly believed there existed, as Mastronardi asserts, "a firm and delineated reality" in the nineteenth and early twentieth centuries, and that childhood vision of wholeness was severely tested by the adult reality of the 1920s.[19]

Their response to this was outrage, precisely that outrage at being "defrauded," fooled, lied to. The lessons learned from parents, school, church, and political leaders were simply false. This anger, as noted, emerged in the literature, particularly in Boedo but also in Florida, to the extent that it seems writers of both groups believed (or hoped) that outrage itself was enough, that through the simple exposure of wretched social conditions, through the very buffooning of the culture's sacred cows, a change—political, aesthetic, or both—might be wrought. Thus, outrage fades into outrageousness—both deadly serious in Castelnuovo's tremendism and comical in the tweaking and nose-thumbing which characterized not only Florida but Boedo as well. We should not forget, however, that this frivolity arose not only from an appreciation of wit, but from quite profound aesthetic, political, and philosophical questions, and constituted for both groups a weapon in the assault on the dominant vision of the world.

Outrage, however, is a privilege. It implies the anticipation of something different, something better, which, for example, those maturing in the 1930s in Argentina had much less reason to expect. They might be bitter, saddened, lonely, but they were immured against outrage by the infamy which characterized their world. For them, it was more difficult to be *lúdico*, "flip," "happy," in that not only personal circumstances but those of the nation as a whole taught them early of deception. They lacked the naive faith of the *boedistas* in the imminence (or immanence) of revolution, recognizing social upheavel instead as a product of arduous labor, labor which might well lead not to utopia, but to failure and brutal reaction. They lost too the notion that art in and of itself might power radical change, just as the idea of Florida that art somehow transcended politics, somehow constituted a realm distinct from the dominant reality, became less and less viable as the twenties waned, and even more so after 1930.

Beyond these reasons, there was among the Generation of 1922 that sense of unity based on youth, which bound together Barletta and Borges, González Lanuza and Mariani, those with world visions as distinct as their gifts. Ironically, those who never postulated in their work the possibility of successful collectivity surely enjoyed precisely such an experience. It was the interaction, cooperation, dialogue and polemic—the groups, the magazines, the madcap doings at the Royal Keller and the lectures at La Peña—which made the Generation of 1922 such a significant entity in the Argentine literary tradition, gave it an importance that two or three dozen artists working independently could never have achieved. That sense of purpose, of at least conceivable victory in the fight to revolutionize art, society or both, coupled with the youth of the constituents, the relatively progressive history of Argentina in the Radical era, and the general prosperity of the age gave these young writers hope, gave them a happiness which, as they surveyed the national consciousness from their thirties, forties, or fifties, they recognized as lost. They saw their youthful selves as special—unspoiled, outraged, naive, self-assured—qualitatively different from those who came after them, the last men to be happy in quite the same way in this century.

It would seem then that the members of the Generation of 1922, much as they disliked, distrusted, or felt deceived by history—both personal and national—nonetheless had faith in their ability to change it, though this faith emerged less strongly in their fiction than in their lives, which perhaps indicates its tenuousness. They saw some chance of choice, some possibility of the recapturing or creation of a life and art more whole, more profound, more organic than that which had arisen in Liberal Argentina. Nicolás Olivari, that determined *poète maudit* who helped found Boedo only to jump ship to Florida, wrote during the twenties: "Every day that passes, it is more difficult for us to feed ourselves, it is more difficult to breathe, until that moment arrives in which we have no other choice but to resign ourselves to commit all the incests, all the murders, all the outrages, or remain, simply, humbly, victims of the family."[20]

This was not the family of the recollected totality of a mythologized Europe or the *bonissima tellus* of the pampa. It was, rather, the family of Liberal history, the alienating system of life which left the man at Corrientes and Esmeralda alone and waiting. But in that world of *Martín Fierro* and *Claridad,* of *Crítica* and the Café Tortoni, Lugones and Yrigoyen, anarchist picnics and the visit of the Prince of Wales, in that first era of the contemporary age, there was still an option. One could dare to commit all those incests, murders, and outrages imaginable either on paper or in reality, in either the service of aesthetic or social revolution, in the hope of avoiding the victimization of that Liberal system, of history, of time. After 1930, after the end of the age of "the last happy men," there was a disquieting sense that, in spite of any rebellions or outrage, one still remained "the victim of the family"—the pawn, not the master, of history.

Notes

INTRODUCTION

1. Mastronardi's remarks appear in a letter to Juan Pinto written in 1940, which the latter quotes in his book *Breviario de la literatura argentina (Con una ojeada retrospectiva)* (Buenos Aires: Editorial la Mandrágora, 1958), p. 23. Arlt's comments are placed in the mouth of Estanislao Balder, protagonist of his last novel, *El amor brujo* (Buenos Aires: Compañía General Fabril Editora, 1968), pp. 87–88.

2. Julio Mafud, *Psicología de la viveza criolla (Contribuciones para una interpretación de la realidad social argentina y americana* (Buenos Aires: Editorial Americalee S.R.L., 1965), p. 157.

3. One of the most entertaining and valuable sources of information regarding Argentina's various distinguished guests of the decade is Francis Korn, Susana Magarza, Lidia de la Torre, and Carlos Escude, *Buenos Aires: Los huéspedes del '20* (Buenos Aires: Editorial Sudamericana, 1974).

4. See Korn, et al., p. 150. The authors list nineteen different Spanish-language dailies which appeared during the 1920s. This total does not include weeklies and semi-weeklies, nor any of the newspapers printed in foreign languages (including German, Italian, English, Yiddish, and Polish). Regarding *Vogue*, see *Nosotros: Revista mensual de letras, arte, historia, filosofía y ciencias sociales*, no. 164, p. 14.

5. Korn, et al., pp. 82–92; also Juan José Sebreli, *Buenos Aires: Vida cotidiana y alienación* (Buenos Aires: Ediciones Siglo Veinte, 1965), pp. 122–23.

6. Charles S. Sargent, *The Spatial Evolution of Greater Buenos Aires, Argentina, 1870–1930* (Tempe, Arizona: Center for Latin American Studies, Arizona State University, 1974), pp. 82–88.

7. Noé Jitrik, "Ricardo Güiraldes," *Capítulo: La historia de la literatura argentina* no. 30 (Buenos Aires: Centro Editor de América Latina, 1968?), p. 669.

CHAPTER 1—REVOLUTION AND RADICALISM

1. Ysabel F. Rennie, *The Argentine Republic* (Westport, Connecticut: Greenwood Press Publishers, 1975), pp. 28–73.

2. Mafud, p. 234.

3. Germán García, *El inmigrante en la novela argentina* (Buenos Aires: Librería Hachette, 1970), pp. 179–81.

4. Rennie, pp. 53–63, especially 56–57; and Gino Germani, *Política y sociedad en una época de transición: De la sociedad tradicional a la sociedad de masas* (Buenos Aires: Editorial Paidós, 1962), pp. 179–81.

5. The classic documentation of the gaucho existence is, ironically, Domingo F. Sarmiento, *Facundo: Civilización y barbarie* (Buenos Aires: Centro Editor de América Latina, 1973), pp. 6–45. A brief exposition may be found in Rennie, pp. 5–14. An extensive bibliography on the gaucho is included in Madaline Wallis Nichols, *The Gaucho: Cattle Hunter, Cavalryman, Ideal of Romance* (New York: Gordian Press, 1968).

6. Esteban Echeverría, quoted in José Luis Romero, *A History of Argentine Political Thought* (trans. Thomas McGann) (Stanford, California: Stanford University Press, 1963), p. 145.

7. Juan Bautista Alberdi, in Romero, p. 144.

8. Noted in a lecture by James Scobie, Professor of History, University of California, San Diego, October 1977.

9. Rennie, pp. 120–27.

10. See James Scobie, *Buenos Aires: Plaza to Suburb, 1870–1910* (New York: Oxford University Press, 1974). Scobie synopsizes some of this information in his *Argentina: A City and a Nation* (New York: Oxford University Press, 1971), pp. 160–75. Also useful is Sargent, pp. 59–93.

11. Romero, p. 183.

12. Germani, pp. 185–88.

13. Germani, p. 185.

14. Romero, pp. 165–82.

15. Germani, pp. 200–202.

16. Romero, p. 182.

17. García, p. 16.

18. Germani, pp. 203–204.

19. Romero, p. 177.

20. Germani, p. 205.

21. Romero, pp. 183–213.

22. David Rock, *Politics in Argentina 1890–1930: The Rise and Fall of Radicalism* (London: Cambridge University Press, 1975), p. 54.

23. David Rock, "Radical Populism and the Conservative Elite, 1912–1930," in David Rock (ed.), *Argentina in the Twentieth Century* (Pittsburgh: University of Pittsburgh Press, 1975), p. 73.

24. Rock, "Radical Populism," p. 68.

25. Romero, pp. 213–26.

26. Rock, "Radical Populism," p. 71.

27. Romero, pp. 196–200.

28. Romero, pp. 200–203.

29. Rock, *Politics in Argentina*, pp. 59–60; Rennie, pp. 204–205.

30. Rock, "Radical Populism," p. 75.

31. Romero, p. 196.

32. The city's first subway line, running beneath Plaza de Mayo and then Calle Rivadavia, carried its first passengers in 1913.

33. Scobie, *Buenos Aires*, pp. 13–14, 35–36.

34. Mafud, p. 68.

35. Mafud, p. 96; Pedro Orgambide, *Yo, Argentino* (Buenos Aires: Jorge Alvarez

Editor, 1968), p. 14.

36. Mafud, p. 89.

37. From a Radical manifesto dated March 3, 1916, quoted in Rock, "Radical Populism," p. 79.

38. Rock, "Radical Populism," pp. 75–76.

39. Romero, p. 224.

40. Rock, "Radical Populism," p. 77.

41. Regarding the Semana Trágica, see García, p. 96; Orgambide, p. 26; Rock, *Politics in Argentina,* pp. 157–200; Rock, "Radical Populism," p. 73; and Romero, p. 223.

42. Orgambide, p. 52.

43. Rock, "Radical Populism," pp. 80–81.

44. Rock, "Radical Populism," p. 81.

45. Romero, pp. 218–26.

CHAPTER 2—THE LITERATURE OF LIBERALISM

1. Adolfo Prieto, "La generación del ochenta: La imaginación," *Capítulo: La historia de la literatura argentina* no. 20 (Buenos Aires: Centro Editor de América Latina, 1968?).

2. García, p. 16.

3. Lugones remarked: "A really balanced and intelligent man passes through three stages: at eighteen, he breaks windows . . . at thirty, he ought to be installing windows; at forty, he should be making windows." See Guillermo Ara, "Leopoldo Lugones," *Capítulo: La historia de la literatura argentina* no. 26 (Buenos Aires: Centro Editor de América Latina, 1968?), p. 615.

4. Ara, "Leopoldo Lugones," p. 624.

5. Myron L. Lichtblau, *Manuel Gálvez* (New York: Twayne Publishers, 1972), pp. 15–49, 72–83.

6. Jorge B. Rivera, "Realismo tradicional: Narrativa urbana," *Capítulo: La historia de la literatura argentina* no. 37 (Buenos Aires: Centro Editor de América Latina, 1968?), pp. 601–605.

7. Rivera, p. 867.

8. Rivera, pp. 871–72.

9. Héctor René Lafleur, Sergio D. Provenzano, and Fernando Pedro Alonso, *Las revistas literarias argentinas (1893–1960)* (Buenos Aires: Ediciones Culturales Argentinas, 1962), p. 28. For samples of the prose and preoccupations of such magazines, see Korn, et al., pp. 53–55, 59–60.

10. Lafleur, et al., p. 67.

11. Lafleur, et al., p. 40.

12. *Nosotros* nos. 168–72.

13. *Nosotros* no. 173, p. 259.

CHAPTER 3—THE CITY AND THE AGE

1. Eduardo González Lanuza, *Los martinfierristas* (Buenos Aires: Ediciones Culturales Argentinas, 1961), p. 17.

2. Mafud, pp. 63–66.

3. Mafud, p. 66.

4. González Lanuza, *Los martinfierristas*, p. 17.

5. Rock, "Radical Populism," pp. 82–83.

6. Rock, "Radical Populism," p. 82.

7. Rock, "Radical Populism," p. 83.

8. Rivera, pp. 866–67.

9. Scobie, *Argentina*, pp. 160–61, 176–82.

10. Ezequiel Martínez Estrada, *Radiografía de la pampa* (Buenos Aires: Losada, 1968), p. 194.

11. Sargent, pp. 66–72.

12. Some information regarding *porteño* theatrical life may be gleaned from Osvaldo Sosa Cordero, *Historia de las varietés en Buenos Aires, 1900–1925* (Buenos Aires: Ediciones Corregidor, 1978). It is probably more enlightening, however, simply to thumb through the major dailies of the era—*Crítica, La Razón*, or one of the others.

13. Sebreli, pp. 119–21; Conrado Nalé Roxlo, *Borrador de Memorias* (Buenos Aires: Editorial Plus Ultra, 1978), p. 210.

14. Sebreli, pp. 134–35; Korn, et al., pp. 83–90, 140.

15. Sebreli, pp. 75–86.

16. Korn, et al., pp. 113–14.

17. Castelnuovo was particularly disturbed by the common identification of the *"mala vida"* of liquor, sex, and crime with the working class, as he makes clear in "Literatura maleva," *Claridad: Revista de arte, crítica y letras. Tribuna de pensamiento izquierdista,* November 1926, p. 2.

18. This description of Buenos Aires comes from the title of Lucio V. Lopez' 1884 novel, *La gran aldea*.

19. Nalé Roxlo, pp. 174–76; Korn, et al., pp. 128–29.

20. The declaration of Madrid as the intellectual meridian of the Hispanic world was originally made in the Spanish magazine *Nueva Gaceta*. Some examples of the Argentine response are reproduced in Adolfo Prieto, *El periódico "Martín Fierro"* (Buenos Aires: Editorial Galerna, 1968), pp. 71–78.

21. For an analysis of this terror of homosexuality see Sebreli, pp. 79–86. For an example of an impassioned denial of an effeminate sensibility, see Eduardo González Lanuza, *Aquelarre* (Buenos Aires: J. Samet, Editor, 1928), pp. 7–8. For an illustration of how ridiculous this sort of debate could become, see the battle in print which developed between Leónidas Barletta and Juan Carlos Paz regarding Honegger's music in *Claridad* (July 1, 1927, pp. 5–7) and *La campana de palo* (no. 15, p. 6; no. 17, pp. 14–15). Finally, note Borges' remarks on the subject in his essay "Nuestras imposibilidades" in *Discusión* (Buenos Aires: Gleizer-Editor, 1932), pp. 16–17. This essay was removed from the collection after the first edition and has never been republished.

22. Rivera, pp. 866–67.

23. Korn, et al., p. 145, pp. 170–86.

24. Rivera, pp. 866–67.

CHAPTER 4—THE MOVEMENTS

1. González Lanuza, *Los martinfierristas*, p. 100.

2. There are almost as many different lists of the constituents of each group as there

were writers, and a few writers—Roberto Arlt, the brothers González Tuñón, Nicolás Olivari—either defy categorization or moved between the two camps. It seems generally agreed that Florida included the following: Ricardo Güiraldes, Macedonio Fernández, Evar Méndez (all older), Jorge Luis Borges, Eduardo González Lanuza, Alfredo Brandán Caraffa, Pablo Rojas Paz, Francisco Luis Bernárdez, Leopoldo Marechal, Oliverio Girondo, Francisco López Moreno, Roberto Ledesma, Carlos Mastronardi, Horacio Rega Molina, Conrado Nalé Roxlo, Alberto Hidalgo, Ricardo Molinari, Jacobo Fijman, Luis Franco, Cayetano Córdova Iturburu, José Pedroni, Eduardo Mallea, Ernesto Palacio, Ernesto Espinosa (Samuel Glusberg), Ulises Petit de Murat, and Norah Lange.

Boedo's members were Elías Castelnuovo, Leónidas Barletta, Lorenzo Stanchina, Alvaro Yunque (Arístides Gandolfi Herrero), César Tiempo (Israel Zeitlin), Enrique Amorim, Abel Rodríguez, Alberto Pineta, Gustavo Riccio, Roberto Mariani, Pedro Juan Vignale, Julio Fingerit, Marcos Fingerit, Aristóbulo Echegarray, Luis Emilio Soto, Juan de Cendoya, J. Salas Subirat, Juan Carlos Paz, Juan Guijarro (Augusto Gandolfi Herrero), and Ernesto L. Castro.

Another figure difficult to place in either camp is Santiago Ganduglia, while such writers as Roberto Ortelli, Roberto Smith, and Homero Guglielmini, significant early in the decade, seem to have largely vanished from the scene by the time the clash between Boedo and Florida erupted. Those writers and intellectuals associated with the Ateneo Universitario (José Gabriel, for example, or Jorge Max Rohde) generally remained outside the fray.

3. Leónidas Barletta, *Boedo y Florida: Una visión distinta* (Buenos Aires: Ediciones Metrópolis, 1967).

4. Borges continues to voice the opinion that the conflict between Boedo and Florida, and indeed the groups themselves, were an "invention" of Roberto Mariani and Ernesto Palacio, and that the "joke" was gradually adopted by other young writers of the day (personal interview, July 5, 1979). Less extreme variants of this version of history are not uncommon among the survivors of Florida. However, those of Boedo, without exception, insist on the existence of and real differences between the two groups.

5. Adolfo Prieto, "Boedo y Florida," *Estudios de literatura argentina* (Buenos Aires: Editorial Galerna, 1969), pp. 50–53.

6. Marta Scrimaglio, *Literatura argentina de vanguardia (1920–1930)* (Rosario, Argentina: Editorial Biblioteca, 1974), pp. 14–15.

7. Lafleur, et al., p. 81.

8. The Borges family left Argentina before the outbreak of hostilities in 1914, and in preference to braving the sealanes, remained on the continent after the war began. Young Jorge Luis thus completed his education in Switzerland, in French.

9. Guillermo de Torre, *Historia de las literaturas de vanguardia* (Madrid: Editorial Guadarrama, 1965), pp. 582–85.

10. Carlos Mastronardi, "El movimiento de *Martín Fierro*," *Capítulo: La historia de la literatura argentina* no. 39 (Buenos Aires: Centro Editor de América Latina, 1968?), p. 920.

11. Prieto, "Boedo y Florida," p. 37.

12. Mastronardi, p. 920.

13. González Lanuza, *Los martinfierristas*, pp. 40–43.

14. Mastronardi, p. 921.

15. Guillermo de Torre (p. 583) says all poems in the first issue of *Prisma* were Spanish. However, in the photograph of the broadside which appears in Rodolfo Borelo, "La narrativa fantástica: Borges," *Capítulo: La historia de la literatura argentina*, no. 48 (Buenos Aires: Centro Editor de América Latina, 1968?), there appears to be one poem by Borges

("Aldea"), one by González Lanuza ("El tren"), and one by Guillermo Juan ("Puerto")—this on p. 1145.

16. *Proa: Revista de literatura* nos. 1–3. Sergio Piñero died in 1922.

17. Jorge Luis Borges, "Ultraismo," *Nosotros* no. 151, pp. 466–71.

18. "Poemas ultraístas," *Nosotros* no. 160, pp. 52–62.

19. The declared *ultraístas* represented were Borges (*Nosotros* no. 168), Roberto Smith (no. 168), Roberto Ortelli (no. 169), Guillermo Juan (no. 169), and Eduardo González Lanuza (no. 170), though Smith insists he only sympathized with the movement.

20. "Nuestra encuesta sobre la nueva generación," *Nosotros* nos. 168–172 (May–September 1923). On p. 6 of no. 168, the questions of the inquiry are set forth. All of the forty-two respondents were under thirty years of age. The youngest questioned was Guillermo Juan, seventeen; the oldest, José Gabriel, Ernesto Laclau, and Schendy Arecelus, were all twenty-seven. A list of respondents and their ages appears in LaFleur, et al., pp. 78–79, along with mention of young writers not included. Of those who were at least briefly associated with Boedo, only four figure in the *encuesta:* Nicolás Olivari (no. 171), Lorenzo Stanchina (no. 171), Santiago Ganduglia (no. 172), and Enrique Amorim (no. 168). At the time, only the first two seem to show a leftward tilt in their ideas. Later prominent Floridians, in addition to the aforementioned ultraists, include Brandán Caraffa (no. 169), Córdova Iturburu (no. 170), and Leopoldo Marechal (no. 170).

21. *Valoraciones* published from September 1923 to May 1928. Its full title indicates its roots in the university reform: *Valoraciones: Revista Bimensual de Humanidades, Crítica y Polémica—Organo Estudiantes Renovación de La Plata.*

22. "Manifesto de *Inicial,*" *Inicial: Revista de la nueva generación* no. 1, pp. 3–6.

23. Alfredo Brandán Carrafa, "Hildebrando Pizzetti y el Díos único," *Inicial* no. 1, pp. 9–12.

24. Alfredo Bianchi, "Inicial," *Nosotros* no. 173, pp. 259–62.

25. Eduardo González Lanuza (personal interview, October 10, 1979).

26. For philosophical influences on *Inicial,* see Scrimaglio, p. 38. For examples indicating that anti-Semitism infected Boedo as well as Florida, see *Claridad,* August 30, 1927 ("¡Asesino!"), September 15, 1927 ("Los sinónimos de judio"), and September 25, 1927 ("De los judios"), an exchange arising from the first article's virulent assault charging Jews with being part of the international power structure which condemned Sacco and Vanzetti.

27. "Enrique Ferri and el facismo," *Inicial* no. 2, pp. 44–46. Note, however, that in *Inicial,* no. 1, the editors begin their political commentary with "Outside of Italy, Europe seems to us at the end of its rope . . ." (p. 36).

28. Jorge Luis Borges, "Acerca del expresionismo," *Inicial* no. 3, p. 16.

29. Roberto Ortelli was not in Buenos Aires at the time of the split in *Inicial,* at least according to Brandán (personal interview with Alfredo Brandán Caraffa, October 6, 1979). Thus, his name appears in both editions of *Inicial* no. 5 (April 1924).

30. *Inicial* no. 5 dated April 1924 is the renegade publication. In the copy of the magazine in the collection of the heirs of Sergio Provenzano, there appears on the inside cover the penciled notation: "Number published by the dissidents. It was the only one published." The "official" magazine is *Inicial* no. 5, May 1924. Its only allusion to any dissension in the ranks is an announcement on page 74 which states: "Mr. Alfredo Brandán Caraffa no longer belongs to the editorial board of *Inicial.*"

31. *Inicial* nos. 6–10.

32. Brandán, in the interview, refused to reveal the source of the fascist offer to Guglielmini, allowing only that the potential sponsor did have the funds to make good his promise.

33. Roberto Mariani, *"Martín Fierro y yo," Martín Fierro,* no. 4. This article is reproduced in Prieto, *Martín Fierro,* pp. 39–43.

34. *Proa* (second series, hereafter "II"), no. 1 for Soto's "El sentido poético de la ciudad moderna: A propósito de 'Versos de la calle' por Alvaro Yunque" (p. 20); no. 3 for Mariani's "Un arbitrario apunte sobre Alfonso Reyes" (pp. 57–60); no. 14 for Neruda's "Poesía escrita de noche" (pp. 24–25) and selections from César Tiempo's "Entre Ríos 1583" (pp. 26–28). Mallea's "¿Y?" appeared in *Proa* no. 4, while Bernárdez became a member of the editorial board for issue no. 13, when Güiraldes resigned to devote more time to the preparation of *Don Segundo Sombra.* Borges' translation of the first fifty or so lines of Molly's soliloquy in *Ulysses* was published in *Proa* no. 6 (pp. 3–6). The two selections from Arlt's "Vida puerca" came from chapter 4 ("Judas Iscarote"), here called "El Rengo" (no. 8, pp. 28–35), and "El poeta parroquial" (no. 10, pp. 34–39). The latter was dropped from the text of *El juguete rabioso* before it was published as a novel.

35. Lafleur, et al. indicate (pp. 101, 159) that *Revista de América* printed six issues between December 1924 and July 1926, though the one copy of the magazine in possession of the Biblioteca Nacional in Buenos Aires carries neither date nor number, and no copies are listed as part of the Provenzano collection. *Síntesis* published forty-one issues between June 1927 and October 1930. *Sagitario (Revista de Humanidades)* was a product of the intellectuals of La Plata, a competitor of *Valoraciones.* It published twelve numbers (including two combined issues) from 1925 to 1928 and included contributions by various members of Florida (Lafleur, et al., pp. 114–15, 160). For information on the *Revista Oral,* see Lafleur, et al., pp. 100–101.

36. *Martín Fierro* had been the title of two earlier journals. The first, an aggressively progressive periodical, was directed by Alberto Ghiraldo, publishing forty-eight numbers in 1904–1905 (Lafleur, et al., p. 52). The second, which published three issues in 1919, was also political, and satirical in a way similar to its more famous successor. Unsurprisingly, one of its directors was Evar Méndez.

37. Lafleur, et al., pp. 92–94.

38. The manifesto appeared in *Martín Fierro* no. 4 (May 15, 1924). It is reproduced in many sources, including González Lanuza, *Los martinfierristas,* pp. 34–35, and Prieto, *Martín Fierro,* pp. 13–14.

39. Alberto Prebish, himself an architect, was the architecture critic for *Martín Fierro.*

40. Prieto, "Boedo y Florida," p. 37.

41. Though European influences on the young generation were by no means universally condemned: see Bianchi's remarks in *Nosotros* no. 203, p. 159.

42. Scrimaglio, pp. 53–73.

43. Mastronardi, p. 917; David Viñas, *Literatura argentina y realidad política: De Sarmiento a Cortázar* (Buenos Aires: Ediciones Siglo XX, 1964), pp. 57–62.

44. Leopoldo Lugones, *El estado equitativo (Ensayo sobre la realidad argentina)* (Buenos Aires: La Editora Argentina, 1932), p. 31.

45. Lugones, p. 67.

46. Lugones, pp. 40–55.

47. Juan Antonio Villodo, "Temas políticas: La revisión fascista," *Nosotros* no. 190. Also note Villodo's reply to Borges' defense in his letter published in *Nosotros* no. 193, p. 284.

48. Borges, in a letter to *Nosotros* (no. 191), insists he cannot understand Villodo's attack on a "purely literary" magazine like *Proa.* He takes several shots at Lugones, and concludes: "I am just not made for patriotic exaltations and lugonistics: visual comparisons

bore me, and rather than the national anthem, I much prefer hearing the tango 'Loca.'" (p. 547).

49. The question of fascism and intellectuals in the 1920s is one insufficiently explored. A rather disappointing treatment of the topic may be found in Alastair Hamilton's *The Appeal of Fascism: A Study of Intellectuals and Fascism, 1919–1945* (New York: The Macmillan Company, 1971). In view of Bolshevism's various crises in the decade, Mussolini's apparent success, and the Italian extraction of many members of the new generation and their largely petit bourgeois origins, it is perhaps surprising so few of them fell under fascism's spell.

50. Mastronardi, p. 928.

51. The morning that the last, complete edition of *Martín Fierro* (nos. 44–45) appeared in Buenos Aires (November 15, 1927), its directors, along with other dignitaries, were assembled on Platform 3 of the Retiro Station, preparing to board the funeral train carrying the remains of Ricardo Güiraldes to his grave at San Antonio de Areco (Lafleur, et al., p. 99).

52. Romero, p. 217.

53. Giordano, p. 963.

54. Alvaro Yunque, *La literatura social en la Argentina: Historia de los movimientos literarios desde la emancipación nacional hasta nuestros días* (Buenos Aires: Editorial Claridad, 1941), p. 323.

55. For information regarding the class background of the various members of Boedo and Florida, see González Lanuza's *Los martinfierristas*, p. 100; Elías Castelnuovo, *Memorias* (Buenos Aires: Ediciones Culturales Argentinas, 1974), p. 128; César Tiempo, *Clara Béter y otras fatamorganas* (Buenos Aires: A. Peña Lillo, Editor, 1974), pp. 11–14; and Raúl Larra, *Leónidas Barletta: El hombre de la campaña* (Buenos Aires: Ediciones Conducta, 1978), pp. 17–24. That Boedo was a purely proletarian phenomenon while Florida was composed purely of *señoritos* is a popular but inaccurate perception. The constituents of both groups arose largely from various strata of a very broadly defined middle sector, though certain members (Güiraldes, Amorim) were surely of highly privileged backgrounds, while others (Castelnuovo, for example) came from truly appalling poverty. On the average, those of Florida were probably more financially secure than those of Boedo, though there were exceptions on both sides.

56. Yunque, *Literatura social*, p. 323.

57. Barletta, *Boedo y Florida*, p. 41.

58. Prieto, "Boedo y Florida," p. 46; Viñas, *De Sarmiento a Cortázar* p. 22; Giordano, p. 966.

59. Adolfo Prieto, "La literatura de izquierda: El grupo Boedo," n.p. (in my possession in the form of mimeographed notes prepared for students of the Facultad de Filosofía y Letras, Universidad Nacional de Cuyo, Mendoza, Argentina, 1974).

60. Larra, *Leónidas Barletta*, p. 47.

61. For example, the sculptor Riganelli and Mariani probably knew each other as early as 1921, when the former illustrated the latter's *Las acequias y otros poemas*. Such figures as Alfredo Bufano and Eduardo Suárez Danero, both writers, may have greater literary-historical significance in their roles as young editors of such publications as Juan Mantecón's *Nueva Era* or *Caras y Caretas*. In the former journal, both Mariani and Castelnuovo were publishing extensively by 1920–21, and it seems probable that, at some point, Bufano may have introduced them. Also, the slightly older poet, Rafael de Diego, was a good friend of Mariani's and apparently close to Antonio Zamora, this according to Alberto Pineta, *Verde memoria: Tres décadas de literatura y periodismo en una autobiografía (Los*

grupos de Boedo y Florida) (Buenos Aires: Ediciones Antonio Zamora, 1962), p. 98. The likelihood, then, is that the paths of writers who were eventually to compose Boedo had already crossed, at least casually, in the early years of the decade, though they themselves may not have struck up real friendships until later.

62. As noted, both Mariani and Castelnuovo contributed extensively to *Nueva Era* early in the decade, and the latter, as early as 1918 or 1919, was publishing pieces in such leftist organs as *La Protesta, Bandera Roja,* and *El Trabajo* (Castelnuovo, *Memorias*, p. 82). Stanchina had obviously achieved considerable prominence by 1923, sufficient to be included in *Nosotros'* poll of young writers. Barletta, meanwhile, in *La Montaña* itself, published poetry in the newspaper's issues of January 6 (p. 6), January 28 (p. 5), and February 2 (p. 6), 1922. Yunque published "Cascotes (Preguntas y respuestas)" in *La Montaña* on March 8, 1922 (p. 6).

63. The literary contest, advertised throughout the summer of 1921–22, offered a thousand pesos and four gold medals as prizes. Pseudonymous entries in prose and verse were accepted up to February 28, 1922. Stories were limited to 4,500 words, and all winners in both categories were guaranteed publication in *La Montaña*. On March 20, 1922, the decisions of the jury (composed of the Argentine writers Juan Pedro Calou and Julio R. Barcos, plus the Mexican Minister Plenipotentiary, A. Médiz Bolio) were announced on page one of the paper. In addition to Castelnuovo, Barletta, and Mariani, the prose winners were the Chilean writer Manuel Rojas (second place) and Germán Bernales (fifth place). The winners in poetry, in order, were Marcos Fingerit, Adela Mella Laina, Mariano de Juan Ibáñez, Luby Guevara, and Pedro Herreros.

64. Giordano, p. 965; Castelnuovo, *Memorias*, p. 127.

65. "Nuestra encuesta sobre la nueva generación," *Nosotros* no. 171, pp. 525–527. Enrique Amorim and Santiago Ganduglia, as mentioned before, were also included in the *encuesta*, but neither had, at that point, evidenced any interest in a leftist aesthetic.

66. Larra, *Leónidas Barletta*, pp. 51–52.

67. *Nosotros* no. 171, p. 527.

68. Boedo seems to have published at least one other journal before *Extrema Izquierda, Dínamo,* though there are apparently no extant copies of it (Lafleur, et al., p. 104). The only evidence of its existence, aside from remarks of writers of the era, is a cartoon in *Martín Fierro* (nos. 4–5), satirizing the journal (reproduced in Lafleur, et al., plate opposite p. 104). There are allusions (e.g., in Castelnuovo's "Reseña sobre el movimiento de Boedo" carboned typescript given me by the author on March 15, 1979, p. 5) to another "magazine," *Izquierda,* but this was likely simply the Monday literary supplement to the evening daily, *El Telégrafo,* which bore that title. *Extrema Izquierda* itself appeared in August of 1924 and ran for two (possibly three) numbers (Lafleur, et al., p. 105).

69. César Tiempo, *Clara Béter*, pp. 12–13. It must be emphasized again that information available on "who knew whom when" is so scant and/or contradictory that it makes developing a definite chronology virtually impossible. Despite César Tiempo's assertion, it seems unlikely Yunque and Castelnuovo were not acquainted before 1925, given that the latter and his brother "Juan Guijarro" (Augusto Gandolfi Herrero) were codirectors of the literary page of the official socialist organ, *La Vanguardia,* at least according to Lubrano Zas in *Gustavo Riccio: Un poeta de Boedo* (Buenos Aires: Editorial Buenos Aires Leyendo, 1969), p. 32. Ganduglia, meanwhile, was given an inscribed copy of *Las acequias y otros poemas* by Mariani in April of 1922 (presented to me by the former in July 1979), while Ganduglia also was obviously well acquainted with other members of the young generation who were interviewed along with him in the *encuesta* in *Nosotros*. Mariani went whoring with José Gabriel of the Ateneo Universitario, which would indicate he probably also knew

other members of that circle (Eduardo Suárez Danero, *Recuerdos de Roberto Mariani* [Buenos Aires: Ediciones Propósitos, 1969], pp. 12–13). Barletta, meanwhile, was quite the protégé of Juan Pedro Calou, a poet active in leftist and artistic circles and one of the judges of the contest at *La Montaña* (Larra, *Leónidas Barletta*, pp. 25–44). Soto was part of the renegade *Inicial* no. 5 editorial board which published Yunque, and also reviewed the latter's *Versos de la calle* in *Proa* (II) no. 1, pp. 11–12.

70. Pineta, pp. 97–102.

71. Personal interview with Alvaro Yunque (July 17, 1979).

72. González Lanuza (personal interview) indicates that editions of many of Florida's members were printed wholly or partly at the authors' expense.

73. Roberto Arlt, *El juguete rabioso* (Buenos Aires: Editorial Latina, 1926), p. 5; Castelnuovo, "Reseña," p. 7.

74. In her afterward to *Versos de una . . .* (Buenos Aires: Editorial Rescate, 1977), Estelle Irizzary mentions a sales figure for the book of 100,000 copies (p. 50). Castelnuovo claims sales of 200,000 copies ("Reseña," p. 7). For more about Clara Béter (alias César Tiempo, alias Israel Zeitlin), see his *Clara Béter*, pp. 11–24. The three ellipsis points in *Versos de una . . .* are part of the book's original title, stand-ins for the word *ramera*, "harlot."

75. Zas, *Gustavo Riccio*, p. 176.

76. Personal interview with Elías Castelnuovo, March 19, 1979.

77. Lafleur, et al., pp. 105–106, which also explains *Claridad's* peculiar numeration.

78. See Barletta's accusatory letters in *El Telégrafo* (October 24, 1927) and *La Libertad* (October 25, 1927), to which the editors of *Claridad* respond in their issue of November 15, 1927.

79. See *Claridad*, February 1927 and November 15, 1927.

80. *Claridad*, September 1926; April 30, 1927; June 10, 1927, and August 30, 1927.

81. Giordano notes that editions of 20,000 copies of the "Colección Los Nuevos" were not unusual (p. 963). The ten titles published between 1924 and 1928 were *Tinieblas* (reprint of Castelnuovo's 1923 collection of stories published by Editorial Tognolini), *Versos de la calle* (Yunque), *Malditos* (Castelnuovo), *Cuentos de la oficina* (Mariani), *Los pobres* (Barletta), *Tangarupá* (Amorim), *Las bestias* (Abel Rodríguez), *Versos de una. . .* ("Clara Béter"), *Desventurados* (Juan I. Cendoya), and *Miseria de 5° edición* (Alberto Pineta).

82. Lafleur, et al., pp. 147–48.

83. Giordano, pp. 973–74. *La campana de palo* also had a short-lived book-publishing venture, which printed Yunque's *Zancadillas* and Gustavo Riccio's *Un poeta en la ciudad*, both in 1926.

84. Lafleur, et al., p. 107.

85. Alvaro Yunque, "Un crítico irresponsable: Pablo Rojas Paz," *La campana de palo*, no. 13, p. 5. One other publication of the *boedistas* was the *Revista del Pueblo*, directed by Julio Fingerit, which ran from April 1926 to June 1927. Perhaps its most notable contribution to the literary polemic of the day was Fingerit's own "Leopoldo Lugones: Enemigo de la civilización." See Lafleur, et al., p. 108.

86. For examples, see Sabajanes, *Martín Fierro*, pp. 97–98, or *Claridad*, March 1927 (comments on Borges' projected translation of *Leaves of Grass*) and October 25, 1927 (regarding González Lanuza's *Aquelarre*).

CHAPTER 5—THE WRITERS

1. Two serviceable surveys of the development of Argentine poetry are Guillermo Ara's *Suma de la poesía argentina, 1538–1969* (Buenos Aires: Editorial Guadalupe, 1970),

and Angel Mazzei's *La poesía de Buenos Aires* (Buenos Aires: Editorial Ciordia, 1962). Scrimaglio, as mentioned, presents a good defense of the originality of the *martinfierristas* in her *Literatura argentina de vanguardia* (pp. 55–73).

2. Ara, *Poesía argentina,* p. 76.

3. Borges produced two books of essays in the 1920s, *El tamaño de mi esperanza* and *Inquisiciones,* both of which he has since disowned. He began publishing stories in the 1930s. Martínez Estrada achieved renown for his *Radiografía de la pampa* and *La cabeza de Goliat,* produced in 1933 and 1940 respectively, while Marechal's most important work is the modernist novel *Adán Buenosayres* of 1948.

4. Castelnuovo, Mariani, and Arlt, for example, were all children of European-born parents. César Tiempo (Israel Zeitlin) was born in Odessa, while González Lanuza arrived in Buenos Aires from Spain at age nine.

5. Eduardo González Lanuza, *Aquelarre* (Buenos Aires: J. Samet, 1927), p. 8. The substitution of "j" for "g" (e.g., *"imájines"* for *"imágines")* is an orthographic idiosyncracy González Lanuza exhibits throughout the text. For a while, the vanguardists apparently felt these spellings were more "authentic." For other examples, see *Proa* (II) no. 5, p. 55, where Borges is identified as "Jorje Borges" and then as "Jorje Borjes," or the whole of that author's *El tamaño de mi esperanza* (Buenos Aires: Editorial Proa, 1926).

6. Regarding the "sissified sensiblity," see chapter 4, note 21.

7. For a further example of González Lanuza's metaphysical concerns in his early work, see his poem "Apocalipsis" in Guillermo Ara, *Los poetas de Florida: Selección* (Buenos Aires: Centro Editor de América Latina, 1968), p. 19.

8. Eduardo Mallea, *Cuentos para una inglesa desesperada* (Buenos Aires: M. Gleizer, Editor, 1926), p. 19.

9. It would be difficult for someone unfamiliar with Chaplin's film to understand "Seís poemas a Georgia." Mallea's use of it so recently after its premiere indicates both his assumptions about the sophistication of his audience and the popularity the cinema had already achieved in Buenos Aires at this early date.

10. César Tiempo, quoted in Pedro Orgambide and Roberto Yahni, *Enciclopedia de la literatura argentina* (Buenos Aires: Editorial Sudamericana, 1970), p. 289.

11. Orgambide and Yahni, p. 289.

12. González Lanuza, *Los martinfierristas,* p. 102.

13. Orgambide and Yahni, p. 289.

14. Among the famous tangos alluded to are "Entra nomás," "Fea," "Callecita de mi barrio," "Corazón de arrabal," and "Viejo amigo."

15. The orthography indicates the speaker is Italian. Quotations are from Enrique González Tuñón, *Tangos* (Buenos Aires: M. Gleizer, Editor, 1926).

16. All the commentaries regarding the author appear in an unsigned prologue in Elías Castelnuovo's *Tinieblas* (Buenos Aires: Editorial Claridad, 1941), pp. 4–5.

17. Castelnuovo, *Tinieblas,* p. 6.

18. Castelnuovo, *Tinieblas,* p. 6.

19. Note, for example, the opening pages of the story "Tinieblas," set in a linotype shop, in Castelnuovo, *Tinieblas,* pp. 29–39.

20. For information regarding Castelnuovo's truly remarkable (and sometimes nightmarish) early life, see his *Memorias,* pp. 7–51.

21. Castelnuovo, quoted in Prieto, "La literatura de izquierda" (mimeographed reproduction).

22. Personal interview with Lubrano Zas (July 16, 1979) and Raúl Larra (July 12, 1979).

23. César Tiempo, *Clara Béter,* pp. 14–15. For another attractive portrait of Yunque,

see Raúl Larra's *Mundo de escritores* (Buenos Aires: Ediciones Sílaba, 1973), pp. 7–10.

24. *Diccionario de la literatura lationoamericana: Argentina (Segunda Parte)* (Washington, D.C.: Unión Panamericana, 1960).

25. Alvaro Yunque, *Ta-Te-Ti* (Buenos Aires: Editorial Futuro, 1959).

26. Giordano, pp. 974–75.

27. Leónidas Barletta, *Los pobres: Cuentos ilustrados con grabados en madera por Juan Arato* (Buenos Aires: Editorial Claridad, 1925), p. 11.

28. Leónidas Barletta, *Royal Circo* (Buenos Aires: Editorial Deucalión, 1966), p. 127. Barletta himself traveled briefly with a circus during the late 1920s, according to Raúl Larra (personal interview).

29. González Lanuza, *Los martinfierristas*, p. 101.

CHAPTER 6—IN THE HEART OF THE BEAST, OF THE BEAST IN THE HEART

1. See Eduardo Suárez Danero, pp. 11–12, 18–19, 24–25; Osvaldo Soriano, "Un gran olvidado de la literatura argentina: Roberto Mariani bajo la cruz de cada día," in "La Opinión Cultural: Literatura, Artes, Espectáculo" [Sunday cultural supplement], *La Opinión* (Buenos Aires), November 26, 1972, pp. 4–5.

2. The only source to mention Mariani as a truckdriver is Leónidas Barletta's introductory essay, "Roberto Mariani" in Roberto Mariani, *Cuentos de la oficina* (Buenos Aires, Editorial Universitaria de Buenos Aires, 1965), p. 8.

3. Suárez Danero, p. 7.

4. Juan Pinto, *Roberto Mariani y su generación* (Buenos Aires, Cuadernos de La Boca del Riachuelo, 1964), p. 10.

5. *Claridad*, April 30, 1927.

6. Miranda Klix, *Cuentistas argentinas de hoy (1921–1928)* (Buenos Aires: Editorial Claridad, 1929), pp. 138–39.

7. César Tiempo, *Clara Béter*, p. 15. Also note Soriano, p. 3. On p. 2 of the article, Mariani's eulogy for Arlt is reproduced.

8. Suárez Danero, p. 11; Soriano, p. 2. Mariani's copy of *A la recherche de temps perdu*, with his penciled marginalia, is in the hands of Rosa Eresky of the Teatro del Pueblo.

9. Soriano, p. 4.

10. Pinto, *Roberto Mariani*, p. 9.

11. Castelnuovo, personal interview.

12. Suárez Danero, p. 18.

13. Mariani published his "Un arbitrario apunte sobre Alfonso Reyes" in *Proa* (II), no. 3, pp. 57–60. His "Introducción a Marcel Proust," published in *Nosotros*, no. 215, pp. 16–23, was originally delivered as a conference at La Peña at the Tortoni. Mariani's 1930 collection of stories, *La frecuentación de la muerte* (p. 2) indicates Mariani also presented a conference entitled "Los problemas del teatro de Pirandello" at La Peña in 1927, which was later published in *La Vanguardia*. This apparently was actually "Los principales problemas pirandellianos," which the newspaper printed on July 3, 1927, indicating that it had been presented as a lecture on June 25, 1927.

14. "Ellos y nosotros" appeared in *Claridad*, March 1927. The prologue appears in César Tiempo and Pedro Juan Vignales' *Exposición de la poesía argentina contemporánea* (Buenos Aires: Editorial Minerva, 1927), pp. 10–11.

15. Exact dates and places of Mariani's residence are difficult to trace. See Suárez Danero, p. 22; Soriano, p. 4; Barletta, "Roberto Mariani," p. 8.

16. These *"aventuras prostibularias"* are recounted rather tamely by Suárez Danero (pp. 12–13), and rather more graphically by Soriano (p. 3).

17. See *Las acequias y otros poemas* (Buenos Aires: Editorial de la revista *Nosotros*, 1921); "Culpas ajenas," *La Novela Semanal* (Buenos Aires), May 1, 1922; "Me llamo Alfonso Fernández y soy español y tendero," *Nueva Era* (Buenos Aires), May 9, 1922, p. 5; and *El amor agresivo* (Buenos Aires: M. Gleizer, Editor, 1926).

18. Raúl Larra, "Roberto Mariani," a chapter in his unpublished memoirs presented to me on July 12, 1979 (p. 6).

19. As indicated, Mariani's personal life is shrouded in mystery, and its sexual component is even murkier. His friends and biographers go to great and peculiar lengths to explain his failure to marry, variously ascribing it to his homeliness (Soriano, p. 3), self-denial (Pinto, *Roberto Mariani*, p. 10), or an impossible love (Larra, unpublished memoirs, p. 6). Castelnuovo (personal interview) explains things by saying that, about Mariani, "there was nothing erotic, nothing sexual." Suárez Danero, meanwhile, remarks rather cryptically: "Mariani lived a relative bohemia, that is, without debauches, drunks, whoring. One doesn't know how to express it really. Something inside him had broken long ago" (p. 8).

Rafael de Diego, however, did know how to express his theory. A boon companion of Mariani during the 1920s, de Diego (personal interview, August 21, 1979) asserts flatly that Mariani was impotent, a condition which grew from a sporadic to a chronic problem as he aged. This constituted "the great drama of Mariani's life," converting itself into "an obsession" which increased his mystical bent and with which he lived "as with an ulcer." De Diego goes so far as to suggest that Mariani, like Borzoni, a central character in his novel, *Regreso a Dios* (Buenos Aires: Editorial Argentinas, 1943), poisoned himself.

In view of the key role of sexuality in Mariani's texts, especially those of the 1920s, the investigation of this issue in his personal life might provide much more than a source of idle gossip.

20. For all practical purposes, there is no serious criticism of Mariani's work.

21. See *La Montaña*, March 20, 1922 and April 9, 1922; for examples of Mariani's work in *Nueva Era*, see the editions of December 10, 1920, p. 27; April 10, 1921 (signed "R.M."), in "Bibliografía"; October 25, 1921 (signed "Máximo Lagos"), p. 16; July 25, 1922 (signed "Roberto Lagos"), p. 4, and March 20, 1923, pp. 2–3.

22. "Me llamo Alfonso Fernández . . ." is, for example, essentially the same in *Nueva Era* in 1922 as in *El amor agresivo* four years later. "María Agustina," in that same collection, and "En la oficina," which became "Toulet" in *Cuentos de la oficina*, were, on the other hand, both extensively reworked in the time between their first and second publications.

23. "Culpas ajenas" was Mariani's only known attempt to produce a piece acceptable to the lucrative "pamphlet fiction" trade of the early 1920s. The first part of "El amor grotesco" appeared in *Nueva Era*, February 22, 1922, p. 5. Part II presumably was published in the edition of March 5, 1922, which is missing from the collection of the newspaper in the Biblioteca Nacional. A two-part "novel" entitled "El amor triunfa a pesar de todo" by Roberto Lagos was published in *Nueva Era*'s editions of July 25 and August 1, 1922. It is virtually certain it is also Mariani's work.

24. In this text, "The Office" refers to that institution personified and with all its metaphorical resonances. When mentioned simply as a site of action, "the office" appears uncapitalized.

25. Olmos y Daniels may be based upon the now-defunct *porteño* department store Gath y Chaves, which operated its main facility on the corner of Florida and Cangallo. The name, in any case, combining an English and Iberian-Jewish surname, seems almost certain

to have inspired Mariani.

26. Roberto Mariani, p. 11.

27. Normally, an Argentine addressing someone in the second person singular, telling him or her to come in, would say *"Vení"* or *"Entrá,"* the understood pronoun being *vos*. The imperative with *vos* takes an accent on the final syllable: *comé, pará, andá, tomá,* etc.

28. One must admit the possibility that Mariani was simply "writing correctly" here (Castelnuovo, *Memorias,* p. 136), though if this is the case, it was for nought. M. López Palermo, *Nosotros'* reviewer of *Cuentos de la oficina* (no. 196, p. 102–103), attacks Mariani's use of localisms: "He feels himself excessively *'porteño,'* and, we should note, those adverbial oddities of our daily conversation are not particularly grammatical."

29. Mr. Daniels' name is mentioned twice in the text, on p. 40, where Santana alludes to "Mr. Daniels' son living it up in Paris," and on p. 70, where the name of the department store appears, which also constitutes the sole reference to Olmos. This would seem to reinforce the distance between the workers and the owners, and, indeed, the "divine" hierarchy of the business. Olmos and Daniels are, for all practical purposes, here "unspeakable names."

30. Sigmund Freud, *The Ego and the Id* (ed. James Strachey) (New York: W. W. Norton and Company, 1960), pp. 18–29, 38–49.

31. Claudio Preti, a member of the Psychoanalytic School of Argentina, has been at work for several years on a history of the spread and influence of the writings and ideas of Freud in Argentina before the founding of the Argentine Psychoanalytic Association in 1942. The appearance of his book should provide systematic evidence of the impact of psychoanalysis on the nation's intellectual life in the early decades of the century. Still and all, a brief perusal of virtually any serious publication of the period, plus a consciousness of *porteño* cosmopolitanism of the era, surely indicates Freud's theories were as much in the air in Buenos Aires as in New York or Paris.

32. Herbert Marcuse, considering Freudian theory from a position informed by Hegel and Marx in his *Eros and Civilization: A Philosophical Inquiry into Freud* (New York: Vintage Books, 1962), expresses this idea felicitously: "The development of a hierarchical system of social labor not only rationalizes domination but also 'contains' the rebellion against domination. . . . Freud's hypothesis on the origin and the perpetuation of guilt feelings elucidates, in psychological terms, this sociological dynamic: it explains the 'identification' of those who revolt with the power against which they revolt. The economic and political incorporation of the individuals into the hierarchical system of labor is accompanied by an instinctual process in which the human objects of domination reproduce their own repression. . . . In retaining the individuals as instruments of labor, forcing them into renunciation and toil, domination no longer merely or primarily sustains specific privileges but also sustains society. . . . The revolt against the primal father eliminated an individual person who could be (and was) replaced by other persons; but when the dominion of the father has expanded into the dominion of society, no such replacement seems possible, and the guilt becomes fatal. . . . Rebellion now appears as the crime against the whole of human society and therefore beyond reward and beyond redemption" (pp. 82–84).

33. Regarding the homosexual subculture of Buenos Aires, see Sebreli, pp. 79–86.

34. Marcuse, expanding on Freud, goes to the heart of this "radical significance": "Freud questioned why the taboo on the perversions is sustained with such extraordinary rigidity. He concluded that no one can forget that the perversions are not merely detestable but also something monstrous and terrifying—'as if they exerted a seductive influence; as if at bottom a secret envy of those who enjoyed them had to be strangled.' The perversions

seem to give a *promesse de bonheur* greater than that of 'normal' sexuality. What is the source of their promise? Freud emphasized the 'exclusive' character of the deviations from normality, their rejection of the procreative sex act. The perversions thus express rebellion against the subjugation of sexuality under the order of procreation, and against the institutions which guarantee this order" (*Eros*, pp. 44–45).

Sebreli touches upon homosexuality's "seductiveness," particularly with relation to the highly repressed petit bourgeoisie, on p. 85 of his book, and throughout the section cited in note 32 he lends sociological evidence to support Marcuse's theoretical stance.

35. At various points Mariani switches to the present tense, apparently to draw attention to and intensify the moment described. Note, later in the text, Guerrero's accidental observation of Toulet's attempted theft.

36. Lagos, of course, is also striking out against himself: "The superego attains these objectives [of repression] by directing the ego against the id, turning part of the destruction instincts against a part of the personality—by destroying, 'splitting' the unity of the personality as a whole; thus it works in the service of the antagonist of the life instinct" (Marcuse, *Eros*, p. 48).

37. Toulet's personality fits well with those analyzed by René Girard in his comments on Proust in *Deceit, Desire and the Novel: Self and Other in Literary Structure* (Baltimore: Johns Hopkins University, 1965), pp. 67, 70.

38. Korn, et al., pp. 92–109.

39. Sigmund Freud, *Totem and Taboo: Resemblances Between the Psychic Lives of Savages and Neurotics* (New York: Vintage Books, 1946), pp. 182–200.

40. Regarding the homoeroticism of the gauchesque, see chapter 8 concerning *Don Segundo Sombra*.

41. Raúl Scalabrini Ortiz, *El hombre que está solo y espera* (Buenos Aires: Editorial Reconquista, 1941).

42. Payró quotes his own review in a letter to Robert Mariani of January 10, 1927, printed as "Carta inédita de Roberto J. Payró" in Roberto Mariani, *Cuentos de la oficina* (Buenos Aires: Editorial Deucalión, 1956), p. 10.

43. Santiago Ganduglia's review of *Cuentos de la oficina* appeared in *Martín Fierro*, no. 19, reproduced in Sabajanes, pp. 97–99.

44. The prize went to Ernesto Morales' *Leyendas Guaraníes*.

45. Larra (unpublished memoir, p. 1) relates that when he first met Mariani in 1940, the latter was toying with nationalism. To demonstrate nonetheless "that he retained the unconformity and rebelliousness of his youth, he told me: 'If somebody had to push a button to blow up this society and change it, I swear to you I'd push it, I would push it . . .' "

46. "In 1945, we [writers of the Left] were all in the demonstration celebrating the liberation of Paris, which had been called by the S.A.D.E. and was held in front of the Congress. Raúl González Tuñón, who had just returned from Chile, confronted him:

"'What? You? Here?'

"And Mariani, violent before the disbelief of his questioner, answered him:

"'And where should I be but here?' " (Larra, unpublished memoir, p. 7).

47. Mariani's obituary appeared in the major dailies in Buenos Aires the day after his death on March 3, 1946. All praised his literary efforts, with the exception of *La Prensa*, whose evaluation of him was decidedly (and unsurprisingly) lukewarm. The oration at Mariani's funeral was delivered by Julio Aramburu, who, along with Borges, Barletta, and Alberto Prando, officially represented the SADE. Borges (personal interview), when asked about Mariani, replied vaguely, "He was a journalist, wasn't he? He did something else. A critic?" He claimed to have no recollection, in 1979, of having attended the funeral.

CHAPTER 7—TREASON AND TRANSFORMATION

1. Stasys Gostautas, *Buenos Aires y Arlt (Dostoyevski, Martínez Estrada y Escalabrini Ortiz)* (Madrid: Insula, 1977), pp. 98–119, 188–189.

2. Raúl Larra, *Roberto Arlt: El Torturado* (Buenos Aires: Editorial Anfora, 1973).

3. Eduardo González Lanuza, *Roberto Arlt (La historia popular, Vida y milagros de nuestro pueblo, #35)* (Buenos Aires: Centro Editor de América Latina, 1971), pp. 15–18. See also Gostautas, pp. 51–57.

4. Some of Arlt's periodistic pieces have been collected in *Aguafuertes porteñas* (1933), *Nuevas aguafuertes porteñas* (1960), and *Aguafuertes españolas* (1936). For a list of other anthologies published posthumously, see Gostautas, p. 310.

5. Larra, *Roberto Arlt*, pp. 132–35; "Calki" (Raimundo Calcagno), *"El Mundo" era una fiesta* (Buenos Aires: Editorial Corregidor, 1977), pp. 63–66.

6. David Viñas, "La mentira de Arlt," originally published in *Contorno* 2 (May 1954), is reproduced in *Punto de Vista: Revista de Cultura* 4 (November 1978), pp. 7–8.

7. Larra, *Robert Arlt*, pp. 61–74.

8. Castelnuovo, *Memorias*, p. 134.

9. The working title of *El juguete rabioso* was apparently "Vida puerca," as that was the name given by *Proa* (II) when it published selections from the manuscript (no. 8, pp. 28–35, and no. 10, pp. 34–39). Nonetheless, it is variously referred to as "La vida puerca" (*Claridad*, February 27, 1927) or "De la vida puerca" (Castelnuovo, *Memorias*, p. 134). The expression "vida puerca" would be equivalent to the English "a dog's life" or, more literally, "a pig's life."

10. César Tiempo, *Clara Béter*, p. 15.

11. González Lanuza, *Roberto Arlt*, p. 19.

12. Roberto Arlt, p. 6.

13. Gostautas, pp. 72, 81.

14. Larra (personal interview) showed me a copy of *Tribuna Libre* in which Arlt's piece appeared, that of January 28, 1920.

15. González Lanuza, *Roberto Arlt*, p. 17.

16. Leónidas Barletta, "*El juguete rabioso* por Roberto Arlt," *Nosotros*, no. 211, p. 554.

17. "Notas Bibliográficas," *Claridad*, November 1926. For Arlt's own declining opinion of *El juguete rabioso* after the publication of *Los siete locos*, see Gostautas, p. 84.

18. There is no book-length study of *El juguete rabioso*, and the bulk of those critics who deal with the work of Arlt relegate it to very minor status. For an example, see Gostautas, who devotes perhaps twenty scattered pages to the novel's analysis in a study three hundred pages in length.

19. Gostautas, pp. 187–89.

20. Korn, et al., pp. 16–29.

21. Ricardo Güiraldes, *Raucho* (Buenos Aires: Centro Editor de América Latina, 1968), p. 115.

22. Scalabrini Ortiz, p. 116.

23. "Roberto Arlt..." (interview), *La literatura argentina* (Buenos Aires), August 1929, p. 27.

24. Roberto Arlt, p. 101.

25. González Lanuza, *Roberto Arlt*, pp. 80–81.

26. What finally occurs between Silvio and the homosexual in the hotel room remains (likely intentionally) obscure. There is the implication (pp. 117–18) that Silvio, in a

kind of trance, has some sort of sexual contact with the homosexual, with the latter leaving him ten pesos when he leaves. Arlt's reticence at this point in the text perhaps indicates that there were certain taboos which even he was not willing to challenge overtly.

27. González Lanuza, *Roberto Arlt*, p. 81.

28. Gostautas, p. 114. These categories are based on those developed by R. W. B. Lewis in his *The Picaresque Saint: Representative Figures in Contemporary Fiction* (New York: Lippincott, 1959).

29. The first edition of *El juguete rabioso* bears the following dedication: "To Ricardo Güiraldes: All near to you must feel the overwhelming need to cherish you. And they must treat you kindly and, lacking anything more beautiful, render up words to you. And so I dedicate to you this book" (*El juguete rabioso*, p. 7). The dedication was cut from the second edition, issued by Claridad in 1931, and all subsequent editions.

CHAPTER 8—THE FAILURE OF MYTH

1. The house, which was that of Güiraldes' maternal grandparents, the Goñi family, was located at Corrientes 537. A photograph of its parlor appears in Noé Jitrik, p. 698.

2. Jitrik, p. 701.

3. Jitrik, pp. 702–704.

4. Güiraldes, responding in *Martín Fierro* (nos. 5–6) to an *encuesta* by the magazine ("Do you believe in the existence of an Argentine sensibility or mentality? If so, what are its characteristics?"), replied affirmatively, adding: "If this [Argentine identity] did not exist within us, it would be our obligation to invent it by the moral law of love and the physical law of the terror of the void." Reproduced in Sabajanes, p. 37.

5. Jitrik, p. 699.

6. Viñas, *De Sarmiento a Cortázar*, pp. 182–89.

7. Jitrik, pp. 718–19; see also "Notas Bibliográficas," *Claridad*, September 1927. For one of the few negative commentaries on the novel, see Ramón Doll's "Segundo Sombra y el gaucho que ve el hijo del patrón" in *Nosotros* 223, pp. 270–81.

8. Ricardo Güiraldes, *Obras completas* (Buenos Aires: Emecé Editores, 1962), p. 350.

9. The passage does continue in a somewhat more equivocal vein: "Did my godfather mean to tell me that I myself, in the new situation I was facing, would come to know this evil? Was there a certain deprecation in his augury?" (p. 487).

10. Mafud, pp. 68–73; Orgambide, p. 14.

11. Mafud, pp. 68–69, 96–98.

12. Mafud, p. 56.

13. Mafud, pp. 62–65.

14. Mafud, p. 98.

15. The wrestling to earth of animals oddly parallels the single episode of overt heterosexual activity in the novel, the rape of Aurora (p. 371).

16. Orgambide, p. 14.

17. García, p. 20.

18. Mafud, p. 96.

19. Horacio Jorge Becco, *Antología de la poesía gauchesca* (Madrid: Aguilar, 1972), pp. 23–52.

20. Mafud makes some interesting comparisons between *Martín Fierro* and *Don*

Segundo Sombra on pp. 346ff.

21. Edward Layton Tinker, *The Cult of the Gaucho and the Creation of Literature* (Worchester, Massachusetts: Proceedings of the American Antiquarian Society, 1947), p. 28.

22. Becco, pp. 50–52.

23. Tinker, p. 32.

24. Nichols, p. 62.

25. Orgambide, pp. 17, 144.

26. Quoted in Nichols, p. 63.

27. Sigmund Freud, *The Interpretation of Dreams* (New York: Avon Books, 1965), pp. 294–97; Sigmund Freud, *New Introductory Lectures* (New York: W. W. Norton and Co., 1965), pp. 59–71.

28. Sigmund Freud, *The Standard Edition of the Complete Psychological Works of Sigmund Freud*, volume 9 (London: Hogarth Press, 1959), pp. 237–41.

29. In a personal interview with Roberto Gowda (May 2, 1979), who holds the private library of Güiraldes and Adelina del Carril, he said he could not remember any texts of Freud's in the collection, though it seems likely that Güiraldes was conversant with psychoanalysis in view of the intense interest in the subject in Paris during the decade. Gowda is an Indian by birth, unofficially "adopted" by Adelina del Carril during her sojourn there in the 1930s and 1940s. He accompanied her to Buenos Aires in 1949 and was the principal executor of her estate.

30. On a more reductionist psychoanalytic level, the length of the poncho may be interpreted symbolically as a commentary on the superior virility of the gauchos, the poncho standing stead for the penis.

31. Freud, *New Introductory Lectures*, pp. 60–65.

32. Freud, *Totem and Taboo*, pp. 182–200.

33. Rock, *Politics in Argentina*, pp. 21–24.

34. Mafud, p. 90.

35. Jitrik, pp. 701–702.

36. Jitrik, p. 707.

37. Wilhelm Reich, in *The Mass Psychology of Fascism* (New York: Farrar, Straus and Giroux, 1970), deals with the links between mysticism and fascism, particularly in chapters 6 and 7. Still, the precise manner in which mystical yearnings may be manipulated by fascism (or any other fanatical movement) remains insufficiently explored. The important point is that mysticism and fascism should not be interpreted here as equivalent terms, but rather as two phenomena which, under peculiar circumstances and via a series of complex transformations, may intertwine with one another.

38. Güiraldes' own desire for a more optimistic finale may explain the fact that, having written the first ten chapters of *Don Segundo Sombra* in Paris in 1920, and the bulk of the rest of the book in 1923–24, he was unable to conclude it until 1926. Perhaps he hoped some other, more encouraging denouement might come to mind. But in view of his advancing (and ultimately fatal) illness, Güiraldes set down the final chapters in the months before his death in 1927.

CHAPTER 9—THE LAST HAPPY MEN

1. Indeed, Yrigoyen's overthrow was generally met with approbation by most sectors of society, including the young generation. The response of the editors of *Síntesis* (no.

41, October 1930, p. 193) is typical: "Given the situation in the country, that requires the sacrifices of everyone for the work of the reconstruction of institutions, SINTESIS now suspends operations after more than three years of uninterrupted labor. It is possible that this suspension may not be definitive. In any case, we invite the writers who have contributed to SINTESIS to remain united, for the good of Argentine letters, that is, as well, part of the Motherland.—N.[ota] de la R.[edacción]."

2. Rennie, pp. 222–26.

3. Rennie, pp. 224–28; Rock, *Politics in Argentina*, pp. 262–64.

4. Sebreli, pp. 137–38. Castelnuovo (personal interview) was among those hauled off the stage of the Teatro del Pueblo for using the expression "hijo de puta" in performance.

5. Uriburu's government was the first to establish a special section of the police to deal with "communist subversion," and also the first in the modern history of the nation which systematically employed torture. See Osvaldo Sabino, "Argentina: Bastard Child of the Inquisition," *Rolling Stock* (Boulder, Colorado), May–June 1982, p. 1.

6. Rennie, pp. 259–61.

7. Rennie, pp. 316–33.

8. For examples, see *Conducta* numbers 2, 3, 4, 6, 7, 8, and 10 (June 1931 through February 1932).

9. Rosa Eresky (personal interview, July 16, 1979), describes various long afternoons at the Teatro del Pueblo during which Rega Molina discussed life and art with his former arch-nemeses—Arlt, Mariani, and Barletta. For more information on the participants in the Teatro del Pueblo, see Larra, *Leónidas Barletta*, pp. 249–50.

10. Herbert Marcuse, *One Dimensional Man: Studies in the Ideology of Advanced Industrial Society* (Boston: Beacon Press, 1964), p. 63.

11. Fredric Jameson, *Marxism and Form: Twentieth Century Dialectical Theories of Literature* (Princeton: Princeton University Press, 1971), p. 82.

12. Marcuse, *One Dimensional Man*, p. 59.

13. See, for example, Viñas, *De Sarmiento a Cortázar*, pp. 194–96. Viñas' own sprawling *Dar la cara* (1962) probably best illustrates what he envisions as true *literatura comprometida*.

14. The whole question of "young literatures," of homoeroticism and the rejection of heterosexual relations in these literatures, is explored as regards the North American production in Leslie Fiedler's *Love and Death in the American Novel* (Briarcliff Manor, New York: Stein and Day, 1975). These elements certainly point the way to a comparatist consideration of Argentine and North American letters and perhaps other hemispheric literatures as well.

15. *Royal Circo*, of course, does present a successful instance of heterosexual attachment, that of John Geeps and Elena, Salustiano's stepdaughter. Notably, however, this is probably Barletta's novel's least convincing moment. Also, Mariani dealt during the twenties with heterosexual attachment in his short story collection with the disquieting title *El amor agresivo* (1927). Neither provides a very satisfying portrait of romance and marriage.

16. Mafud, p. 84.

17. Quoted in Prieto, "Boedo y Florida," p. 54.

18. See particularly Mafud, p. 117 (nt.).

19. Pinto, p. 23.

20. Quoted in Ara, "Florida y la vanguardia," p. 994.

Bibliography

PERSONAL INTERVIEWS

Barcia, José. Buenos Aires, Argentina. July 14, 1979.
Borges, Jorge Luis. Buenos Aires, Argentina. July 5, 1979.
Brandán Caraffa, Alfredo. Buenos Aires, Argentina. October 6, 1979.
Calí, Américo. Mendoza, Argentina. November 28, 1979.
Castelnuovo, Elías. Buenos Aires, Argentina. March 19, 1979.
de Diego, Rafael. Buenos Aires, Argentina. August 21, 1979.
Ereski, Rosa. Buenos Aires, Argentina. July 16, 1979.
Ganduglia, Santiago. Buenos Aires, Argentina. July 14, 1979.
Goldar, Josefa. Buenos Aires, Argentina. July 16, 1979.
González Lanuza, Eduardo. Buenos Aires, Argentina. March 19, 1979.
Gowda, Roberto. Buenos Aires, Argentina. May 2, 1979.
Larra, Raúl. Buenos Aires, Argentina. July 15, 1979.
Levinson, Luisa Mercedes. Buenos Aires, Argentina. August 5, 1979.
Tiempo, César (Israel Zeitlin). Buenos Aires, Argentina. May 30, 1979.
Tudela, Ricardo. Mendoza, Argentina. November 30, 1979.
Villabuena Welsh de Pinto, Celia. Buenos Aires, Argentina. August 26, 1979.
Yunque, Alvaro (Arístides Gandolfi Herrero). Buenos Aires, Argentina. July 17, 1979.
Zas, Lubrano. Buenos Aires, Argentina. July 16, 1979 and October 22, 1979.

JOURNALS

Magazines

La campana de palo: Periódico mensual. Bellas artes y polémica (second series). Unnumbered first issue–no. 17 (September 1926–September/October 1927).

Claridad: Revista de arte, crítica y letras. Tribuna del pensamiento izquierdista.
    July 1926–December 1930.
Extrema Izquierda: Revista de crítica, no. 2.
Inicial: Revista de la nueva generación. Nos. 1–10 (October 1923–August 1926).
Inicial: Revista de la nueva generación. No. 5 (dissident publication, April 1924).
Insurrexit: Revista literaria. Nos. 1, 6 (September 8, 1920; no date).
Martín Fierro: Periódico quincenal de artes y crítica libre (second series). Nos. 1–
    44/45 (February 1924–November 15, 1927).
Nosotros: Revista mensual de letras, arte, historia, filososía y ciencias sociales.
    Nos. 117–248 (January 1919–January 1930).
La Novela Semanal. Nos. 1–262 (November 19, 1917–November 20, 1922).
Los Pensadores. Nos. 1–100 (February 1922–November 1924).
Proa: Revista de literatura. Nos. 1–3 (August and December 1922; July 1923).
Proa (second series). Nos. 1–14 (August 1924–December 1925).
Revista de America (no date; no number).
Sagitario: Revista de humanidades. Nos. 1–10 (June 1925–August 1926).
Síntesis: Artes, ciencias y letras. Nos. 1–41 (September 1927–October 1930).
Valoraciones: Humanidades, crítica y polémica. Nos. 1–12 (September 1923–May
    1928).

Newspapers

Collections of all newspapers listed below are incomplete in both the Biblioteca
Nacional (Buenos Aires) and the Biblioteca del Congreso (Buenos Aires).

Crítica (1920–1930)
La Montaña (1919–1925)
La Nación (1920–1930)
Nueva Era (1919–1922)
La Vanguardia (1920–1930)

PRIMARY SOURCES

Arlt, Roberto. *El amor brujo.* Buenos Aires: Compañía General Fabril Editores,
    1968.
———. *El juguete rabioso.* Buenos Aires: Editorial Latina, 1926.
———. *Los siete locos/Las lanzallamas.* ed. Adolfo Prieto. Caracas: Biblioteca
    Ayuacucho, 1978.
Barletta, Leónidas. *Los pobres: Cuentos ilustrados con grabados en madera por
    Juan Arato.* Buenos Aires: Editorial Claridad, 1925.
———. *Royal Circo.* Buenos Aires: Editorial Deucalión, 1966.

Béter, Clara (Israel Zeitlin). *Versos de una....* Buenos Aires: Editorial Rescate, 1977.

Borges, Jorge Luis. *Discusión.* Buenos Aires: M. Gleizer Editor, 1932.

———. *Obra poética, 1923–1967.* Buenos Aires: Emecé Editores, 1967.

———. *El tamaño de mi esperanza.* Buenos Aires: Editorial Proa, 1926.

Castelnuovo, Elías. *Larvas.* Buenos Aires: Editorial Cátedra Lisandro de la Torre, 1959.

———. *Tinieblas.* Buenos Aires: Editorial Claridad, 1941.

Girondo, Oliverio. *Veinte poemas para ser leídos en el tranvía/Calcomanías/ Espantapájaros.* Buenos Aires: Centro Editor de América Latina, 1967.

González Lanuza, Eduardo. *Aquelarre.* Buenos Aires: J. Samet, Editor, 1928.

González Tuñón, Enrique. *Camas desde un peso.* Buenos Aires: Editorial Deucalión, 1956.

———. *Tangos.* Buenos Aires: M. Gleizer, Editor, 1926.

Güiraldes, Ricardo. *Obras completas.* Buenos Aires: Emecé Editores, 1962.

———. *Raucho.* Buenos Aires: Centro Editor de América Latina, 1968.

Mallea, Eduardo. *Cuentos para una inglesa desesperada.* Buenos Aires: M. Gleizer, Editor, 1926.

Mariani, Roberto. *Las acequias y otros poemas* (Dibujos de Riganelli). Buenos Aires: Editorial de la Revista *Nosotros*, 1921.

———. *El amor agresivo.* Buenos Aires: M. Gleizer, Editor, 1926.

———. *La cruz nuestra de cada día.* Buenos Aires: Editorial Ariadna, 1955.

———. *Cuentos de la oficina.* Prol. Leónidas Barletta. Buenos Aires: Editorial Universitaria de Buenos Aires, 1965.

———. *La frecuntación de la muerte.* Buenos Aires: Talleres Gráficos Argentinos L. J. Rosso, 1930.

———. *Regreso a Dios.* Buenos Aires: Editorial Argentinas, 1943.

———. "Ventanas de la soledad: Antipoemas con asunto." Manuscript in the hands of Rosa Eresky, Teatro del Pueblo, Buenos Aires.

Yunque, Alvaro (Arístides Gandolfi Herrero). *Bichofeo.* Buenos Aires: Editorial Claridad, 1929.

———. *Ta-Te-Ti.* Buenos Aires: Editorial Futuro, 1959.

———. *Versos de la calle.* Buenos Aires: Editorial Claridad, 1924.

ANTHOLOGIES

Ara, Guillermo (ed.). *La poesía gauchesca.* Buenos Aires: Centro Editor de América Latina, 1967.

Ara, Guillermo (ed.). *Los poetas de Florida: Selección.* Buenos Aires: Centro Editor de América Latina, 1968.

Becco, Horacio Jorge (ed.). *Antología de la poesía gauchesca.* Madrid: Aguilar, 1972.

Giordano, Carlos (ed.). *Los escritores de Boedo: Selección*. Buenos Aires: Centro Editor de América Latina, 1968.

———— (ed.). *Los poetas sociales: Selección*. Buenos Aires: Centro Editor de América Latina, 1968.

Gobello, José and Jorge A. Bossio (ed.). *Tangos: Letras y Letristas*. Buenos Aires: Editorial Plus Ultra, 1969.

Lafleur, Héctor René and Sergio Provenzano (ed.). *Las revistas literarias: Selección de artículos*. Buenos Aires: Centro Editor de América Latina, 1968.

Miranda Klix (Guillermo Klix Miranda) (ed.). *Cuentistas argentinas de hoy: Muestra de narradores jóvenes*. Buenos Aires: Editorial Claridad, 1928.

Prieto, Adolfo (ed.). *El periódico "Martín Fierro."* Buenos Aires: Editorial Galerna, 1968.

Sabajanes, Beatriz Sarlo (ed.). *Martín Fierro (1924–1927)*. Buenos Aires: Carlos Pérez Editor, 1969.

Tiempo, César (Israel Zeitlin) and Pedro Juan Vignale. *Exposición de la poesía argentina contemporánea*. Buenos Aires: Editorial Minerva, 1927.

SECONDARY SOURCES

Ardissone, Elena and Nélida Salvador. *"Nosotros," 1907–1943* (index). Buenos Aires: Fondo Nacional de las Artes, 1971.

Ara, Guillermo. *Introducción a la literatura argentina*. Buenos Aires: Editorial Columba, 1966.

————. *Ricardo Güiraldes*. Buenos Aires: Editorial La Madrágora, 1967.

————. *Suma de la poesía argentina, 1538–1969*. Buenos Aires: Editorial Guadalupe, 1970.

Barcia, José. *El lunfardo en Buenos Aires*. Buenos Aires: Editorial Paidós, 1973.

Barletta, Leónidas. *Boedo y Florida: Una visión distinta*. Buenos Aires: Editorial Metrópolis, 1967.

Bordelois, Ivonne. *Genio y figura de Ricardo Güiraldes*. Buenos Aires: Editorial de la Universidad Nacional de Buenos Aires, 1966.

Brenan, Gerald. *The Spanish Labyrinth*. New York: Cambridge University Press, 1962.

Calki (Raimundo Calcagna). *"El Mundo" era una fiesta*. Buenos Aires: Corregidor, 1977.

Capítulo: La historia de la literatura argentina (Adolfo Prieto, General Editor). Buenos Aires, Centro Editor de América Latina, 1968. Vols. II and III.

Castelli, Eugenio and Rogelio Barafalde. *Estructura mítica e interioridad en "Don Segundo Sombra."* Santa Fe, Argentina: Librería y Editorial Colmegna, 1968.

Castelnuovo, Elías. *Memorias*. Buenos Aires: Ediciones Culturales Argentinas, 1974.

————. "Reseña sobre el movimiento Boedo." Carboned typescript.

Chatwin, Bruce. *In Patagonia*. New York: Summit Books, 1977.

Cortázar, A. R. *Poesía gauchesca argentina: Interpretación con el aporte de la teoría folklórica*. Buenos Aires: Guadalupe, 1969.

Diccionario de la literatura latinoamericana, Argentina (in two parts) Washington, D.C.: Unión Panamericana, 1960.

Fiedler, Leslie. *Love and Death in the American Novel*. Briarcliff Manor, New York: Stein and Day, 1975.

Fillol, Tomás Roberto. *Social Factors in Economic Development: The Argentine Case*. Cambridge, Massachusetts: MIT Press, 1961.

Freud, Sigmund. *The Ego and the Id*. New York: W. W. Norton and Company, 1960.

————. *General Psychological Theory: Papers on Metapsychology*. New York: Collier Books, 1963.

————. *The Interpretation of Dreams*. New York: Avon Books, 1965.

————. *New Introductory Lectures*. New York: W. W. Norton and Company, 1965.

————. *The Standard Edition of the Complete Works of Sigmund Freud*. London: The Hogarth Press, 1969. Vol. IX.

————. *Totem and Taboo: Resemblences Between the Psychic Lives of Savages and Neurotics*. New York: Vintage Books, 1946.

García, Germán. *El inmigrante en la novela argentina*. Buenos Aires: Librería Hachette, 1970.

————. *La novela argentina*. Buenos Aires: Editorial Sudamericana, 1952.

Germani, Gino. *Política y sociedad en una época de transición: De la sociedad tradicional a la sociedad de masas*. Buenos Aires: Editorial Paidós, 1962.

Ghiano, Juan Carlos. *Ricardo Güiraldes*. Buenos Aires: Editorial Pleamar, 1966.

————. *Testimonio de la novela argentina*. Buenos Aires: Ediciones Leviatán, 1959.

Girard, René. *Deceit, Desire and the Novel: Self and Other in Literary Structure*. Baltimore, Maryland: Johns Hopkins University Press, 1965.

González Lanuza, Eduardo. *Los martinfierristas*. Buenos Aires: Ediciones Culturales Argentinas, 1961.

————. *Roberto Arlt (La historia popular: Vida y milagros de nuestro pueblo)*. Buenos Aires: Centro Editor de América Latina, 1971.

Gostautas, Stasys. *Buenos Aires y Arlt (Dostoyevski, Martínez Estrada y Escalabrini Ortiz)*. Madrid: Insula, 1977.

Guglielmini, Homero. *Fronteras de la literatura argentina*. Buenos Aires: Editorial de la Universidad Nacional de Buenos Aires, 1972.

Güiraldes, Ricardo. *Semblanza de nuestro país*. Privately printed, 1972.

Hamilton, Alastair. *The Appeal of Fascism: A Study of Intellectuals and Fascism, 1919–1945*. New York: Macmillan, 1971.

Iusem, Miguel. *Diccionario de las calles de Buenos Aires*. Buenos Aires: Instituto Rioplatense de Ciencias, Letras y Artes, 1971.

Jameson, Fredric. *Marxism and Form: Twentieth Century Dialectical Theories of Literature*. Princeton, New Jersey: Princeton University Press, 1971.

Korn, Francis, Susan Mugarza, Lidia de la Torre, and Carlos Escudé. *Buenos Aires: Los huéspedes del veinte*. Buenos Aires: Editorial Sudamericana, 1974.

Lichtblau, Myron L. *Manuel Gálvez*. New York: Twayne Publishers, Inc., 1972.

Lugones, Leopoldo. *El estado equitativo (Ensayo sobre la realidad argentina)*. Buenos Aires: La Editora Argentina, 1932.

Lukács, Georg. *Theory of the Novel: A Historico-Philosophical Essay on the Form of Great Epic Literature*. Cambridge, Massachusetts: MIT Press, 1952.

Lafleur, Héctor René, Sergio Provenzano, and Fernando Pedro Alonso. *Las revistas literarias argentinas (1893–1960)*. Buenos Aires: Ediciones Culturales Argentinas, 1962.

Larra, Raúl. *Leónidas Barletta: El hombre de la campaña*. Buenos Aires: Ediciones Conducta, 1978.

———. *Mundo de escritores*. Buenos Aires: Editorial Sílaba, 1973.

———. *Roberto Arlt: El torturado*. Buenos Aires: Editorial Anfora, 1973.

———. "Roberto Mariani." Unpublished memoir.

Mafud, Julio. *Psicología de la viveza criolla (Contribuciones para una interpretación de la realidad social argentina y americana)*. Buenos Aires: Editorial Americalee S.R.L., 1965.

Marcuse, Herbert. *Eros and Civilization: A Philosophical Inquiry into Freud*. New York: Vintage Books, 1962.

———. *One Dimensional Man: Studies in the Ideology of Advanced Industrial Society*. Boston: Beacon Press, 1964.

Martínez Estrada, Ezequiel. *Radiografía de la pampa*. Buenos Aires: Losada, 1968.

Masotta, Oscar. *Sexo y traición en Roberto Arlt*. Buenos Aires: Jorge Alvarez Editor, 1965.

Mazzei, Angel. *La poesía de Buenos Aires*. Buenos Aires: Editorial Ciordia, 1962.

Meyer, Doris. *Victoria Ocampo: Against the Wind and the Tide*. New York: George Braziller, 1979.

Mullahy, Patrick. *Oedipus, Myth and Complex: A Review of Psychoanalytic Theory*. New York: Hermitage Press, 1952.

Murena, H. A. *El pecado original de América*. Buenos Aires: Editorial Sudamericana, 1965.

Naipul, V. S. *The Return of Eva Peron, With the Killings in Trinidad*. New York: Vintage Books, 1981.

Nalé Roxlo, Conrado. *Borrador de memorias*. Buenos Aires: Editorial Plus Ultra, 1978.

Nichols, Madeline Wallis. *The Gaucho: Cattle Hunter, Cavalryman, Ideal of Romance*. New York: Gordian Press, 1968.

Nuñez, Angel. *La obra narrativa de Roberto Arlt*. Buenos Aires: Editorial Nova, 1968.

Orgambide, Pedro. *Yo, Argentino*. Buenos Aires: Jorge Alvarez Editor, 1968.

Orgambide, Pedro and Roberto Yahni. *Enciclopedia de la literatura argentina*. Buenos Aires: Editorial Sudamericana, 1970.

Paullada, Stephan. *Rawhide and Song: A Comparative Study of the Cattle Cultures of the Argentine Pampa and North American Great Plains.* New York: Vantage Press, 1963.

Pinto, Juan. *Breviario de la literatura argentina (Con una ojeada retrospectiva).* Buenos Aires: Editorial La Mandrágora, 1958.

————. *Roberto Mariani y su generación.* Buenos Aires: Cuadernos de La Boca del Riachuelo, 1964.

Pineta, Alberto. *Verde memoria: Tres décadas de literatura y periodismo en una autobiografía (Los grupos de Boedo y Florida).* Buenos Aires: Ediciones Antonio Zamora, 1962.

Prieto, Adolfo. *Boedo y Florida (Estudios de la literatura argentina).* Buenos Aires. Editorial Galerna, 1969.

————. *Diccionario básico de la literatura argentina.* Buenos Aires: Centro Editor de América Latina, 1968.

————. "La literatura de izquierda: El grupo Boedo." Mimeographed material provided to students by the Facultad de Filosofía y Letras, Universidad Nacional de Cuyo, Mendoza, Argentina, 1974.

————. *Sociología del público argentino.* Buenos Aires. Editorial Leviatán, 1956.

Rank, Otto. *The Myth of the Birth of the Hero and Other Writings.* New York: Vintage Books, 1964.

Reich, Wilhelm. *The Mass Psychology of Fascism.* New York: Farrar, Straus and Giroux, 1970.

————. *Sex-Pol: Essays, 1929–1934.* New York: Vintage Books, 1972.

Rennie, Ysabel F. *The Argentine Republic.* Westport, Connecticut: Greenwood Press Publishers, 1975.

Rock, David (ed.). *Argentina in the Twentieth Century.* Pittsburgh: University of Pittsburgh Press, 1975.

Rock, David. *Politics in Argentina, 1890–1930: The Rise and Fall of Radicalism.* London: Cambridge University Press, 1975.

Romano, Eduardo. *Análisis de "Don Segundo Sombra."* Buenos Aires: Centro Editor de América Latina, 1967.

Romero, José Luis. *A History of Argentine Political Thought* (trans. Thomas F. McGann). Stanford, California: Stanford University Press, 1963.

Sargent, Charles S. *The Spatial Evolution of Greater Buenos Aires, Argentina, 1870–1930.* Tempe, Arizona: Center for Latin American Studies, Arizona State University, 1974.

Sarmiento, Domingo F. *Facundo: Civilización y barbarbie.* Buenos Aires: Centro Editor de América Latina, 1973.

Scobie, James. *Argentina: A City and a Nation.* New York: Oxford University Press, 1971.

————. *Buenos Aires: Plaza to Suburb, 1870–1910.* New York: Oxford University Press, 1974.

Scrimaglio, Marta. *Literatura argentina de vanguardia (1920–1930).* Rosario, Argentina: Editorial Biblioteca, 1974.

Sebreli, Juan José. *Buenos Aires: Vida cotidiana y alienación.* Buenos Aires:

Ediciones Siglo Veinte. 1965.

Soboleosky, Marcos. *El amor en la literatura argentina*. Buenos Aires: Ediciones Culturales Argentinas, 1966.

Soriano, Osvaldo. "Un gran olvidado de la literatura argentina: Roberto Mariani bajo la cruz de cada día," "La Opinión Cultural: Literatura, Artes, Espectáculo" (Sunday Cultural Supplement). *La Opinión* (Buenos Aires). November 26, 1972.

Sosa Cordero, Osvaldo. *Historia de las varietés en Buenos Aires, 1900–1925*. Buenos Aires: Ediciones Corregidor, 1978.

Suárez Danero, Eduardo. *Recuerdos de Roberto Mariani*. Buenos Aires: Ediciones Propósitos, 1969.

Teruggi, Mario E. *Panorama del lunfardo*. Buenos Aires: Editorial Cabargón, 1974.

Tiempo, César (Israel Zeitlin). *Clara Béter y otras fatamorganas*. Buenos Aires: A. Peña Lillo, Editor, 1974.

Timerman, Jácobo. *Prisoner Without a Name, Cell Without a Number*. New York, Alfred A. Knopf, 1981.

Tinker, Edward Layton. *The Cult of the Gaucho and the Creation of Literature*. Worchester, Massachusetts: Proceedings of the American Antiquarian Society, 1947.

de Torre, Guillermo. *Historia de las literaturas de vanguardia*. Madrid: Editorial Guadarrama, 1965.

Viñas, David. *Literatura argentina y realidad política: De Sarmiento a Cortázar*. Buenos Aires: Ediciones Siglo Veinte, 1964.

Yunque, Alvaro (Arístides Gandolfi Herrero). *La literatura social en la Argentina: Historia de los movimientos literarios desde la emancipación nacional hasta nuestro días*. Buenos Aires: Editorial Claridad, 1941.

———. *Síntesis histórica de la literatura argentina*. Buenos Aires: Editorial Claridad, 1957.

Zas, Lubrano. *Gustavo Riccio: Un poeta de Boedo*. Buenos Aires: Editorial Buenos Aires Leyendo, 1969.

———. *Palabras con Elías Castelnuovo*. Buenos Aires: Carlos Perez Editor, 1969.

de Zuleta, Emilia. *Guillermo de Torre*. Buenos Aires. Ediciones Culturales Argentinas, 1962.

Index

Alberdi, Juan Bautista, 3, 4–5
Alem, Leandro, 8
Almafuerte (Pedro B. Palacios), 18, 46; influence on Boedo of, 38
Alvear, Marcelo de, 14, 23–24, 66, 144
Amorim, Enrique, 41, 170n55, 171n65; *Amorim*, 43
Anarchism, 9–10, 13, 34, 38, 57–58
Andreiev, Leonid: influence on Boedo of, 38, 71
Anti-Personalist Radical Civic Union, 24, 144. See also Radical Civic Union
Anti-Semitism: in Argentina, 13, 15; in Boedo and Florida, 168n26; of Leopoldo Lugones, 37; of literary journal *Inicial*, 33
Argentina: economy of, 6–7, 9, 10, 125, 151, 152–53; foreign economic interests in, xvii, 7, 10, 12, 152; historical background, 3–14; in the 1920s, xvi–xviii, 23–28; land ownership in, 6–7; leftist politics in, 39; publishing in, 18–19, 27; traditional culture of, 7, 11, 133. See also Argentine literature, Gaucho, Immigration, Magazines, Middle Class, Newspapers, Oligarchy, Urban proletariat
Argentine literature: fictional tradition in, 46–47; in the 1930s, 153–55; of the Liberal era, 15–20; lyric tradition in, 46; women in, x–xi. See also Argentine theater, Generation of 1880, Generation of 1922, Poetry
Argentine Patriotic League, 12, 53, 146

Argentine theater: of the early 1900s, 18. See also Teatro del Pueblo
Argentinidad, 11, 121, 158, 179n4
Arlt, Roberto, xv, 30, 45, 57, 65, 71, 95–117, 157, 173n4; dramas of, 153; *Las lanzallamas*, 97, 99; life of, 95–97; *Los siete locos*, 72, 97, 99; relationship of to Boedo and Florida, 97; relationship of with Ricardo Güiraldes, 97–98. See also *El juguete rabioso*
Artistas del pueblo, 40
Ateneo Universitario, 31, 93n69, 167n2

Bandera Roja, 171n62
"Barbarism" (Sarmentine notion of), 3–4, 10
Barbusse, Henri, 42
Barletta, Leónidas, 19, 39, 43, 45, 47, 62–65, 72, 93, 157, 171n62, 171n69; and the beginnings of Boedo, 40–41; *Boedo y Florida: Una visión distinta*, 30; *Canciones agrias*, 43, 62; in the 1930s, 153; *Los pobres*, 62; reviews *El juguete rabioso*, 99; *Royal Circo*, 49, 62–65, 72; and the Teatro del Pueblo, 62, 153
Baroja, Pío, 71, 103
Barrett, Rafael, 38
Bernárdez, Francisco Luis, 34
"Béter, Clara" (Israel Zeitlin), x, 172n74; *Versos de una…*, 42, 172n74
Bianchi, Alfredo, 19, 33, 37
Blomberg, Héctor, 18

191